Moving a Battleship with Your Bare Hands

Governing a University System

Laurence A. Weinstein

MAGNA
PUBLICATIONS, INC.

Moving a Battleship with Your Bare Hands

Printed in the United States of America.

First Edition.

Library of Congress Cataloging-in-Publication Data

Weinstein, Laurence A., 1923-

Moving a battleship with your bare hands : governing a university system / Laurence A. Weinstein. — 1st ed.

   p. cm

Includes bibliographical references and index.

ISBN 0-912150-27-0

University of Wisconsin System — Administration — Case Studies. 2. College adminstrators — Wisconsin —Attitudes — Case Studies.

I. Title.

LD6096.W45 1993   93-22814

                                              CIP

Cover Design by Tamara Cook

Magna Publications, Inc.
2718 Dryden Drive
Madison, WI 53704-3086
608/246-3580

I dedicate this work to all of my University of Wisconsin System regent colleagues, past, present, and future, and to the University of Wisconsin System and campus administrators, faculty, and staff, who in so many ways serve the citizens of the state by being advocates for one of the world's preeminent systems of public higher education. I especially dedicate this to the students, who must remind us all, from time to time, that it is for them that public universities exist.

Contents

Foreword

Anthony S. Earl, governor of Wisconsin (1982 - 1986)

Anyone concerned about the problems facing public higher education will profit from reading *Moving a Battleship with Your Bare Hands*. Although this book is focused on the University of Wisconsin System, it deals with problems confronted by public higher education in general.

The author thoughtfully discusses many topical issues, such as the conflict between access and quality; concerns about the lack of emphasis placed on undergraduate education; and the implications of increasing reliance on tuition to meet shortfalls in government support. But at least as important is his treatment of the deeper underlying problems bedeviling public higher education. Not the least of those problems is governance. The author points out that although citizens and public officials frequently identify public universities as "our greatest assets," attention paid to governance is casual — indeed, in many cases, careless. As the title of this book suggests, far too much is left to inertia and far too little effort is made to confront the status quo; to identify problems facing our universities; and to fashion solutions to those problems.

Men and women chosen to govern our public universities confront that obligation in a variety of ways. For some, such a position is merely honorific. For others, it is an avocation. For still others, it is the most serious responsibility a citizen can perform — to protect and enhance public higher education and all that it means to our society. Fortunately, for the University of Wisconsin System, Laurence Weinstein chose the latter route. His book is an extension of his sense of responsibility to public higher education. It offers wise and prudent counsel for those who value higher education.

i

Words of Thanks

It is always dangerous to enumerate those to whom one should give thanks. Nonetheless, there are those without whose help this book would not have been possible.

First and foremost, I wish to thank my wife, Fran, who has been a source of unending encouragement. She has been more than patient in listening to my endless conversations about the subject matter of this book and understanding the countless evening and weekend hours spent at my desk absorbed in this project. She always provided a needed sense of humor. She placed over my personal computer a cartoon that shows a man busy at work. His wife is behind him exclaiming, "I need a hug."

I owe a special thanks to former Governor Anthony S. Earl, who nominated me to the University of Wisconsin Board of Regents in 1984.

Diane Bailiff, Ph.D., provided invaluable help with research and editing. I am deeply indebted to Marilyn Annucci of Magna Publications, who contributed enormously in finalizing the manuscript for publication.

University of Wisconsin System President Katharine C. Lyall encouraged me without attempting to influence my observations or conclusions in any way.

University of Wisconsin Extension Chancellor Patrick G. Boyle was most helpful in sharing with me his knowledge of the history of UW Extension services in Wisconsin as well as his visions for the future.

University of Wisconsin System Senior Vice President Stephen Portch helped me fill the gaps in my files, as did Associate Vice President Jennifer B. Presley, Regent Executive Assistant Fredi-Ellen Bove, and Regent Secretary Judith A. Temby. I am especially grateful to Secretary Temby and Program Assistant Beverly Zimmerman, both of whom assisted me in carrying out the duties of the regent president.

Senior Vice President Ronald C. Bornstein served as an invaluable guide and confidant while he accompanied me as I travelled the state as regent president.

I want to add a special word of thanks to those regents who served with me on the board and twice elected me president. They provided me the opportunity to serve the UW System, an experience I will always cherish.

About the Author

Laurence A. Weinstein served on the University of Wisconsin Board of Regents from May 1984 to June 1991. He was elected president for two terms (1986-1988), was chair of the board's Business and Finance Committee, a member of the Education Committee, the Executive Committee, and the governor's Higher Educational Aids Board. He is a member of the University of Wisconsin Hospital and Clinics Council of Trustees.

He received his B.B.A. degree (1945) from UW-Madison's School of Business, and his J.D. degree (1947) from UW-Madison's School of Law. He served on the *Law Review* and was inducted as a member of COIF, the honorary legal scholastic society.

Since 1951, he has served as CEO of distribution businesses in Madison, Oshkosh, Eau Claire, and Barron, Wisconsin. He is the only person in the United States to have been elected president of two national trade associations related to his business endeavor.

Among his awards are the *Time* magazine Distinguished Wholesaler Award, the University of Wisconsin-Madison School of Business Distinguished Business Alumnus Award, the Friend of Extension Award, and the Distinguished Service Award in Trusteeship from the Association of Governing Boards of Universities and Colleges. He has been recognized for Distinguished Service as the University of Wisconsin System Board of Regents President by a joint resolution of the Wisconsin Assembly and Senate.

Glossary

ADL — Anti-Defamation League of B'nai Brith

AGB — Association of Governing Boards

AIA — Accuracy in Academia Comprehensive Universities — Non-doctoral universities in the UW System

DOA — Department of Administration

DPI — Department of Instruction

ECB — Educational Communications Board

FTE — Full-Time Equivalent (Full time plus part time converted to full time. Used in counting staff or students.)

GPR — General Purpose Revenue (state tax revenue)

Headcount — Full time plus actual number of part time. Used in counting staff or students.

HEGIS — Higher Education General Information Survey

JACAP — Joint Administrative Committee on Academic Programs (VTAE/UWS)

JACCE — Joint Administrative Committee on Continuing Education (VTAE/UWS)

JACPF — Joint Administrative Committee on Physical Facilities (VTAE/UWS)

JCOF — Joint Committee on Finance

LAB — Legislative Audit Bureau

LFB — Legislative Fiscal Bureau

MATC — Milwaukee or Madison Area Technical College

MIC — Minority Improvement Council

NCATE — National Center for Accreditation of Teacher Education

NIH — National Institute of Health

OPAR — UW System Office of Policy Analysis and Research

PELL — Pell Grants (formerly Basic Education Opportunity Grants)

SERC — Satellite Educational Resources Consortium

TAUWF — The Association of University of Wisconsin Faculty. The organization's name has been changed to The Association of University of Wisconsin Professionals (TAUWP).

UTIC — Undergraduate Teaching Improvement Council (UW System)

UWS — University of Wisconsin System

VTAE — Vocational, Technical and Adult Education

I

Conclusions and Introduction

The University of Wisconsin System is committed to providing *quality* in teaching, in research, and in public service. The University of Wisconsin System is also committed to providing *access* to its quality programs and resources. To ensure maximum quality and to provide access within the resources available, the University of Wisconsin System must also be *efficient*. However, when faced with a choice between maintaining educational quality and decreasing access to its programs and resources, the University of Wisconsin System must choose to maintain quality. For if academic programs, research, and public service are not first rate, access to the institutions will be of little value.[1]

On February 16, 1984, Governor Anthony S. Earl nominated me to serve a seven-year term as a member of the University of Wisconsin System (UW System) Board of Regents, to begin May 1, 1984. One of the earliest reports I received from the System was several hundred pages long. I could not locate the conclusion because it was buried about half way into the report. I expressed my annoyance and insisted that conclusions be stated "up front," followed by the reasons that led to such conclusions.

Conclusions

Consistent with this view, let me state my conclusions:

While this book focuses on educational and administrative issues facing the University of Wisconsin System, the problems confronting Wisconsin are not unlike those challenging public colleges and universities nationwide. The UW System's proclaimed goal to preserve and enhance the quality of its mission is certainly a reflection of the purpose of American higher education. The effort to maintain quality has become so important that it now takes precedence over access. We know that future funding will be limited, making it necessary to reassess the hope for increasing budgets through state taxation or substantially increased tuition. Therefore, in order to meet the commitment to quality, we will need new and creative approaches.

Unfortunately, instead of facing funding realities and adopting needed changes, the approach is to continue to emphasize obtaining more funds, either from the state or from students through large tuition increases. Neither is likely to occur. Administrators and the board need to seek and implement other solutions.

1

My experience leads me to conclude that the governing boards, working with administrators, need to adopt new strategies. Past experience has shown that governing boards can govern responsibly if they assume leadership and institute needed changes. They must insist that their initiatives be implemented and that normally accepted management principles be adopted.

Regardless of available funds, quality issues must be addressed. Generalizations will not do. Governing boards need to define quality and break it down into its elements. And for each element, there must be a recognition of the problems, so that governing boards can find solutions. The quality issues, as I see them, are:

Quality of governance. The UW System Board of Regents is given governing authority by statute. The board must accept that authority and govern boldly, regardless of challenges to their power. Problems facing the UW System will not be solved by looking for consensus through endless meetings of systemwide committees. The board must identify and deal with internal and external obstacles to change. In this role, the board must make clear that it is the advocate for the System.

The process by which regents are appointed needs major overhauling. The governor nominates, but the state senate confirms after public hearings. The confirmation process should determine the "mental baggage" that nominees bring to the board and whether that mental baggage is consistent with the role regents must play if quality is to be preserved. It makes a difference who serves as regents.

Quality of administrators. For too long, it has been accepted practice that university administrators must come from the faculty. That attitude unnecessarily limits the pool of qualified candidates and should be changed. Once appointed, administrators must be paid competitively. It is time for legislators to face this issue squarely.

Quality of faculty. Currently, the faculty define their quality through control of the tenure process. Tenure is awarded by the board on a pro forma basis. Yet the qualifications of tenure and the entire reward system need to be challenged if faculty are to carry out the three missions of the university — research, instruction, and community service. Compensation of faculty is unnecessarily burdened because it has been tied to that of academic staff.

Quality of undergraduate instruction and Extension programs. It does little good to discuss the quality of undergraduate education and Extension programs without realizing that the doctoral campus faculty, by their own standards for awarding tenure and post-tenure review, diminish the importance of both. The regents must insist that all faculty carry out these missions. Further, Exension budgets must be controlled centrally in order to ensure program quality and minimize duplication.

Quality of students. Based on current graduation rates, it is clear that qualifications for admission to UW System campuses are substantially lower than requirements to graduate. The result is too many underprepared students in the System. Facilities are strained, and the state is spending too much on students who are not qualified. The university can address underpreparation constructively through cooperative efforts with the Vocational, Technical and Adult Education (VTAE) system.

Quality of facilities. While the state has provided funds for new construction, it has failed to allocate funds for maintenance. "Crumbling Academia" is not a theory. The state needs to put money into maintenance as well.

Quality of the campus environment. There is much talk of creating a quality campus environment that is inclusive. Yet, there is discrimination against women and minorities in the faculty. Those who discriminate are not punished. That, in my view, is unacceptable. The minority recruiting program is being threatened by regents. Regents need to remember who they represent — a diverse community.

The quality issues will not be resolved unless adoption and implementation of solutions receive support from the governing board, administrators, faculty, political leaders, and the media. That will require a change in attitudes.

I will address each of these conclusions and provide a number of suggestions and options for resolving the issues of quality. Some come from the literature, while many are the result of my own experience. Most do not depend on additional funding.

Moving the Battleship

The reluctance to change is caused not only by an unwillingness to overcome internal and external obstacles but by an acceptance by some that there is little one can do to change a large bureaucracy. But the quality of the university depends on dealing with quality issues. Let me explain by beginning with my feelings about my appointment to the UW System Board of Regents.

I considered this appointment to be among the most important and prestigious events of my life. I had earned undergraduate and graduate degrees from the University of Wisconsin-Madison. My wife had also graduated from UW-Madison. The opportunity to serve as a regent was a time for celebration in our family. I viewed this appointment as a chance to give back to the university a small token of my appreciation for the tremendous contribution it had made to my life and to the lives of my wife, our siblings, children, and extended families.

With that said, you can imagine my disappointment when, shortly after my confirmation by the Wisconsin State Senate, a member of the UW-Madison faculty told me not to expect to make any changes. Why? Because, he said, a university is a large bureaucracy. It is like a battleship at rest. And I, as an individual, would have about as much effect on bringing about change as I would in attempting to move a battleship with my bare hands. I resented his advice. My idea of public service was to make a difference, to foster and support needed change.

Some months later, I found myself becoming discouraged. The board had listened to what seemed to be endless testimony and had received numerous written reports, none of which contained any conclusions or recommendations. At a meeting of the board, I heard myself blurt out, "Moving this System is about as easy as moving a battleship with your bare hands!" That frustrated outburst became a challenge for me. I was determined to move the "battleship."

What about my faculty friend's assertion? Was he correct? Was my frustration well-founded? This brings me to the major motivation for writing this book, to show that we both were wrong. During my seven years on the board, regents did make substantial differences by governing responsibly, by supporting and promoting change. The "battleship" was moved, with difficulty I admit, but it was moved nonetheless. Despite the numerous obstacles to change, the years I served on the board were incredibly productive years for me. My hope is that my insights may help those who follow keep the "battleship" moving.

At the end of my term as president of the board, System President Kenneth A. Shaw paid me a high compliment. He presented me with a cap from the "SS Wisconsin" and said, "You proved that you could move a battleship with your bare hands!" A year later, upon my retirement from the board, Executive Vice President Katharine C. Lyall wrote me: "You showed that complex organizations can, nonetheless, command their own fate if they have the courage to try and the will to persist." What was so special about those years for me and my colleagues on the board? It was during that time that the board began to understand its statutory authority to govern. Major change was possible because of that recognition. To illustrate what I mean, here is a list of major board initiatives adopted during the period from 1984 to 1991.

1. Planning the Future," a strategic plan that was designed to project UW System development 10 years into the future. It was this policy document that raised admission standards, instituted an enrollment management plan, and set policies for the transfer of credits from the Vocational Technical Adult Education (VTAE), as well as intra-institutional transfers of credit.

2. "Design for Diversity," a multifaceted initiative addressing the issues of minority student recruitment and retention and recruitment of

women and minorities as faculty. The board also directed UW System Administration to implement the minority initiative by hiring a special assistant to the president for minority affairs, an administrative level position.

3. A systemwide leave of absence policy that allowed faculty to be absent from the classroom in pursuit of personal rather than institutional goals, and incorporated clearly defined and monitored guidelines.

4. A policy statement outlining the role of Extension and its relationship to UW System campuses. New language acknowledged integration of UW Extension programs into the 13 UW System institutions. The language made it clear that UW Extension would continue to be in charge of its own budget, ensuring control and quality of outreach programs, and strengthening the mission of UW Extension.

5. A policy on "Competition with the Private Sector." The policy set out broad definitions of activities that were consistent with the mission of the UW System without being unnecessarily competitive with the private sector. The policy included procedures for hearings and appeals.

6. A salary structure for senior executives that was more competitive with that of peer institutions.

7. A compensation catch-up for faculty and academic staff.

8. A revised course drop/add policy that more accurately reflected academic calendars and student access to courses.

9. Implementation of a strategic plan for the schools of Business and business programs.

10. An improved process for evaluation of the UW System president and campus chancellors.

11. Policies that provided a framework for campuses to deal with developing and offering students remedial education and skill-development opportunities.

12. Creation of an intergovernmental Task Force on Supplies and Expenses.

13. Institution of annual agendas for each board committee, including a schedule for reports and follow-up.

14. Development of plans for improving undergraduate education.

15. Development of a plan for systemwide proficiency testing in math and English after the sophomore year.

16. Entry into a formal agreement between the UW System and VTAE that clearly defined each institution's missions.

17. Adoption of a UW System biennial budget proposal, reduced by the regents *before* being sent to the governor. (This may have been the first biennial budget proposal held to such scrutiny.)

18. Creation of tenure and post-tenure review guidelines.

19. Adoption of plans to eliminate programs considered to be substandard.

Moving the "battleship" meant confronting these issues as well as others and then formulating and implementing new policies. It meant that regents had to exercise their authority. Change did not come easily. There were many challenges from administrators, faculty, and some regents. The institution for which we were advocates too often saw us as being too involved in internal management, or simply disagreed with the conclusions we reached and ignored regent mandates.

Most of us who were serving on the board knew that we were changing the institutional culture by exercising our authority. I was, therefore, amused by the conflicting observations made by media editorial writers, legislators, faculty, and even some regents. What follows is a sampling of those conflicting observations:

On the one hand and on the other hand:

- Why aren't the regents in charge?
  - How can you trust the regents?
- Why do the regents micro manage?
  - Why don't the regents manage?
- Why is the System so secretive?
  - Why does the System produce so many reports?
- Why is the System so elite in setting standards?
  - Why is the graduation rate so low?
- Why should my son or daughter have to travel to get the courses required for the major?
  - Why is there so much duplication of course offerings between campuses?
- We need to be competitive in compensating the faculty.
  - In Wisconsin, we don't pay state employees in the six figures.
- We want to be competitive in order to attract excellent faculty.
  - We don't have to pay our faculty the same as the "competition" does because of our state's superior quality of life.

- The regents have the statutory authority to close a campus.
  - The regents better not close any campuses.
- ROTC discrimination against gays and lesbians violates regent policy.
  - ROTC serves a greater good by graduating officers with college degrees.
- Tuition is a real bargain.
  - Student debt is a real burden.
- Why doesn't the System take charge?
  - Who can trust the System?

In addition, there were many allegations from inside and outside the System:

- Why is the faculty so arrogant? Do they think they own the place? Why don't the faculty trust anyone who isn't faculty?
- We should not be spending so much time recruiting minorities. If they work hard, like the rest of us, they can make it.
- Why isn't everyone held accountable for their failure to carry out established policy or for actions that are contrary to established policy?
- Why can't the media ever get it right?

My "Mental Baggage"

I will be discussing the importance of attitudes that regents bring with them. It makes a difference. I bring to this writing my own "mental baggage," attitudes that come from my home environment and my training as an accountant, attorney, CEO in the private sector, and grateful alumnus, and concerned citizen.

When I was an undergraduate student at the University of Wisconsin-Madison (1941-1945), Professor Selig Perlman was lecturing about the upcoming Yalta Conference. That conference brought together the heads of state of the World War II Alliance (the United States, Great Britain, France, and the Soviet Union) to discuss the ftermath of the war. Professor Perlman began by telling us that in order to comprehend what was happening at Yalta, we must first understand the "mental baggage" each participant brought to the meetings. He examined the mindset and assumptions of the participants — how they differed and how they were the same.

Likewise, in order to have an idea of how potential regents will deal with issues that confront the UW System, one must understand their assumptions, their world view, the mental baggage that they bring to the deliberations. Their mental baggage will have an impact on how they analyze problems and construct solutions to those problems.

I am no different. While this book is a reflection of the seven years I served as a member of the board, you are entitled to know the mental baggage I believe I brought to the board and to this writing.

There are several major pieces of mental baggage that come with me. At home, I learned the importance of public education, a disdain for intolerance, and a commitment to the disadvantaged in our society. At the University of Wisconsin-Madison, I acquired a boundless appreciation and respect for education that is shared by the members of my family. And then there is my experience as a CEO in the private sector. All of this had an impact on how I viewed my role as a regent.

Home Influence

My wife and I are the children of immigrants who came to this country in the early years of this century. Our parents were among the millions of Jews who fled eastern Europe, refugees from religious persecution and economic hardship. In addition, government schools were often closed to them, because they were Jews. Universities had strict quotas for admission of Jewish students.

My father was 11 years old when he came to this country with his father. They worked as peddlers and saved enough to send for my father's mother and five siblings. My mother came to the United States with her oldest brother. Her father had preceded them. Her mother and seven siblings arrived 10 years later, having been caught in the Russian revolution, which prevented them from leaving earlier.

Our parents told us a great deal about the stifling life of the "shtetl," small isolated villages of eastern Europe. In 1989, my wife and I travelled to the then USSR and visited the villages where our parents had spent their early childhood. It appeared to us that nothing had changed in the last 100 years. The streets were muddy, the people were dressed poorly, and the houses looked very much like the old photos we had seen. There was one major change. There were no Jews living in those tiny villages in 1989. Most had been murdered by the Nazis. We were surprised to learn that the universities still maintained quotas for Jews. We came home, more impressed than ever by the remarkable commitment those immigrants had made to their own education as well as to that of their children, despite the formidable economic obstacles and the social and language barriers they encountered in this country.

My parents' experiences in eastern Europe influenced their views of the "new world." They felt strongly that their children must take full advantage of an open and free society's educational opportunities that had been denied to them. My appreciation for the outstanding public universities of Wisconsin was reinforced by the number of baccalaureate, masters, and doctoral degrees earned by members of our families.

Our parents considered education to take precedence over all else. At our graduation ceremonies, their tears of joy were testimony to that. They believed that public education was the foundation of our democracy. My father's only formal education had been attending a "cheder" (Jewish religious school). Although our parents did not have the opportunity to receive a formal education in this country, they were self-educated, mostly in Yiddish, their native tongue. My parents maintained an extensive library and were avid readers. They learned English on their own. Dad was always a bit concerned about his English spelling skills. Were he alive today, I would tell him that his second-oldest son, even after seven years of college, still relies on the spell check of the word processor for accuracy!

With the rise of the Nazis in the 1930s, many Jewish writers fled Eastern Europe and made their way to the United States. When they were in Madison, they came to our home. I recall very well the spirited discussions that took place in the library, Dad's favorite room, between my father and those visitors as they addressed the issues of the day. We children were always invited and encouraged to join in the discussions.

Dad established a successful business, yet he never forgot his origins. He knew religious persecution and economic and educational deprivation first-hand. He would be labeled a "liberal" today. I am sure he would have worn it as a badge of honor. My parents would never blame the victims of poverty for their condition. They would never subscribe to the "boot strap" theory espoused by many in recent years. They never grew weary of trying to better the conditions for all. They had no patience with those who were bigoted or intolerant toward others because of their race or ethnicity. They believed in the admonition of the ancient Jewish scholar, Hillel, "If I am not for myself, who will be for me? Yet if I am for myself only, what am I? And if not now, when?"

Since my parents did not take for granted that their children would fully understand the vast differences between the "new world" and the "old," nor could they assume that their children would accept their value system, they helped found a school for Jewish children that met five afternoons each week after regular public school. There we read poetry of Yiddish writers who decried the oppression of the New York "sweat shops" and learned about the pioneers of the labor movement. I vividly recall a poem by I. L. Peretz where he declared that learning in and of itself was not enough. What a tragedy, he wrote, that a scholar would devote endless hours studying *The Talmud* but would not apply his knowledge to helping improve the lot of humankind. Not a bad idea for today's scholars. Our childhood heroes were the ancient Hebrew prophets who spoke out against poverty, intolerance, government corruption and the uselessness of war.

Our dinner table discussions, led by Dad, centered on world affairs. He taught us about the economic, physical, and human destruction of war. He forcefully expressed his views about tolerance, government corruption, and the importance of education. We were taught that none of us live in a vacuum. If one person suffers, we all suffer. Poverty is a disease that will infect us all no matter how fortunate our economic circumstances happen to be.

In our household, it was considered an honor to be included in the dinner table discussions and to be asked to express one's views. My oldest brother was an active participant long before I was. The proudest moment of my early childhood came the evening Dad turned to me and asked, "Well, Laurence, what do you think?" Those dinner table discussions also included a report by the children of their day's activities at school. My parents were genuinely interested in hearing from us.

Because they believed that, for each individual, education was the most important liberating force, they made it clear to us that we were expected to be good students and study hard. Going to school was our "job," and we were expected to do our job well. Every report card was carefully scrutinized. One of our family jokes relates to a comment Dad made upon reviewing my oldest brother's high school report card, which contained all A's. After looking it over he asked, "Is there anything better?" He knew that one could also achieve A pluses!

While we were tempted to complain occasionally about a teacher, we knew that such complaints would fall on deaf ears. Our parents believed that since the teachers were imparting knowledge, they deserved a special place in our society and were to be respected. This was true of all "educated" people. We were to be grateful for the opportunity to receive a formal education. It was an opportunity not to be trivialized. After high school graduation, my parents expected us to enroll at the University of Wisconsin- Madison and live at home. Living "on campus" was wasteful in their view. Fraternities were out of the question, unless they were scholastic fraternities.

I brought to the UW System Board of Regents an attitude about the role of public education and tolerance and an understanding of the stifling effect of poverty and ghetto life. I had learned this at home listening to my parents' remembrances of their lives in eastern Europe. Outside of the comfort of our home, I experienced anti-Semitism and exclusion from some of the high school clubs. In the 1930s Father Coughlin preached his hatred of the Jews every Sunday over the radio. Being called a "Christ killer," "dirty Jew," "shenie," and "kike" were not novel experiences for me.

In debates that took place at regent board meetings around issues concerning discrimination, economically disadvantaged students, access to public higher education, the importance of adequate state funding for public higher education, and tuition policies, I found myself expressing views that I had learned as a child — lessons not easily forgotten. Many children of immigrants had similar home experiences. Our childhood was obviously quite different than children's whose middle-class parents were born in the United States and were members of the Christian majority.

Private Sector Influence

From my private sector experience, I had reached some conclusions about management responsibility, effectiveness, accountability, control, and achieving goals in a timely manner. I believe that the public sector can learn a great deal from the private sector.

My experience taught me that in order to get things done, one had to have a commitment to the process of management. Management in the academy is sometimes referred to as "governance." It was clear to me that any effective management system had to understand and incorporate three steps. None could be short-circuited.

Step 1: Management must establish goals, policies, and standards as well as timetables for performance.

Step 2: Goals must be implemented. In order for that to occur, someone must be assigned responsibility. I knew only too well that everyone's business was no one's business. Those affected by the goals, policies, or standards must also understand them as well as the timetable for completion.

Step 3: There must be a control mechanism in place to ensure completion of and compliance with the established goals, policies, or standards. Timely reviews of accomplishments are necessary so that corrective action can be undertaken when necessary. There should be no last-minute surprises.

My experience in the private sector did cause me to be frustrated with the apparent lack of adherence to these three steps and the lack of urgency at the UW System and campus levels to implement needed change.

My Attitudes About My Role as a Regent

Before assuming my responsibilities as a regent, I read Chapter 36, Wisconsin Statutes. It seemed straightforward enough to me. Having earned a law degree from the University of Wisconsin-Madison, I was familiar with statutory language. I recalled the warning of my faculty friend, that there was little I could do to change the university. However, as I read Chapter 36,

Wisconsin Statutes, it seemed to me that this much was clear about the authority vested on the board to move the "battleship:"

1. The legislature and governor had passed a merger bill (1971) that brought the former two systems of public higher education under one board of regents.

2. The board of regents was the governing body of the *entire* System: it hired the System president, the vice presidents, and the chancellors.

3. The chancellors, deans, department heads, and faculty were duty-bound to carry out *all* of the policies of the board, not just those with which they agreed.

4. The faculty had certain powers which were *delegated* to them subject to the powers of the chancellor, System president, and the board.

5. The board of regents had an obligation to govern the UW System.

What They Didn't Tell Me, and What I Learned Very Early

All this seemed straightforward to me early on. I was more than surprised to learn that many regents had never read Chapter 36, Wisconsin Statutes, and that others had simply ignored it. How else could one explain:

1. That 12 years after merger legislation was passed there were still chancellors who did not "get along" with the System president, and felt no compunction about going directly to the legislature to propose action contrary to regent resolutions.

2. That there were chancellors and some faculty who thought the merger was a bad idea and promoted legislation to undo the merger.

3. That there was tremendous jealousy between UW-Milwaukee and UW-Madison, the two doctoral campuses. If Madison had it, Milwaukee wanted it.

4. That there was open disdain expressed between UW-Oshkosh and UW-Green Bay, one referring to the other as inferior.

5. That because the System president held tenure at the UW-Madison Law School and at no other campus, there was suspicion among other campuses about his ability to be impartial.

6. That there were rumors that some campuses wanted to dismantle UW-Extension by taking over its budget.

7. That academic staff on some campuses felt that they were second-class citizens and threatened to organize a union, which the UW System and campus administrators opposed unionization, since they thought it would seriously complicate staffing needs.

8. That some of the VTAE district directors said that since the UW System was in open competition with them, they wanted to become community colleges and offer two-year degrees that would be the same as those offered by UW Centers.

9. That some UW-Madison administrators wanted to discontinue undergraduate education on their campus.

10. That some legislators were convinced the UW System was out of control; that there was no functioning central governing authority; and that faculty were overpaid, underworked, and spent too much time out of the classroom doing private consulting.

11. That some regents did not understand, or were unwilling to exercise, the authority granted them in Chapter 36, Wisconsin Statutes, and characterized regent action as "micro managing."

How I Saw My Role

Once I understood what lay below the surface, I had to decide what my role would be. I decided that the following 10 principles would guide my tenure on the board:

1. I would oppose anyone who was not prepared to uphold the merger.

2. I believed that insubordination from any UW System employee, chancellors included, was not acceptable and deserved discipline, up to and including dismissal, if necessary.

3. I knew that the idea proposed by some that UW-Madison should become a graduate school was ludicrous. The citizens of the state had poured hundreds of millions of dollars into buildings for the campus on the assumption that it would treat undergraduate instruction as a key part of its mission.

4. I would openly oppose any attempts by VTAE to set up programs parallel to the UW System's two-year campuses. That idea was contrary to the provisions of Chapter 36, Wisconsin Statutes, which forbade duplications between the two systems that did not exist at the time of the merger.

5. I firmly believed in maintaining central control of the UW Extension budget in order to ensure that statewide planning would be maximized and duplication of programs between campuses would be minimized.

6. I was concerned that UW-Milwaukee had an identity crisis. I believed that rather than try to mimic UW-Madison, it should develop its unique strengths. It has, for example, the only School of Architecture in the state.

7. I did not believe there was anything to be gained by ignoring the unhappiness expressed by academic staff. I did not believe they should be treated like faculty. I thought that those who wanted to unionize ought to. I saw no point in devoting energy to fighting it. However, I would not support their attempts to become part of management at the same time they were talking about organizing a union.

8. I was committed to conducting myself according to the authority mandated to the regents in Chapter 36, Wisconsin Statutes, regardless of who opposed me. Many did oppose me, among them chancellors, faculty, and some regents. I kept a copy of Chapter 36, Wisconsin Statutes in my regent brief case and quoted from it often.

9. I believed there was a distinction between practical shared governance and total confusion or inaction by a decision-making process that often seemed endless and indecisive.

10. I was determined, to the extent possible, to be an advocate for the faculty, academic staff, and particularly students, who, after all, were the reason we maintained the universities. That meant being available to them as well as to the governor, legislators, and the media. I was especially concerned about students. They were on campus for a limited number of years and did not have the political clout of faculty and staff. Changes that were implemented after their graduation did them no good. It was on their behalf that I felt an urgency to implement change.

Regardless of my "mental baggage," I hope to contribute to maintaining and improving the quality of the University of Wisconsin System, to which my family and I and the citizens of the state owe so much. I believe that accepting the nomination to serve as a regent for one of the nation's most prestigious educational systems requires a serious commitment to encouraging and accepting change by governing wisely through thoughtful stewardship. My approach to this important responsibility is here, on these pages. So, let us begin.

II.

A Short Guide to the UW System

Conclusion #2: Regents and others will more easily understand the process of change if they have: an overview of recent history of public higher education in Wisconsin; an understanding of the significance of the UW System's three-part mission (instruction, research, outreach); an appreciation of the budget; and an insight into public higher education's governance structure. This includes fostering a more meaningful relationship between the University of Wisconsin System (UW System) institutions and the Vocational, Technical and Adult Education (VTAE) system, while maintaining an appreciation of the differences inherent in the two systems.

University systems are complicated organizational structures. Yet they must be governed. Before dealing with issues of governance and change, we must understand the structure of the UW System, the statutory governance structure, and the UW System's relationship to the VTAE system.

During my term on the board I visited each baccalaureate campus and several of the UW System's Center campuses. As president, I spoke on behalf of my regent colleagues and the UW System to legislators, governors, faculty, staff and student leaders, media representatives, and alumni groups. From these experiences, I concluded that many people inside and outside of the UW System did not know enough about post-secondary public education in Wisconsin.

In an attempt to remedy that situation, I offer my "short guide." The purpose of the guide is to briefly describe: Wisconsin's two publicly funded systems of post-secondary education, the UW System and the VTAE system; the merger of Wisconsin Statutes Chapter 36 (University of Wisconsin) and Chapter 37 (Wisconsin State University System) institutions; the composition of the UW System campuses; financial resources, size, and institutional missions; and the various roles governance plays in policy development. Understanding these issues is not only the responsibility of regents, but all those who are interested in the quality of public higher education.

Contrasting Wisconsin's Two Systems
of Public Higher Education

Vocational, Technical and Adult Education System

Some understanding of the VTAE system will help you understand the differences in missions and funding of the two systems, as well as their relationship to one another.

Chapter 38, Wisconsin Statutes established the VTAE system. The VTAE's governance structure, board authority, and institutional missions are quite different from those of Chapter 36, Wisconsin Statutes, which established the UW System. Chapter 38.001[1] describes the duties of the state board of the VTAE system. "The board shall be responsible for the initiation, development, maintenance and supervision of *programs with specific occupation orientation below the baccalaureate level, including terminal associate degrees, training of apprentices and adult education below the professional level.*" (emphasis added)

Section 38.001[2][b]provides that the district boards of the VTAE system shall "... actively coordinate, with the institutions and centers within the University of Wisconsin system, the sharing of programs and facilities, including the collegiate transfer program, adult education and evening courses and part-time student and associate degree programs, *in order to reduce the duplication of such programs and facilities*" (emphasis added).

Each VTAE institution is governed by a district board. Section 38.12 provides that the district boards "... shall have exclusive control of the district schools established by it and the property acquired for the use of such schools." This limits the role of the state board.

Section 38.08 defines the makeup of district boards. Members must be residents of the district where the VTAE campus is located and the appointment is made in their district. These individuals, representing their district's tax payers, set the funding level for their campus. For the period 1985-86, the principal funding sources for the districts were:[1]

Property Tax	54%
State Aid	22%
Tuition and Fees	13%
Federal Aid	11%

District boards establish the property tax mill rate. It may not exceed the statutory maximum. For the period above, the maximum was 1.5 mills.

The state board consists of members appointed by the governor, the president of the UW System Board of Regents, and the state superintendent of public instruction. All new programs of the districts must receive approval from the state board.

University of Wisconsin System

In 1971, the University of Wisconsin System came into being with enactment of Chapter 36, Wisconsin Statutes. The UW System is different from the VTAE system in almost every respect. Governance of the UW System is vested in a board of regents that has authority over policy development and controls budgets of all System institutions. This is not true of the VTAE state board.

Unlike the VTAE, the UW System does not have taxing authority. It derives its income from state taxes, tuition, federal, state, and private research grants and gifts.

The mission of the UW System is to grant two-year associate and baccalaureate, professional, and graduate degrees, to conduct research, and to do outreach through a network of UW Extension offices. This is substantially different from the VTAE system's mission, which is to provide non-baccalaureate occupational programs to its students.

Relationship of the Two Systems

Cooperation between the two systems is an extremely important matter of public policy and is achieved in the following ways:

1. The president of the UW System Board of Regents serves on the VTAE board, and the president of the VTAE board serves on the board of regents.

2. The missions of the two systems differ in order to ensure the unique character of each post-secondary option for students. Chapter 36.31, Wisconsin Statutes, does not allow the UW System to add programs that offer training for semi-professional or skilled-trade occupations beyond those offered in 1972-73 without the approval of the VTAE board. The VTAE board, on the other hand, has no authority to expand its college parallel programs without the approval of the board of regents.

3. In addition to the distinct missions and limitation on the expansion of programs beyond those that existed at the time of the merger, three sections of the Wisconsin Statutes reinforce cooperation between the two systems:

   - Section 20.901[4] requires state agencies to cooperate in the exchange of information and in the "... performance and execution of state work. ..."

- Section 38.001[1] applies specifically to the VTAE system, and provides that the VTAE system will function "... cooperatively with other educational institutions ..."

- Section 38.12[8][b] states that the VTAE district boards "... shall actively coordinate ..." with the UW System "... in order to reduce the duplication of such programs and facilities." The reference is to "... collegiate transfer programs, adult education and evening courses, and part-time student and associate degree programs. ..."

4. Three standing committees were established by the two systems to ensure oversight of these mandates:[2]

- The Joint Administrative Committee on Academic Programs (JACAP). JACAP is charged with the responsibility of ensuring that programs "... being initiated by either system do not encroach on the other system."

- The Joint Administrative Committee on Continuing Education (JACCE). This committee reviews non-credit courses of each system in order to eliminate duplication.

- The Joint Administrative Committee on Physical Facilities (JACPF). This committee deals with "... possible common facilities use."

5. Councils for Inter-institutional Cooperation were established wherever VTAE and UW Center campuses located in the same community. They are charged with cooperating relative to programs, usage of facilities, and long-range planning.[3]

It would appear that structures are in place for cooperation between the VTAE system and UW System. In practice it does not work very well. These committees and councils are staffed by employees of the two systems. Members of the lay boards are not involved, which I see as a major weakness. There is no oversight of the discussions. In addition, the district institutions of the VTAE system have not agreed to be bound by these committees and councils.

Merger of the Wisconsin Public Universities[4]

Prior to October 1971, Wisconsin had two public systems of higher education: "University of Wisconsin" and "Wisconsin State Universities." The University of Wisconsin was created in 1848, the year Wisconsin became a state. The state constitution provided for "establishment of a state university at or near the seat of state government."[5] The University of Wisconsin consisted of the land-grant university at Madison, established in 1849, the University of Wisconsin-Milwaukee, established in 1956, UW-Green Bay and UW-Parkside, both established in 1969, 10 freshman-sophomore centers, and statewide Extension.

The Wisconsin State Universities System began in 1857, when state law established the Board of Regents of Normal Schools. In 1927, the normal schools were given authority to grant baccalaureate degrees in education, and they became State Teachers Colleges. Liberal arts programs were added in 1951, and Wisconsin State Colleges came into existence. In 1964, Wisconsin State Colleges became Wisconsin State Universities.

There had been proposals going back to the early part of the 1900s to merge all of Wisconsin's public higher education to be governed by a single board.[6] It was not until the adoption of Chapter 36, Wisconsin Statutes, which was signed into law on October 8, 1971, by Governor Patrick J. Lucey, that the two systems were finally merged, and two great institutions of public higher education became the University of Wisconsin System.

Merger legislation passed in the Senate by a vote of 17-16. The idea of a merger was hotly debated then and the debate continues. Institutions, not unlike individuals, resist change. When I became a member of the UW Board of Regents in 1984, I was told by some members of the UW-Madison faculty and administration that the merger threatened UW-Madison because its budget was part of the entire System's budget. Others, including Governor Lucey, told me the exact opposite. In a "showdown" between the former "University of Wisconsin" and "Wisconsin State Universities," the latter had more political clout and would have prevailed.

Milton E. Neshek, who served on the original UW System Board of Regents, believed merger was a necessity and that it would save state taxpayers "millions and possibly billions of dollars" in its first 20 years. Neshek said that, "The two systems were operating independent of one another. Each was negotiating and lobbying its own budget directly with the legislature. I also became very concerned when I saw plans and heard ideas of law schools, medical schools and so on being talked about for campuses all over the state. It became apparent to me that the state of Wisconsin could not afford it all. We needed centralized planning and better coordination. Merger was the answer."[7]

In 1986, 15 years after the merger legislation was signed, Kenneth Shaw was hired as the UW System president. The board instructed him to complete the merger. He was to make it clear that chancellors reported to the UW System president and he would speak to legislators and the governor for all of the campuses. I believe that the merger, as it related to the relationship between the System and campus administrations, was completed during Shaw's tenure. Two factors were involved in the merger's completion. First, Shaw made it clear to chancellors, with support of the board, that the organizational structure of the merger was to be respected. Second, many of the chancellors and top campus administrators, who had negative responses to merger, retired. Their replacements had no pre-merger experience and accepted the merger as a fait accompli.

Institutions within the UW System and Their Missions

There is general agreement that the merged systems reflect long-standing public policy that geographic access should be maximized by maintaining campuses throughout the state. There are now 27 campuses in the UW System:

- Two doctoral campuses, located in Madison and Milwaukee. UW-Madison is the home of the UW System's research and teaching hospital and the only medical and law school in the System. UW-Milwaukee has the state's only School of Architecture.

- Eleven "comprehensive" campuses, conferring baccalaureate degrees and some master's degrees, are located in Eau Claire, Green Bay, La Crosse, Oshkosh, Kenosha, Platteville, River Falls, Stevens Point, Menomonie (Stout), Superior, and Whitewater.

- UW Centers has 13 two-year freshmen-sophomore centers located in Baraboo, Rice Lake, Fond du Lac, Menasha, Manitowoc, Wausau, Marinette, Marshfield, Richland Center, Janesville, Sheboygan, West Bend, and Waukesha. UW Centers campuses award two-year associate degrees. The associate degree may become the terminal degree. Those with or without the degree may transfer credits to other System institutions. Transfer of credit is worked out through agreements reached with each campus, pursuant to a regent mandate that such transfers should be allowed, encouraged, and facilitated.

- UW Extension has offices in every county of the state, and on each campus in the UW System.

Mission Statements

Chapter 36.09[1][b] grants authority to the board after public hearings, to establish a mission statement for each institution "... delineating specific program responsibilities and types of degrees to be granted." There is no requirement that there be uniformity in mission statements.

Chapter 36.01[2], Wisconsin Statutes, provides that the mission of the UW System is threefold: instruction, research, and outreach through extension services. Chapter 36.01[1] states that "undergraduate teaching" shall be the "main priority" of the UW System.

It Is a Huge and Complicated System

Not only is the UW System complicated (made up of 27 institutions with differing missions, plus UW Extension with offices in every Wisconsin county), it is also huge in terms of budget size, number of employees, real estate holdings, and number of students.

Budget and Funding Sources

The breakdown of the UW System budgeted revenue sources for 1991-92 was:

State appropriations	34.92%
Federal appropriations	13.77%
Private gifts and trusts	7.12%
Academic student fees	14.82%
Auxiliary enterprises and services	14.25%
University Hospital and Clinics Revenue	10.88%
All other	4.24%
TOTAL	100.00%

The UW System budget for 1991-92 was $2,175,109,432.[8] There are two major misconceptions about the budget. First, since the media presents the budget as a total figure, little is understood about its components. That often leads the public to conclude that Wisconsin taxpayers contribute $2 billion-plus annually in support of the System. In fact, the state contributes about one-third of that total. Second, the state's share of the System's total budget has been declining over the years from 42.76% in 1981-82 to 34.92% in 1991-92.[9] For the period 1992-93, the state's share dropped further, to 34.2% of the total UW System budget.[10]

It is important to note that state appropriations are not evenly divided among campuses in proportion to their total budgets. For 1989-90 to 1991-92, state appropriations accounted for 27.78% of UW-Madison's budget. For 1991-1992, state appropriations constituted only 25.96% of UW-Madison's budget. The difference was made up in increased private gifts and grants: federal and private gifts and grants amounted to 27.17% of its budget.[11] Still, someone quipped that UW-Madison was not a state-supported institution, but a state assisted institution! (The state currently funds about two-thirds of the resident undergraduate instructional costs and none of the out-of-state undergraduate instructional costs.)

Federal grants and contracts plus private gifts amounted to 20.89% of revenues. This systemwide average did not accurately reflect the vast differences between campuses. UW-Madison accounted for 70.94% of the total, or $310 million, which made it the premier research institution in the System. The second largest single recipient of federal and private grants was UW-Milwaukee, with $26.6 million, or 6.07% of the System total. Each of the other campuses generated federal and private funds amounting to a low of

$4 million to a high of $11.5 million for the same time period. Auxiliary enterprises and services include student resident halls, student unions, and student athletic facilities, and are basically funded through user fees.

The UW-Madison Hospital and Clinics, considered to be among the top 25 teaching and research hospitals in the nation, produced revenues of $224.8 million. The state contributed a mere $2 million, an amount that had remained constant for many years. Despite its very minor contribution to the budget, the state maintained rigid control over the purchasing, compensation, and acquisition of facilities of the hospital. This has raised many concerns regarding operating efficiencies. At the time of this writing, a plan was being considered that would restructure the Hospital and Clinics so that there would be more flexibility in purchasing, compensation, and the acquisition of facilities.

Economic Contribution of the System to the State

While addressing the UW Board of Regents at its September 1991 meeting, then Acting System President Katharine Lyall said, "If the UW System were a private enterprise, we would rank 208th among the Fortune 500 — in Wisconsin, we would be the second largest enterprise. ..."[12]

The UW System has made an enormous economic contribution to the state of Wisconsin. In economic terms, the accepted multiplier used to determine how many dollars an enterprise brings into the state is 2.25.[13] For every non-state dollar the System brings into the state, there is a total spending increase of $2.25. Non-state revenues amounted to $1.4 billion for fiscal year 1991-92. Using a multiplier of 2.25, the UW System contributed about $3.3 billion dollars in spending increases in the state. In the private sector, we would hail that as a very good return on investment.

Real Estate

As of July 1990, the UW System owned 17,728 acres of land, 1,600 buildings of 42,189,133 gross square feet, with a replacement cost including contents of $5.9 billion.[14]

Employees[15]

The state uses FTE or full-time equivalents to count individuals employed by System institutions. For the 1990-91 fiscal year, the UW System had budgeted 27,778 full-time equivalent positions in the following categories:

Faculty	7,332
Other Unclassified	8,301
Classified	12,145
TOTAL	27,778

("Other unclassified" refers to non-faculty employees who are not part of the civil service system. "Classified" refers to civil service employees.)

Size of the Student Body[16]

Total fall semester student enrollment peaked at 164,518 in 1986. The Board of Regents' enrollment management policy reduced that number to 159,979 by 1990.

Purpose

The UW System's purpose is to carry out its three-part mission of instruction, research and outreach. Both Chapter 36, Wisconsin Statutes and board policy make it clear that quality is to be given precedence over access.[17] A strategic plan for the 1990s, "Planning the Future" was adopted by the board in 1986: "The major objective of the study was to find ways to ensure the continued quality of education in the System. ... When faced with a choice between maintaining educational quality or providing free-market access for students, the regents place priority on quality."[18] The board has been consistent in maintaining that access without quality is not a worthy goal. The challenge that faced the board while I served and the challenge that will face future boards is to put the study's findings into practice.

Governance Structure

Chapter 36, Wisconsin Statutes, the Administrative Code, regent policy statements and bylaws, and faculty, academic staff and student rules constitute the governance structure of the UW System and its institutions.

Chapter 36, Wisconsin Statutes

The basic document that set out the governance structure and purpose of the UW System is Chapter 36, Wisconsin Statutes. I was surprised that most board members, administrators, faculty, and media representatives did not understand the vast authority granted to the board in Chapter 36, Wisconsin Statutes.

Regents cannot fully carry out their responsibility, nor can campus and system administrators, faculty, and others relate meaningfully to regent action, unless Chapter 36, Wisconsin Statutes is understood. Chapter 36, Wisconsin Statutes established the order of responsibility for governance of the UW System. First, section 36.09[1][a] provided, "The *primary responsibility* for governance of the system shall be vested in the board [of regents] which shall enact policies and rules for governing the system, plan for the future needs of the state for university education, ensure the diversity of quality undergraduate programs while preserving the strength of the state's graduate training and research centers and promote the widest degree of institutional autonomy within the controlling limits of system-wide policies and priorities established by the board" (emphasis added).

To further strengthen the board, Chapter 36, Wisconsin Statutes was amended to provide that the board of regents be given the authority to close a campus. Section 36.09[1][g] had provided that the board could not "create nor discontinue any university or center unless specifically authorized by the legislature in each case." This section was repealed in 1987.

Next, section 36.09[2] provided that the president of the system "... shall be the president of *all the faculties* and shall be vested with the responsibility of administering the system *under board policies* ..." (emphasis added).

Next, section 36.09[3] described the role of the chancellors. "The chancellors shall be the executive heads of their respective faculties and institutions and shall be vested with the *responsibility of administering board policies under the coordinating direction of the president and be accountable and report to the president and the board. ... Subject to board policy* the chancellors of the institutions in consultation with their faculties shall be responsible for designing curricula and setting degree requirements; determining academic standards and establishing grading systems; defining and administering institutional standards for faculty peer evaluation and screening candidates for appointment, promotion and tenure ..." (emphasis added).

This was followed by section 36.09[4], which dealt with the faculty. "The faculty of each institution, *subject to the responsibilities and powers of the board, the president and the chancellor* of each institution, shall be vested with responsibility for the immediate governance of such institution and shall actively participate in institutional policy development. As such, the faculty shall have the primary responsibility for academic and education activities and faculty personnel matters" (emphasis added).

Section 36.09[5] detailed the role of the students. "The students of each institution or campus *subject to the responsibilities and powers of the board, the president, the chancellor and the faculty* shall be active participants in the immediate governance of and policy development of such institutions. As such, students shall have primary responsibility for the formulation and review of policies concerning student life, services and interests. Students in consultation with the chancellor and *subject to the final confirmation of the board* shall have the responsibility for the disposition of those student fees which constitute substantial support for campus student activities" (emphasis added).

Chapter 36, Wisconsin Statutes set up an understandable hierarchy of authority:

- The board is responsible to the legislature and through it to the citizens of Wisconsin.
- The president of the System is hired by the board and is responsible to the board.

- The chancellors are hired by the board and responsible to the System president and the board.
- The faculty is responsible to the chancellor, the System president, and the board.
- The students are responsible to the faculty, the chancellor, the System president and the board.

The UW System Board of Regents has been vested with primary and ultimate authority and responsibility. Others *derive* their authority from the board and remain subject to the control of the board. It follows that the board may revoke *delegated* authority, and it has done so from time to time. Chapter 36, Wisconsin Statutes emphasizes this point. For example: section 36.09 gives the board authority to:

- establish and discontinue educational programs;
- establish policies to ensure that programs are consistent with missions;
- establish missions of each campus;
- establish the type of degrees to be granted by each campus;
- appoint the president, chancellors, and deans of the Centers;
- establish the number of officers, faculty, academic staff, and other employees;
- delegate and rescind authority granted to chancellors, officers, faculty and students;
- allocate funds and adopt budgets;
- establish salaries for persons not in the classified (civil service) staff;
- sell or dispose of property;
- have concurrent police power with other authorized peace officers over all property within its jurisdiction;
- establish policies of admission and transfer of credits within the system or from other educational institutions outside the system;
- confer degrees, and
- grant sabbatical leaves.

Only section 36.13[1] limited the board's powers by providing that tenure may be granted "... by the board upon the affirmative recommendation of the appropriate chancellor and academic department or its functional equivalent within an institution." This has been interpreted to mean that the board may not grant tenure without the "affirmative recommendation" above referenced, but it is clear that the board may deny tenure. Further, in speaking of tenure, section 36.13[3] provided, "The board and its several faculties after consultation with appropriate students shall adopt rules for tenure and probationary appointments, for the review of faculty perform- ance and for the non retention and dismissal of faculty members. Such rules shall be adopted under ch.227 (Chapter 227, Wisconsin Statutes)." These rules are contained in the Administrative Code.

Tenure, hitherto considered to be hallowed ground, is now the subject of legislative action. Assembly Bill 561, introduced on October 17, 1991, was adopted by the legislature, and signed into law on March 6, 1992. It amended Chapter 36.13[1][b], Wisconsin Statutes and created 36.13[2][a] and 36.13[2][b]. It gives the board of regents authority to grant tenure *without* an affirmative recommendation of an appropriate academic department pro- vided the following is true: the negative recommendation is found to be based on impermissible factors, and there is an affirmative recommendation of an ad hoc committee, appointed at the institutional level and authorized to review the faculty member's record against the criteria for tenure published by the institution. Impermissible factors include constitutionally protected conduct, expressions, or beliefs; prohibited factors of state or federal law regarding fair employment practices; "ignoring available data that bears materially on the quality of performance, making unfounded, arbitrary or irrelevant assumptions of fact about work or conduct." Denying tenure because of race, gender, sexual preference, ethnic background, etc., is prohibited.

Despite the clear language of Chapter 36, Wisconsin Statutes, some administrators and faculty say the board oversteps its authority when it addresses issues such as academic and educational activities, and personnel matters. Yet with the exception of tenure and probation, it is torturing the language of Chapter 36, Wisconsin Statutes to argue that the board's authority is limited by or subject in any way to the consent of the administrators or faculty. This is a threshold issue, because any interpreta- tion that would limit the board's authority obviously could exempt administrators and faculty from complying with board policy. In Chapter 5, I will discuss how, in practice, this interpretation has constituted an obstacle to change. In Chapter 8, I will revisit the subject of tenure and faculty authority as related to the issues of change and the board's authority.

Administration

While the board hires the president of the UW System and the campus chancellors, on a day-to-day basis, the chancellors report to the president. In addition to the president, the UW System has two senior vice presidents (Academic Affairs and Administration), and three vice presidents: Business and Finance, Physical Development and Planning, and University Relations. These officers are responsible for administering Academic Affairs, the Undergraduate Teaching Improvement Council (UTIC), the Credit Transfer Project, Athletics (commissioners for men's and women's athletics), Financial Administration, the Controller's Office, Financial Reporting, Trust Funds, Internal Audit, Information Systems, Budget Planning, Preparation and Analysis, Equal Opportunity Programs and Policy Studies, General Counsel (legal staff), Human Resources, Employee Relations, Personnel Services, Payroll and Staff Benefits, Minority Affairs, Minority Information Center (MIC), Physical Planning and Development, Policy Analysis and Research, and University Relations. The 1991-92 UW System Administrative Directory lists 219 employees (classified and unclassified) at four locations in Madison. The Office of the Board of Regents has a staff of seven and is managed by the secretary to the board. Each of the System vice presidents and unit heads works directly with his or her counterparts on the various campuses and serve as staff to the regent committees.

The legislature amended Chapter 36, Wisconsin Statutes in 1987, giving the System president authority to hire vice presidents and taking that authority away from the board. The rationale was that since the vice presidents reported to the president, they should be hired by the president. This interpretation was based on a misunderstanding of how the board and System work. Vice presidents are the major staff of the board's standing committees. The board members are consulted by the System president in evaluating vice presidents' performances. In practice, therefore, the president hires the vice presidents only after conferring with the board.

At the campus level (including UW Centers), the chief executive officer is the chancellor. The chancellor's cabinet normally includes a vice chancellor for academic affairs and several associate or assistant vice chancellors responsible for student affairs, public relations, minority programs, etc. Course offerings are divided into departments, headed by a department chair, or a school, headed by a dean. UW-Madison, the largest campus, has four vice chancellors: Academic Affairs, Health Sciences, Administration, and Legal Services. These officers are hired by the chancellors after receiving authorization from the board.

Extension is also administered by a chancellor. There are two major divisions in the UW Extension: Cooperative Extension, with offices in every Wisconsin county, and Outreach and Continuing Education Services. In addition, Extension includes WHA Radio and Television, the Center for Instructional Support, Geological and Natural History Survey, Photo Media Center, the Wisconsin Survey Research Lab, and some conference centers.

Because chancellors are hired by the board and function with authority delegated to them by the board, regents may choose to serve on the chancellor's final selection committees for campus deans or department chairs. During my term on the board, I served on such committees for the selection of deans of schools of education and the Law School at UW-Madison. There had been discussion that regent bylaws should be amended to prohibit regents from serving on campus selection committees. I disagreed.

Such limitation on regent authority would give credence to the erroneous idea that Chapter 36, Wisconsin Statutes is not clear in establishing the governance structure of the System.[19]

Wisconsin Administrative Code[20]

"Wisconsin Administrative Code, Rules of the Board of Regents of the University of Wisconsin System" is a supplement to Chapter 36, Wisconsin Statutes. It covers such subjects as faculty and academic staff rules and appointments, procedures for dismissal, due process provisions, student academic and non-academic disciplinary procedures, and the use of university facilities.

Faculty Rules

Individual campus faculty governing bodies (senate) may create rules that are specific to their institutions. These rules are in addition to Chapter 36, Wisconsin Statutes and the Administrative Code. Board approval of Faculty Rules is required.[21]

Regent Policies

Regents adopt resolutions, which in turn become policies for System institutions. The *Regent Policy Book* may be obtained from the secretary of the board of regents. Regent policies cover such diverse subjects as: tenure review, undergraduate education, undergraduate transfer policy, remedial education, drop/add policy, administrative salary range, admission policy, enrollment management, equal employment opportunities, leaves of absence, minority/disadvantaged programs, mission statements, and competition with the private sector. Each institution is responsible for implementing regent policies in accordance with its campus missions.

Regent Bylaws

The regent bylaws provide the organizational outline for selection of officers of the board, terms held, and standing committees of the board: Education, Business and Finance, Physical Planning, and Personnel.

Academic Staff Governance

In 1985, Chapter 36, Wisconsin Statutes was amended to include section 36.09 [4m]. It provides that academic staff, subject to the "responsibilities and powers of the board, the president, and the chancellor and faculty of the institution, shall be active participants in the immediate governance of and policy development for the institution." This addition to Chapter 36, Wisconsin Statutes gives academic staff primary responsibility for policies that affect their particular assignments.

Regent Resolution 3359 directed each chancellor to implement participation of academic staff in campus governance. The Wisconsin Administrative

Code, Section 9.02, codified that fact. "Each chancellor shall provide for the establishment of a committee to advise the administration on policies and procedures for academic staff adopted by the institution. ..."

An example of the change this amendment made possible is at UW-Madison. In 1987, its academic staff adopted Articles of Organization in 1987, which were then affirmed by the Faculty Senate. *Academic Staff Governance, A Brief History, 1992,* reported that academic staff served as voting members on 20 committees that previously had included them only on an ex-officio basis.

Student Governance

Each campus has a student organization, governed by a senate, elected by students. Student governance includes responsibility for allocation of segregated fees — fees that are charged to students over and above tuition. Such fees pay for recreational sports, student centers, student health insurance, daycare, some tutorial services, special programming, and student organizations.

Chapter 36, Wisconsin Statutes included provisions for students to be appointed to campus search and screen committees.

In my opinion, student governance was limited by System President Shaw following a request made by the UW-Madison student government to the chancellor. It asked for a disclaimer to be included in all relevant campus publications stating that ROTC violated university policies prohibiting discrimination. The chancellor denied the group's request. The students appealed the chancellor's decision to the president of the System. He refused to hear the appeal on the grounds that in 1988, the students, faculty and chancellor defined "student life, services and interests" areas in which student governance has primary responsibility to include: registration and regulation of student organizations; non-academic social, cultural, and recreational programs for students; and those services that are initiated and operated by students.[22] This narrow definition of student life, as well as Shaw's adherence to it, was unfortunate.

How Much Time Does It Take to Be a Regent?

Regents volunteer their time. When asked, regents usually state that they spend 20-30 hours per month on board matters. That includes reading materials and attending briefings, committee and board meetings, and public hearings. Board meetings are held the first Thursday and Friday of each month.

What takes up so much time? The average monthly agenda and materials are several hundred pages long. To be prepared to participate in decision-making, the regents must read and understand those materials. Meeting materials include an agenda and backup information for the committees, as well as special reports for all regents to consider. Each committee meets for

3-6 hours the day before the board meeting. The full board meets the next day for 4-5 hours in open session, hearing and acting on committee reports; receiving reports from the president of the System, the Council of Trustees of the University Hospital and Clinics, the president of the VTAE board; and receiving special reports. Following the open session, the board recesses into closed session to discuss personnel and legal issues, as permitted by law. Including travel time, the days regents meet are fully occupied.

Officers of the board and committee chairs devote considerably more time. The regent president is called upon to represent the board at campus functions, to meet with the governor and legislature, and to meet with faculty, academic staff, and student leaders as well as the media, alumni, and friends of the UW System. In addition, the regent president and vice president meet with the System president and System officers before each monthly meeting. Regent committee chairs meet with System staff prior to the monthly meeting and approve the agendas for their committees.

III.

Regents' Mental Baggage
Makes a Difference

Conclusion #3: The attitudes, or "mental baggage," regents bring to governing have a profound effect on policy making. They need to be understood by those who nominate and confirm regents. While we may like to believe that we can approach issues that face the UW System in a purely objective way, we are all a reflection of our own mental attitudes — our "mental baggage." The process used to select regents needs to take into account the nominee's attitudes about education in Wisconsin.

I will examine governance from two points of view. In this chapter, I will discuss the importance of attitudes that regents bring to the table. Those attitudes influence policy. They are not given enough consideration during the selection process. In the next chapter, I will discuss governance in terms of regent authority and management practices.

Nomination, Confirmation, Indoctrination

My Experience: Some Initial Thoughts

Chapter 36, Wisconsin Statutes established the composition of the 17-member UW System Board of Regents. Fourteen members are nominated by the governor, two each year to serve seven-year terms, plus a student regent who is nominated for a two-year term. The Wisconsin Senate Education Committee holds hearings and makes its recommendation to the full senate, which confirms or rejects the nomination. The Superintendent of Public Instruction (the K-12 system) and the president of the board of the Vocational, Technical and Adult Education (VTAE) system also serve on the board by virtue of their offices.

The process used to select and educate regents is in need of improvement. The UW System is a public institution. The process needs to be meaningful. It needs to involve not only the governor, but the legislature, UW System Administration, faculty and staff, students, the media, and the public, as well as the nominee. Currently, only the governor seems to care who serves on the board of regents. All the others behave as though it makes no difference who serves. Here is where our mental baggage resurfaces. Clearly, the attitudes nominees bring to the board have an impact on the direction the System takes. Because of that, those attitudes ought to be known *before* confirmation takes place.

While I basically endorse Wisconsin's method for selecting regents, I believe there are some major improvements that can be made in how board members are selected and educated. I base this on my own experience as a regent.

My experience provides a model of how it should not be done. Here is how it unfolded for me. In February 1984, while my wife and I were on vacation, our son called to inform me that Governor Anthony S. Earl wanted to know if I would be interested in serving on the board of regents. I told him that I would be most anxious to serve. When I returned home, I met with the governor. He did not have a personal agenda for my appointment. His only concern was that I keep an open mind and bring my best judgment to bear on issues after hearing all sides. I told him that I was flattered by his intention to nominate me. He shook my hand and wished me well. The newspapers reported I had been nominated. Everyone else was silent. I was not contacted by anyone — not UW System Administration, campus administrators, faculty, or regents. Later, I learned that it was accepted practice not to interact with the nominee.

Confirmation by the senate was the next step. I did not want to attend my confirmation hearing without having some understanding of the major issues facing higher education in Wisconsin. I naively assumed that I would be asked about those issues by the Senate Education Committee. I called Bryant Kearl, then vice chancellor of UW-Madison, and asked him to brief me. When we met, he told me that the major issue facing the UW System was the ongoing conflict between quality and access as it related to funding. We discussed other issues and then, based on these discussions and reading I had done on my own, I prepared a three-ring note book divided into the following categories:

- My qualifications
- Quality vs. access
- Academic staff concerns
- Collective bargaining issues
- Compensation issues
- Conflict-of-interest issues
- Disclosure of faculty's outside income
- Duplication of departments vs. cost vs. access
- Faculty ethics code
- Fall semester startup
- Independence of the board of regents
- UW-Madison vs. other campuses — the merger issue

- Non-resident tuition exceptions
- My own priorities
- Payment of property tax
- Ph.D. nursing programs — unnecessary duplication?
- Sabbatical leave policy
- Adding a student regent to the board
- Pre- and post-tenure evaluation

Behind each divider I put newspaper articles, copies of pending legislation, pro and con arguments, and my own tentative conclusions. Just prior to the hearing, I visited with members of the Senate Education Committee to learn their concerns and interests.

I came to the hearing prepared to answer questions put to me by the committee. My recollection is that, with the exception of a question about faculty conflict of interest, I was not asked about the issues I had researched. I never opened the three-ring notebook. I was puzzled that no one had asked me about the important issues confronting the UW System. Nonetheless, I was glad to have been prepared. I knew a lot about the System before the first board meeting.

What's Wrong with the Current Process?

Chapter 15, Wisconsin Statutes is titled "Structure of the Executive Branch." Section 15.07 deals with boards. Section 15.07(1)(a) provided that, "If a department or independent agency is under the direction and supervision of a board, the members of the board, other than the members serving on the board because of holding another office or position, shall be *nominated* by the governor, and with the *advice and consent of the senate* appointed ..." (emphasis added). It is clear that the governor does not *appoint* the regents, but *nominates* them. The appointment is reserved for the senate. The senate is free, therefore, to reject nominees. After the hearings held by the Senate Education Committee, senate confirmation takes place and the nominee becomes an appointed regent.

What is wrong with the current process? There is an assumption that it doesn't make much difference who serves on the board. The only people who seem to care are the governor and the nominee. That is wrong for both legal and public policy reasons.

In my view, the senate should not confirm without knowing the nominee's views on important educational issues — issues that face the UW System, such as enrollment management, faculty compensation, retention policies, equity in hiring, recruitment of minorities, undergraduate education, and tuition policy. It is not realistic to assume that nominees have no attitudes nor "mental baggage,"or that they will approach these issues with a completely open mind.

What about the nominee who says at the hearings that he or she has not thought about the issues and has no opinion, but will keep an open mind. In my opinion that is either deceitful or mindless. Why should a nominee be confirmed who hasn't bothered to learn about the major issues? And if he or she had discussed them with those who can identify them, the nominee would obviously begin to think about solutions. But, perhaps, not unlike some federal judicial nominees, the nominee takes the position at the hearing that he or she has no views so that no one can be critical of him or her. The UW System is much too important to the citizens of Wisconsin, and serving on the board of regents is much too serious a responsibility to be treated this way.

The Senate Education Committee has not been careful enough in reviewing nominees. In 1991, the committee actually recommended a nominee for confirmation who did not appear at the public hearing. He was represented by his son and a friend. Not surprisingly, they attested to the nominees worthiness. The public never had an opportunity to hear the nominee's views. The public is entitled to know how the nominee feels about major issues confronting public higher education. And they are entitled to know *before* confirmation.

At the same time, public pressure forced the Senate Education Committee and the full senate to reject a nominee who did appear at the hearing. In this case, the nominee had made his views known through his own newsletter. There was publicly expressed opposition to the nomination by the media, faculty, and students. Those who favored or opposed the nomination were given an opportunity to be heard, and they spoke out at the hearing. The nominee was subjected to thorough questioning by members of the committee. The lesson here is obvious. The public, faculty, staff, and students can make a difference. If they do not participate, they should not complain later.

What about the role of UW System administrators? In my case, there was no contact from the System administration until after the senate confirmed me. UW System President Robert O'Neil called to congratulate me and asked to stop by my office. He arrived carrying several thousand pages of material, arranged in no special order, dropped them on my office coffee table and said, "You might want to look this over." To his surprise, I did. The pile included board minutes and regent policy papers. It was then that I decided, as I struggled through the disorganized pile of papers, that if I ever had the power, I would insist that all regent materials come three-hole punched, so that they could be organized in a notebook. When I became committee chair, I required that it be done. Progress comes slowly, even in small matters.

I asked O'Neil if he had played any role in the regent selection process. He said that he had not, but that the governor had called him, "as a matter of courtesy," before sending the nominee's name to the senate.

Now I was officially a regent of the UW System. Once again I was on my own to figure out how this system of higher education worked and what the major issues were. Frankly, it made me suspicious that administrators hoped I would remain confused. Since the overwhelming number of nominees are accepted by the senate, it would not be unreasonable for the UW System to assume that nominees will be confirmed. Therefore, they should play an active role with the nominee and the Senate Education Committee *before* confirmation hearings are held. Why?

Because most nominees know little about the state's network of educational institutions, about their missions, funding, quality and access issues, etc. I urge the UW System administration to contact nominees immediately after the nomination becomes public. The nominees should be offered as much help as possible. There should be meetings with the System president and vice presidents. Nominees should be given Chapter 36, Wisconsin Statutes as their most important guide in their work as regents. They should be briefed about the issues that confront UW System institutions and administration. In addition, UW System administrators ought to educate the Senate Education Committee so that its members understand the major issues confronting the System and will ask nominees relevant questions.

I don't understand the neutrality of faculty, staff, and students. They should also contact the nominees and explain their concerns. If they believe that the nominee will not be a positive influence on the System, they ought to appear at the confirmation hearing and speak out.

I also fault the nominees who take the position that they are yet too new to have an opinion on the major issues. UW System administrative offices can provide material for nominees to read and discuss with administrators, faculty, staff, students, and regents before their confirmation hearing. A packet would include:

- Chapter 36, Wisconsin Statutes
- Regent policy book (a summary of every regent policy)
- Administrative code
- Regent bylaws
- The most current *Fact Book for the University of Wisconsin System*

Even if none of these subjects is discussed at the hearings, the nominee will have a head start on understanding the System.

One last word. After confirmation and as part of the learning process, there is no substitute for visiting UW System campuses. This is an opportunity to meet with chancellors, faculty, academic staff, and students. I always came away impressed with the overall quality of the institutions and their leadership. I recall showing a UW-Madison faculty member the agricultural facilities of one of the campuses located about 100 miles from Madison. He was genuinely surprised — "I didn't know it was here. Why didn't somebody tell me." I was happy to point out that the UW System had *many* fine campuses.

What Difference Does It Make Who Serves as Regents?

I described the mental baggage I brought to the board and the inadequacy I felt existed in the nomination and confirmation process. Why? Because the existing process seemed to ignore the mental baggage that came with the nominees to the board. It was as though their attitudes about education made no difference. But those attitudes do make a difference. Our mindset as regents determines policy. And that, in turn, determines the kind of university system the state will maintain. If we are confirmed without a proper hearing, then it is too late. It is also too late to complain.

It Makes a Difference When Defining the Role of the Board

Board members have three unique roles: they are managers, advocates, and representatives of the public interest. First and foremost, the board must manage or govern the System pursuant to the authority granted by Chapter 36, Wisconsin Statutes. Earlier I said that policy creation, implementation, and control are what that authority means. When I began my term on the board, few of us fully understood our role in governance. Over the years there has been a slow change in attitude. While more members of the board do understand their role in governance, there remains a missing link. Making policy is only half of the job. Having that policy carried out is the other half. That is the missing link. Regents need to address the importance of implementation. The board has not developed any procedures to ensure institutional compliance with board policy. What is to be done when board policy is not carried out by those who have been assigned the responsibility to do so? There should be a mechanism for monitoring follow-through.

Regents are advocates and must not take on the role of regulators. What does this mean? At the time of this writing, recently confirmed regents are expressing the view that they ought to ensure that the university system does not seek *too* much of the state's total budget. They have failed to understand that monitoring the state's budget is not the task of the board of regents, but the responsibility of elected regulators, the executive and legislative branches of government. Citizens have placed the responsibility for balancing the various needs of the state in their care. It is not appropriate for regents to assume that they represent state government in apportioning state resources. *The charge to the board is to advocate for public higher education to the regulators while representing the broader public interest.* Of course, the board has to be concerned that the money the UW System has been allotted is well spent; that efficiencies are in place and monitored; and that decisions are made in a timely manner.

An example of my concern is a statement made by George K. Steil, Sr., in his speech accepting the board presidency in June 1992. "While we are assisted by the state, and I emphasize not supported by the state, nevertheless, we must be cognizant of other needs of the state of Wisconsin, and that higher education is not the *only* obligation of the State Treasurer." In my view, that confuses the role of the board with the role of the legislature and governor. As citizens of Wisconsin, everyone ought to consider the issue of fiscal priorities. But as regents, we agree to wear a different hat. We accept the responsibility for advancing the needs of public higher education as forcefully as possible. In the end, the governor and the legislature, not the board of regents, will order the state's priorities. "Being cognizant" of demands on the state treasury will not determine the needs of UW System institutions, whose well being is the responsibility of the board. As members of the governing body of the UW System, regents have to state clearly, to those who set the state's fiscal priorities, that if the goal is to have a public university with "X" number of students, "Y" number of programs, and if quality is to be maintained, then "Z" number of dollars are needed. If those dollars are not provided, then the options must be clearly defined, showing the pluses and minuses of each. That is the role of advocacy.

Regents need to understand that they are the *primary* advocates for the UW System. That includes advocating vigorously for:

- Fair compensation for faculty, staff, and administrators.
- Class section access for students.
- Affordable tuition.
- Quality laboratories and research facilities.
- A quality campus environment.
- Adequate state funds to provide educational opportunity to those who are prepared academically but cannot afford the cost.
- Quality education, research, and outreach at every level.

While the administrative professionals of the UW System present the case for public higher education to the governor, the legislature, and the public, unless the board members play an active role in publicly supporting their arguments and their convictions, the message will not be heard. Why is that? Board members have nothing to gain personally by advocating the needs of the System. They are involved because of their commitment to education, and they agree to volunteer their time to play a part in ensuring quality education. Because of that, they have credibility. In his address to the

UW Board of Regents on July 13, 1990, State Senator Robert Jauch urged us to see our primary responsibility as one of identifying the needs of the UW System and becoming advocates for those needs. "It is then up to the Legislature to determine the priorities of overall state spending,"[1] Jauch said.

Even though the governor nominates individuals to be regents, presumably because they are friends who have been politically supportive, once confirmed they must distance themselves from that office. Unless they do, they will not be able to act independently and in the best interest of the System. I do not believe that any governor expects a regent to "check" in with his or her office before every crucial vote. The state is best served when the board and the governor are independent of each other. This independence allows an unbiased dialogue to take place, and then where there are differences of opinion, so be it. In my own experience, there were issues where the governor who appointed me and I disagreed. Yet we reserved the right to be independent in our judgment, and our respect for each other was enhanced.

Advocacy also means sending the right signals to the board's constituents. The most important are the students. In discussing campus environment, I will comment on how harmful it can be when regents send the "wrong message" to students. When regents discuss tuition policy, they must keep the student in mind first and foremost. Obviously, if the students believe that regents are not their advocates, then they have a right to feel alienated. The same is true for faculty, academic staff, and administrators.

As the UW System advocates, regents need to be aware of their public voice. Incautious comments can cause great harm. Examples abound. During an open session, a regent said that voting for a particular resolution would precipitate a call "from the other end of State Street," meaning either from the governor's office or from legislative leaders. The implication here was that the opinion of those bodies had an impact on the direction the board should go. Bad message. Regents are supposed to exercise their independent judgment and not act as if they are the captives of political leaders. Other regents have said that the System should be run like a business without explaining what they meant. That, of course, brought expected snickers. What business did they have in mind? General Motors, with its unprecedented losses? Aren't we about education, not profits, etc.? The regents' roles as advocates will be undermined unless those within the System and the board speak with one voice when they address the public and the state's political leaders. Otherwise there will be chaos and everyone loses. Advocacy should be based on reasonable conclusions reached after considerable deliberations.

As an example of what I mean by "advocacy," consider undergraduate education. Historically, the state has paid approximately two-thirds of the instructional cost for resident undergraduate education, the balance coming from tuition. I see the role of the regents as advocating undergraduate education as follows:

1. First, identify those elements that will maintain and enhance quality instruction on each campus: quality of faculty, students, facilities, and campus environment.

2. Make certain that admission standards of each campus are in sync with campus graduation requirements.

3. Determine the number of in-state high school graduates who can meet admission standards.

4. Decide how many exceptions to those standards should be allowed and how campuses will deal with those exceptions in order to maximize student success.

5. Review and determine the faculty/student ratio without being bound by some "magic" number.

6. Adopt a budget that will provide a quality education for those admitted. That budget should include a tuition level that takes into account the economic circumstances of the citizens of the state as well as the availability of student aid programs, so that tuition never becomes the gate-keeper to admission. (Instructional costs for out-of-state students are not subsidized by the state.)

7. After adopting a tuition schedule, look to the state for the balance. Once determined, advocate for that balance as vigorously as possible with the governor, legislature, media, and public.

8. Be prepared to explain the alternatives that will be adopted if the requested amount of state funding is not forthcoming. Quality education is the goal and the regents must take that goal seriously.

These eight steps illustrate responsibilities that are a far cry from those who see their primary role as ensuring that the UW System does not spend too much of the state's resources. By abdication of their responsibilities to advocate and represent, regents avoid the responsibility of governance that is assigned to them in Chapter 36, Wisconsin Statutes.

After weighing the various demands made by all agencies on total state revenue, the governor and legislature make the decision as to how much of the state's revenues will be allocated to the UW System. In the process, the regents *must* be the advocates for the system because they are also the most credible.

Regents also represent the public interest. This means that the funds provided by the state and students through tuition and fees are used prudently and efficiently, and that there is accountability at every level.

It Makes a Difference When Determining Policy

In November 1991, a newspaper reporter asked for my views about the current board of regents, because it was more conservative than when I served. He wondered whether this was going to make any difference. I told him it was dangerous to generalize. I believed that words such as "conservative" and "liberal" were loaded. Yet it is true that one's views do make a difference in terms of "social issues," and social issues are the centerpiece of what regents are asked to consider in policy formation. Some examples.

Investment policy: Wisconsin law, as interpreted by the attorney general, prevents the UW System and its institutions from investing in South African companies because of Wisconsin's opposition to Apartheid. In 1991, members of the board suggested that the attorney general review the policy because of "reforms in South Africa."[2] The attorney general ruled that the policy would not be changed due to continued discrimination by the South African government.[3] This is a case where political views might make a difference. The board's query about whether or not the UW could begin investing in South Africa caused concern among minority students, who concluded that the board was more interested in return on investment than quality of campus environment.

Programs that enhance multicultural diversity: There has been a growing polarization of views around issues of equal opportunity. When "Design for Diversity," the regents' multifaceted plan to diversify the student body and faculty, was adopted by the board (April 7, 1988, by a vote of 12 to 5), the board felt its action could make a difference for students of color, women, and other disadvantaged groups. Some of us argued that universities have a special obligation to set an example for society, and that universities must be more tolerant and more caring than society at large. On the other hand, some argued that the only way to get ahead was through hard work. Those who didn't make it did not work hard enough and there was little the regents could do. After all, we live in an open society that provides equal opportunity for all, and there is no point in special programs. It follows from that point of view that programs such as Design for Diversity are "social engineering" and are not a responsibility of the university. Again, one's personal values affect board policy.

Student Conduct Code: The board's adoption of a change in the Student Conduct Code (UWS 17), later confirmed by the legislature, is a logical extension of Design for Diversity.[4] Initially, the majority of the board felt that speech demeaning and harassing minority students was not acceptable behavior by university students in an environment where everyone was entitled to an opportunity for an equal education. The board unanimously accepted the resolution on August 9, 1988, and the legislature confirmed. The District Court for the Eastern District of Wisconsin (Case No.: 90-C-328) ruled that the code was unconstitutional because it was too broad. The board countered by adopting a redraft that was believed to be responsive to the court's objections. It passed by a smaller margin than its predecessor, but passed, nonetheless, by a vote of 12 to 5 on June 9, 1989. There had been some concern that the more conservative board members would take the opposite view, but they did not. Finally, on September 11, 1992, the regents voted to repeal the revised code with a vote of 10 to 6. Of course it makes a difference who serves on the board.

ROTC: This issue is an excellent example of regents' attitudes making a difference in the position taken by the board.

What is the precedent for having ROTC in the UW System in the first place? The Morrill Act of 1862 established grants of land to be used for education through sale of the granted land or as a site for an educational institution. UW-Madison is the Land Grant institution in Wisconsin. Among the obligations articulated in the Morrill Act of 1862 is that the study of "military tactics" be included in the choices offered students. It is not essential, however, that ROTC be the means for satisfying this requirement, although that has become the custom.[5] Nine other UW System institutions offer ROTC programs even though they have no obligation to do so.

On the face of it, no one disagrees that ROTC discriminates against gay and lesbian students by denying them federal scholarships and commissions in the armed forces. It is clear that discrimination against students because of their sexual preference violates regent policy[6] and that state law makes such discrimination unlawful.[7] Nevertheless, the board debated the issue of ROTC's discrimination and held hearings to allow public debate.

The board could not bring itself to confront the issue head on, even though a faculty vote at UW-Madison held that ROTC should be discontinued. The furthest the board would go was to instruct the UW System president to do what he could to effect a change in policy at the Department of Defense.[8] Subsequent reports to the board indicated no progress. What will the view of the current board be?

Funding vs. quality: Some argue that individuals with a liberal bent cannot deal with this issue rationally, because they believe in open, unlimited access, unlimited funding, bloating the System, and threatening quality. I consider myself a "liberal," yet, on this fundamental issue, there does not appear to be any difference between "liberal" and "conservative" points of view. The cooperation between the liberal and conservative members of the board brought about a substantial reduction of the System's proposed 1991-93 biennial budget request before submission to the governor.

Tuition policy: Some regents believe that since a university education will produce greater lifetime income, it is worth the "investment," that investment being tuition. They tend to favor higher tuition than those who believe that tuition should not be the gatekeeper to admission. In other words, those with the money to pay get in and those without have the "privilege" of incurring huge debt. Regents, as a board, can help determine the cost of public higher education.

The Selection Process: Is There a Better Way?

The governing board of some state universities is elected by the citizens, or may even have the governor as a member. This approach tends to politicize the university. As much as possible, governing boards need to be free from political pressure so that they can base their decisions solely on what will preserve and enhance the quality of the institutions they govern. In Wisconsin, regents are nominated by the governor and confirmed by the senate.

For contrast, here is how California, Michigan, and Oklahoma select regents. The University of California (Berkeley, Davis, Irvine, Los Angeles, Riverside, San Diego, and San Francisco) is a constitutional university, created by Section 9, Article IX of California's constitution.[9] Its board has seven ex-officio members: the governor, lieutenant governor, speaker of the assembly, superintendent of public instruction, president and vice president of the Alumni Association, and president of the university, along with 18 additional members appointed by the governor and approved by a majority of the senate.[10] The appointed members serve 12-year terms and have full powers of "organization and government."[11] The bylaws describe the appointed regents as individuals who are "broadly reflective of the economic, cultural, and social diversity of [California], including ethnic minorities and women."[12] The governor is required to consult with an advisory committee made up of:

- the speaker of the assembly and two public members appointed by the speaker,
- the president pro tempore of the senate and two public members appointed by the Senate Rules Committee,
- two public members appointed by the governor,
- the chairman of the board of regents,
- an alumnus of the university chosen by the alumni association,
- a student chosen by the University of California Student Association,
- and a member of the faculty chosen by the academic senate.[13]

The president of the board is the governor; all other officers are elected by the board.[14] At the University of Michigan, also a constitutionally created university, the regents are elected by the public.

Of interest is an Oklahoma law, passed in 1990. It requires 15 clock hours of education, including two hours of ethics education for all new higher education board members appointed after January 1, 1991.[15] The education program is being worked out jointly by the State Regents for Higher Education and the attorney general. In addition, any would-be regent is required to complete the "Oklahoma 'Acid Test' for Considering Service as a Regent." Applicants are told to ask themselves whether they are prepared to:

- Commit 10-20 hours monthly.

- Take 15 hours of education about higher education in Oklahoma.

- Accept responsibility for the institution and accountability for the quality of its product, the fiscal and academic soundness of its operation, and its ethical values.

- Accept, understand, and comply with open meeting law, open record law, and ethics and nepotism laws.

- Disclose personal financial information.

- Balance the needs of students, faculty, administration, alumni, business, the institution, government, and the public and withstand pressure to deviate from that course.

- Support the president — with strength, not docility — becoming informed quickly and asking critical questions.

- Argue fiercely in board deliberations ... and then leave individual arguments behind to accept and support board action.

- Think of the office in terms of its responsibility before its honor.

Wisconsin would do well to adopt both the requirement of education as well as the Oklahoma Acid Test.

After my term on the board expired, I was asked by the executive director of The Association of University of Wisconsin Faculty (TAUWF) to write out what I believed would be essential criteria for board membership. My list follows. Regents must be willing to:

1. Spend 20-30 hours per month reading board agendas, student newspapers, a national publication, and correspondence; framing questions; drafting alternate resolutions; and lining up votes of support for positions.

2. Keep an open mind on controversial issues until all sides have been heard.

3. Travel in the state and accept speaking engagements to explain the system to the public and meet with faculty, staff, and student groups.

4. Ask tough and unpopular questions in order to get to the truth.

5. Realize that most public policy issues are more complicated than they may appear at first blush.

6. Attempt to uncover "hidden agendas."

7. Be sensitive to the needs of faculty, staff, students, and the public and balance the role of advocate for the System with advocate for the public.

8. Understand financial realities, and be willing to make the tough decisions necessary to preserve the quality of the System.

9. Withstand intimidation of chancellors, faculty, staff, or students when convinced of one's position.

10. Keep an active follow-up file of issues that are before the board, so that they do not slip between the cracks.

Earlier in this chapter, I said that I basically approved of Wisconsin's selection process. However, I am critical of the lack of interest and involvement of the Senate Education Committee, System Administration, faculty, academic staff, students, and the public. I hear very little criticism of this lack of involvement, although some are quick to complain that the board is becoming "too conservative." In another time, the complaint might have been that the board was becoming too "liberal."

Some criticize the process as being too political, i.e., the governor nominates his friends and supporters and those who share his own political philosophy, which is either too conservative or liberal, depending on who occupies the governor's office. Others criticize the composition of the board because it does not reflect the demographics of the state. For example, there are as many regents from La Crosse as there are from Madison, despite the disparity in the size of the communities and the campuses. Others are critical because there are too many lawyers and business people on the board and that is not reflective of the state's economic structure. Still others complain that there are not enough women and minorities on the board.

Some take a legislative approach to correcting apparent inequities in the process. Assembly Bill 1024, which would amend Chapter 15.91 and create Chapter 15.91[5][1], and 36.08, Wisconsin Statutes, introduced in March 1992, proposed that a board of regents nominating committee be created, similar to California's. The committee would include two state senators, two state representatives, and five members appointed by the governor, including a student member, a faculty member, and a UW System graduate. The public would be notified of vacancies on the board of regents and the committee would screen nominations, evaluate applicants, and submit at least three names to the governor for each vacancy. The governor would either nominate from the list submitted or tell the nominating committee why the nominations were unacceptable. If the latter took place, the nominating committee could resubmit those names or add new ones. Since the governor's appointees would dominate the committee, it is not clear that any substantial change would occur.

I view this as a change in form, not substance. Governors "get their way" not because of statutory authority but because of the inaction of others. The Senate Education Committee is not required to recommend for confirmation people who have not withstood the scrutiny of a public hearing as previously discussed, nor is the senate required to confirm every name it receives from the Senate Education Committee. Furthermore, those whose lives are directly affected by the regents (i.e., administrators, faculty, staff, and students) ought to let their views be known. Finally, the public should have a greater interest in who serves on the board. In a democracy, we truly get what we deserve.

The Attempt at Political Neutrality

The board prided itself on being politically neutral. I was told early on, by a veteran board member, "When we come through the boardroom door, we leave our partisan political loyalties outside." While at board meetings, regents rarely referred to the political party to which they belonged, everyone knew which governor had appointed them. When selecting committee chairs and vice chairs, thought was given to striking a balance between Republicans and Democrats. The same was true for electing a president and vice president of the board. It had been the practice of the board that if the president was a Democrat, then the vice president should be a Republican, and vice versa. In addition to reinforcing the board's non-partisanship, it made good sense, since it was important that both Democratic and Republican members of the legislature, as well as the governor, identify with board leadership. Since I was a member of the Democratic Party, and was nominated by a Democratic governor, my vice president, Paul Schilling, was a member of the Republican Party, and was nominated by a Republican governor.

When Schilling became president, Thomas Lyon, a Democrat, was elected vice president.

When Lyon became president, his vice president was Albert Nicholas, a Republican. As he reflected upon his first year in office, Regent President Lyon remarked at the board meeting of July 13, 1990, "A common theme of the Weinstein and Schilling presidencies was that the board of regents is nonpartisan in its deliberations and advocates what it collectively believes to be in the best interest of its shareholders — the citizens of Wisconsin and the users of its services — 160,000 students. That approach has served us very well, and I will do everything possible to maintain the working climate that I have inherited."[16] And so it went — until recently.

There has been a shift in this approach to non-partisanship. The balance has disappeared. At this writing, there are 13 Republicans and three Democrats who are appointed members of the board. Recently, some of my regent colleagues and I were understandably surprised to hear a newly appointed board member say publicly, "I don't want to offend the governor!" That was not considered good manners. The board is supposed to be concerned with what is good for the System, not what makes governors happy. What will happen to this former posture of political neutrality? At present, the president, vice president and all committee chairs are regents appointed by the sitting governor, and are all of the same political party.

IV.

Regents Must Understand and Exercise Their Authority

Conclusion #4: To move the battleship, or bring about change, regents must understand, accept, and carry out their unique role of governance as defined in Chapter 36, Wisconsin Statutes. In addition, the UW System and UW Board of Regents must have strong leaders who agree on and adopt short- and long-term goals and are willing to implement and vigorously monitor progress toward achievement of those goals.

In the previous chapter I discussed governance and its relationship to regent attitudes and the confirmation process. The attitudes that regents bring with them influence policy. In this chapter, I will discuss governance in terms of regent authority and management practices.

A major challenge that faced the board when I served (and will face the board in the future) was the challenge to recognize that the interpretation of regent authority, as defined by Chapter 36, Wisconsin Statutes, was not universally accepted by faculty and campus administrators. We will see in the following chapters how that lack of acceptance constituted a major obstacle to change, and can stand in the way of regent policy being implemented.

Who governs the University of Wisconsin System? If one were to ask that question of regents, administrators, or faculty, each would respond, "We do." Therein lies the problem. Each can argue its case. Regents will point to Chapter 36, Wisconsin Statutes; faculty know that regents come and go while faculty have tenure; administrators control the departmental budgets, and have the overall campus in mind as well as the expertise.

No organization can be governed effectively in this manner. There has to be an understandable and accepted governance structure with clearly defined lines of authority. While Chapter 36, Wisconsin Statutes clearly defines the UW System's governance structure, it is among the least read and adhered to documents.

Regents must address this issue if they are to govern effectively. An article in the December 1978 issue of *Wisconsin Ideas*, written by several former chairs of the UW-Madison (Faculty) University Committee, concluded: "Faculty governance, like shared governance in the larger view ... assumes that the successful operation and improvement of the university, and of academic activities in general, are a common interest shared by faculty and administrators, as well as by students and society at large. It follows from this assumption that rational investigation and discussion will ordinarily lead to agreement on most issues."[1]

No one would argue with that. Rational investigation and discussion are certainly the smoothest and most effective methods for instituting change. Even smoother would be for the board to adopt plans of action presented by System administration that come with the endorsement of the chancellors, faculty, staff, and students. It is always preferable, in both the private and public sector, for everyone who will be involved with implementation of change to have "bought in" and made the plan their own. That is the ideal. I discovered that finding the elusive consensus rarely happened in the UW System. By the time systemwide committees had finished their studies and made recommendations, what appeared to be consensus was often too bland to be effective.

Another problem facing the board was that the process the former chairs of the Faculty Committee considered acceptable was long and tedious. This ideal approach was often unresponsive to meeting needs. Those of us who came from the private sector wanted to move the decision-making process along at a faster pace. I heard more than one regent say privately that if the private sector took as long to make decisions as the UW System did, "We would go broke" — a reflection on my feelings about moving the "battleship." Citizens and political leaders have a right to expect the UW System to meet needs in a timely and responsive manner. The approach I am urging is that the board and System accept certain basic principles of management and adapt them to the needs of higher educational institutions. This is important because when it is perceived that the System administration or the institutions are not moving to meet the needs of the citizens, then the legislature, in response to public pressure, can move in and mandate change. At that point, the board of regents and System administration would clearly have lost control.

What Does It Mean to Govern (Manage)?

I've described my private sector experience in management and the lessons I learned. It is clear to me that these fundamental ideas are transferable to the management-governance of higher education. The lessons I learned come down to two fundamental ideas about effective management:

1. *The decision-making process must rely on an information system that identifies problems and opportunities in a timely manner.* Once problems and opportunites are identified, individuals can address them by considering various options, each subject to input from relevant sources, so that the pluses and minuses of each can be considered. Those who have the responsibility to manage must make decisions, and those who have the responsibility

to implement the decisions must do so. All of this must take place in a time frame that is responsive to the goals. While there may be dissatisfaction in some quarters with the decision, implementation must go forward. Throwing rocks at the decision cannot be tolerated. It is another form of chaos. No one will know whether the decision was right or wrong or should be adjusted or abandoned unless it is implemented. Everyone's business is no one's business. Responsibility without authority is chaos.

2.   Management decisions of regents are made in three steps:

[1.] *Set standards, goals, and policies.* Since management, in the private sector, has ultimate responsibility, it must set standards, establish goals, and formulate policies for the enterprise. This should not be delegated to others. The university is no different. It is important for regents to understand the basic conflict that surrounds the question: Who should govern? Chapter 36, Wisconsin Statutes provides the answer, although some disagree with its clear language. The regents have ultimate responsibility, ultimate accountability, and therefore, ultimate authority. Others have delegated authority. There can be little accountability to the public if the responsibility to govern is broken into little pieces with no one body exercising overall authority. When state government looks for accountability, it does not turn to the chancellors or faculty, but calls upon the regents and System administrators pursuant to Chapter 36, Wisconsin Statutes.

There is an old story told about the five-year-old child who had never spoken. Suddenly, at breakfast, the child said, "The cereal doesn't taste good." In absolute amazement, the parents asked the child why he had been silent for five years. The child responded, "Up until now, everything was OK."

In public higher education, everything is not O.K. If financial support had continued to increase year after year consistent with enrollment growth, the UW System might have been able to tolerate the view that every major decision had to be by consensus and that the faculty had what amounted to veto power over the board. But higher education has been facing tough times. Diminishing financial resources have already been stretched. If quality is to be maintained, the following issues need to be addressed from a systemwide point of view: decisions regarding enrollment size, tuition, admission standards, retention rates, administrative and faculty compensation, flexibility and efficiency issues, program duplication, campus missions, closing departments, schools, or campuses, quality of facilities, quality undergraduate education, campus environment, relationships between campuses, relationships between UW System and the VTAE, and the continuing role of Extension. This cannot possibly be done department by department, campus by campus, without creating total chaos. Systemwide strategic plans must be developed and implemented by the regents.

Within departments and schools, faculty still decide what courses to offer and how and who should teach them. They also handle the departmental budget and establish tenure tracks and admission and matriculation standards. But the faculty must understand that if they fail to carry out these functions, then the board has no recourse but to exercise its authority. Regents have primary responsibility for the quality of the UW System institutions. While they delegate to administrators and faculty, in the end the board is accountable for the outcome and must be prepared to take action under two general circumstances.

a) When the board determines that those to whom authority has been delegated have not acted in an appropriate manner.

b) When the board determines that certain initiatives must originate at the System level in order to ensure systemwide uniformity and applicability.

This need to act is sometimes misunderstood even by former board members. In a letter to the editor that appeared in the *Wisconsin State Journal*, June 21, 1992, Regent Emeritus Arthur De Bardeleben criticized Regent President George Steil: "His demonstrated interest is in attempting to support further Regent inroads into matters such as class size, educational and other academic programs, and tenure, for all of which, by force of Wisconsin statutes, the faculty have 'primary responsibility.'" De Bardeleben seems to equate "primary" with "exclusive," which is a misreading of Chapter 36, Wisconsin Statutes. I will detail in chapter VI that the board has acted when those charged with the responsibility fail to carry it out. That is not only proper, but essential to the governing process as contemplated in Chapter 36, Wisconsin Statutes. In my response to De Bardeleben (June 22, 1992), I pointed out that this "primary responsibility" of which he spoke, was "... subject to the responsibilities and powers of the board, the president and the chancellor of each institution."[2]

I carried Chapter 36, Wisconsin Statutes to every meeting of the board. My views of regent authority were well-known, and I stated them on more than one occasion. When I met with System President Shaw on June 13, 1986, following my election as president of the board, I discussed the need to deal with the issues of shared governance and regent policy-making authority. Curiously enough, only rarely did anyone say to me, "Wait a minute. You have it all wrong. You don't understand shared governance." However, I did encounter faculty members and administrators who did not believe they were obligated to carry out regent mandates.

[2.] *Implement.* The standards, goals, and policies are implemented by assigning responsibility to appropriate individuals. Sometimes those who have the responsibility to implement board policy do so half-heartedly or not at all. There should be some consequence when board directives are not carried out. The implementation process occurs, ideally, when the goals, standards, policies, etc, are:

a) clearly understood,

b) accepted by those who will implement them,

c) subject to an established timetable for implementing them, and

d) specifically assigned to those who will be given the responsibility to carry them out, in order to avoid "buck passing."

The merging of Wisconsin's two former systems of public higher education was meant to put a stop to in-fighting that had gone on between institutions and had the attention of the legislature. The newly merged system was to speak with one voice. The board of regents was given vast governing authority so that public higher education could be offered to the citizens of the state in the most efficient and effective manner while maintaining quality. Debating proposed policies is healthy for an organization. But at some point, the debate must end and the policy must be implemented.

[3.] *Control.* Results will not occur unless there are control mechanisms in place that measure achievement against established standards, goals, or policies. Timeliness is of great importance. Through regular follow-up reports a determination can be made whether or not goals, standards, etc., are being met and what is being done to meet them. There has been ongoing discussion about cutting back on the number of reports the regents receive from the System as an attempt to "be more efficient." I would caution the regents to be very careful in making changes in this area. It is only through reports that progress being made in carrying out regent policy can be monitored.

I heard it said many times that "universities are not like a business. They are different." There were those who sincerely believed that we "outsiders" could not possibly understand the culture of governance in a university. While I understand the difference in purposes, one being an educational, research, and outreach enterprise and the other for making a profit, I do not buy into the idea that the function of management is different. As a regent, I did not believe that managing a university was so mystical that we "outsiders" could not understand it. What I experienced was a lack of appreciation of well-established management principles — Principles that have proven track records.

I know that this view of governance offends some. However, I am convinced that the principles enunciated here are correct. I am aware of the tradition of "shared governance." As perceived by some it gives the faculty super authority.

Michael H. Walsh, former chairman and chief executive officer of Union Pacific Railroad, served as a trustee of Stanford and Creighton universities. He raised the basic question whether leaders in higher education have the "right stuff" to manage change.[3] "All of our institutions (private or public) are dealing with only one constant and that constant is change," he said. His advice and thoughts apply to academic administrators as well as to regents/trustees:

- Focus on what matters — not the politics and internal lines of authority.

- Push responsibility down.

- Communicate. Talk straight and openly, and let people know what is going on and why.

- Focus on getting it done, on results.

- Recognize that whether you are in a business or a university, the organization frequently conspires to defeat you ...

- Recognize that you manage better if you measure better.

- Be aware that some academics are suspicious, even contemptuous, of anything that smacks of management or administration. ...

Walsh wonders "if higher education leaders, absent crisis, have the skill and the will to mobilize a complacent academic community. I worry about whether the means and mechanisms universities employ are up to the task if we all fall too easily into the shopworn explanations of why universities are somehow different or unique."

Sometimes those who say that those of us in the private sector do not understand the difference between a business and a university cleverly shift the argument by asking whether those with a "conservative mindset" would like the university to be run like the "collapsing domestic auto companies."[4] In my view, labels such as "conservative" or "liberal" are relatively useless when considering issues of governance. What needs to be addressed is the issue of maintaining quality in light of funding realities. The management mindset that Walsh writes about, or the three elements of management that I have discussed, are absolutely essential if the university is to respond to changing circumstances and manage its affairs. It is in that context that universities must be managed like a business. In addition, unless regents understand their authority and exercise it, the System will be in trouble and the public will be badly served. If Regents do not ensure that the three principals of setting goals, implementing them, and controlling them are in place, then their policies will be held hostage to institutional obstacles to change. In at least five instances that I can recall, regent policy was only partially implemented because System administration did not adequately implement those policies at the campus level or follow up so that there was a control process in place to monitor progress. Regent policies that do not follow the three-step process are no more than a wish list.

It is important to point out that by no means is every faculty member interested in being involved in governance issues. Some are critical of those who are active in faculty senates and suggest that they should devote their time to education, research, and outreach. Others have left the private sector in order to get away from administrative chores. One said, "I have 1,500 square feet. I control what goes on inside, who I hire, I raise the research money, and I am my own boss. I left the private sector because I wanted my own shop and did not want to be involved in a bunch of committees."

Seven Principles that Make Change Possible

1. Hire a strong System president.

The board must select a System president who is willing to carry out regent policy, even when that policy is unpopular. Consensus building in any organization is better than a whip. But there has to be a timetable for action, or the opportunities for change will pass. The president must also convey a sense of urgency about policy implementation.

This individual must have a vision of what the System should look like five, 10 years hence, and be able to "sell" that vision to the board. The System's strategic plan must reflect that vision. To the extent that faculty and campus administrators "buy into" the plan, so much the better. However, the plan must be adopted and supported by the board or there will be no progress toward achievement.

The board's support is required to empower the System president. An example of bringing vision and planning together was Shaw's commitment to have merger solidly implemented with everyone singing from the same hymnal. He accepted the empowerment of the board and assumed a strong leadership posture with campus administrators and legislative and executive branches of government. During his interview for the System presidency, Shaw was asked what he would do if the chancellors did not sing from the same hymnal. "I will take away their hymnals," he responded. That made a strong and positive impression on the board.

2. Elect a strong board president.

Regents should carefully select their leader since the president of the board *must* play an active role in developing the agenda for the System. To be successful, the agenda must be one that can be agreed upon by the regent vice president, the System president, and the regent committee chairs. When the president's term is up, it is important for all players to agree that the term in office made a difference. An example of what I mean comes from an exchange I had with Regent Herbert Grover, superintendent of public instruction. I vividly recall soliciting votes from regents after I announced my candidacy for the office of president. I spoke to Grover, for whom I had and continue to have great respect. He had served as president of the board some years before. He asked me, "Do you want to be satisfied to eat shrimp or do you want to get something done? When your presidency is over do you want to look back at the accomplishments or count the number of times you were called 'Regent.' " That was blunt enough to make a point I already agreed with. Leaders need goals to be effective. I had a list of goals I hoped would be accomplished during my term. I discussed them with Paul Schilling, the board's vice president. We agreed on the goals. We then met with the System president and asked him for his goals. Once we all agreed, that shared list became our target for the year.

The agenda: The next step was to assign each goal to a regent standing committee. Among my innovations in support of change was an agenda for each committee that showed the items requiring action and the date for completion of the task. As changes took place, the agendas were updated by the regent secretary. Committee agendas contributed to steady, forward movement.

The president of the board should be willing to devote the time necessary to contribute to the vision and help interpret that vision to the public, legislators, governor, media, and other regents. At the same time, the president of the board must understand the thinking (mental baggage) of the board to advise the System president where changes in specific plans need to be made in order to garner enough votes for passage. The board president must meet with faculty, staff, and student governance groups to receive input from them as well as to interpret board actions. It's a time-consuming job. The time devoted is absolutely essential to the process. During my term as president, Board Vice President Schilling and I were in contact not only weekly, but often daily. We met with the System president on a regular basis. It was a wonderful and productive relationship.

Committee Appointments: Schilling and I agreed on the makeup of committees as well as who we would ask to serve as chairs. Before appointing them, we met with each and reviewed our agendas for that committee. We wanted to make sure that the regent committee chairs were "on board." We appointed Regent Grover, superintendent of public instruction and a non-appointed member of the board, chair of the Education Committee. That appointment met with controversy and raised eyebrows. In previous years, he had been pushed aside. Our thinking was that since he was the superintendent of the Department of Public Instruction [DPI] and was responsible for the K-12 system, he was a logical choice to chair the committee. System teacher training programs prepared future Wisconsin teachers and were of concern to him. In addition, graduates from Wisconsin's elementary and secondary schools ultimately became students in the UW System. It was a great choice. As a result, the UW System and DPI worked more closely together than ever before. All committee assignments would have an impact on what kind of results we were going to have.

3.　**Conduct regular evaluations of those charged with the responsibility to implement regent policies.**

These evaluations of chancellors and System officers should include a detailed report of progress made in carrying out regent policies. There should be rewards for success as well as punitive action for those who do not comply. Regents are in control of compensation for that group of executives, who serve at their pleasure, and should feel free to make that power felt.

4.　**Don't "knock" systemwide committees.**

Just make sure they produce a report that is helpful in formulating policy. Systemwide committees draw representatives from all campuses. While their deliberations may seem endless and their conclusion nebulas, these committees can serve as a way of getting people to "buy in." In order for systemwide committees to be effective, however, regents should instruct them to include in their reports suggestions for fixing responsibility, time tables for completion, and proposed follow-ups for tracking progress. When they are not included it should be understood that either the System or the board *will* add them.

5.　**Nine votes carry the day.**

There will be times when only the board can make a decision. There may be a stronger sense of urgency and accountability by the board than by others. The board may decide that it cannot wait any longer for a consensus to evolve at the System level, and nine votes at a board meeting will pass any resolution. Those regents who feel strongly about an issue should deal with that reality. Getting out the vote is a perfectly respectable way to govern. Schilling and I understood that basic principle, and did not hesitate to divide up the list, make telephone calls, and line up votes.

6.　**Encourage innovative approaches to old problems and challenge old assumptions.**

7.　**Anticipate that there will be objections. Find out in advance what they will be.**

Objections will be discussed in some detail in the next two chapters. For our purposes here, it is useful to remember that public hearings are the usual format used to get input from faculty and others. While this is an appropriate mandated forum in a public university, it should not be the only method used. Often those who appear represent only themselves. To compensate for this, small groups of regents should meet with faculty, staff and student leaders, and chancellors. This is likely to allow for a more honest exchange of views.

V.

Regents Must Recognize Internal and External Obstacles to Change

Conclusion #5: In order to move the battleship, or bring about change, regents must recognize and deal with the internal and external obstacles to change.

I have been comparing the UW System to a battleship at rest. Effecting change was about as easy as moving a battleship with one's bare hands. Yet experience has shown that it can be done quite effectively — changing the System, that is, not moving a battleship. In order to effect change there must be strong leadership at the System and regent levels, and a resolve on the part of the regents to carry out their unique roles of governance and advocacy. In addition, regents must understand the obstacles that exist inside and outside the System. Their statutory responsibility is to formulate policy that will bring about needed change in order to preserve quality.

Obstacles to Change

In this chapter, I will identify the obstacles that stand in the way of change as I encountered them. For if change is to occur, those obstacles must be identified and overcome. The next chapter will provide examples from my own experience on the board to indicate that when the regents understand and exercise their authority, these obstacles can be overcome.

One might expect that scholars would welcome change, since the very nature of research is to forge new frontiers. I found the opposite to be true. Faculty and administrators were generally comfortable with the way things were. There appeared to be acceptance when change came from their ranks. However, they resisted change when it was initiated by the System administration or the regents. They saw for themselves a much greater role in governance than Chapter 36, Wisconsin Statutes conferred on them. Regents, also, resisted some changes. Political leaders also resisted change. They criticized regents for not being more "take charge" on the one hand, but would not give the System more flexibility or incentives to be efficient on the other.

Conflicting Views of Governance

Faculty, administrators, and regents hold vastly differing views of governance. Chapter 36, Wisconsin Statutes clearly gave the board ultimate authority to make policy and set the course for the System. That includes initiating change in order to improve or maintain quality.

What regents called policy, some attacked as "micro managing." If one adopted the view that regents, administrators, and faculty are involved in an equal partnership, with responsibility diffused, then the results are predictable: Regents can adopt policies that mandate certain needed changes, but faculty and administrators may feel free to ignore the mandated policy or the timetable set for implementation and evaluation. Regents need to understand the tension this conflict over governance creates and be willing to deal with it.

An article referred to earlier, authored by several former UW-Madison university committee chairs, discussed the meaning of faculty governance from their perspective. They define faculty governance "... [as] a process of joint decision-making by faculty, administrators, students, and the regents (representing the public), resting on the assumption that the strength of the university lies fundamentally in its faculty." Faculty "... are the people best qualified to chart the educational course of the institution."[1] John J. Corson acknowledged this tension as a dilemma.[2] "On the one hand, it is generally contended that trustees/regents bear the ultimate and full responsibility for the performance of their institutions. Simultaneously, faculties and presidents usually contend that trustees are not competent to make decisions as to admissions, faculty hiring and promotion, or what programs and courses shall be offered."

To be sure, not all faculty members agree on what might be termed the "proper" role of the faculty in governance. I have spent considerable time discussing with faculty their differing views. Some said that if a faculty member becomes involved in doing research, teaching, and service obligations, they will not have time to spend with administrative details and should leave that to others. Some said that those who get involved in administrative details were not adequately discharging their primary obligations of teaching, research, and outreach. And still others have said in so many words, "Why don't you get rid of faculty governance." I was told recently by a faculty member that the best form of governance for a university is a "benign dictatorship." So we have faculty arguing among themselves about their "proper" role in governance. The board of regents has a clear definition in Chapter 36, Wisconsin Statutes of their responsibilities to govern. I believe that there are two general circumstances where the board must exercise its authority:

1. when the regents determine that faculty or administrators have not acted in a timely manner in carrying out the authority delegated to them, and

2. when the regents determine that certain policy decisions are best made at the System level so that there is uniformity among the various institutions.

Examples applicable to the above two circumstances are provided in the next chapter.

Tenure

Tenure can constitute a substantial obstacle to change. The Wisconsin Administrative Code section UWS 3.01(a) defines tenure as "... an appointment for an unlimited period granted to a ranked faculty member." Tenure is granted by the board of regents "... upon the affirmative recommendation of the appropriate academic department ... and the chancellor ..." There are two criteria for dismissal, "just cause" and "financial emergency."

Tenure is regarded as a lifetime appointment. Rarely are tenured faculty members dismissed. I know of no case where refusal to carry out regent policy resulted in the termination of tenure. During my term on the board, I don't recall the issue even being raised. According to section 4.01(1) of the code, dismissal of a tenured faculty member may only be by the board for "just cause" and after "due notice and hearing." "Just cause" is not defined in the code. The burden of proof is on the administration.

The other criteria for dismissal of a tenured faculty member is in the event of "financial emergency."[3] Financial emergency can be declared by the board only if the board concludes that all of the following exist:

> The total general program operations budget of the institution, excluding adjustments for salary/wage increases and for inflationary impact on non salary budgets, has been reduced; Institutional operation within this reduced budget requires a reduction in the number of faculty positions such that tenured faculty must be laid off. ... Such a reduction in faculty positions shall be deemed required only if in the board's judgement it will have an effect substantially less detrimental to the institution's ability to fulfill its mission than would other forms of budgetary curtailment available to the institution. ...

None of this can take place until there has been consultation with the faculty in the search for other ways to find budgetary reductions, including which departments or schools should be eliminated. Then due process must take place for the faculty members affected.

Without declaring a "financial emergency," it is nearly impossible for one department to have the number of tenured faculty reduced while another is expanded in response to changing needs. The major organizational disadvantage here is departments can become entrenched with tenured members. This limits the institution's ability to move positions from departments where demand may be low to those with greater need. Changes, therefore, have to await the retirement of tenured faculty. For this reason, it is also difficult to eliminate duplicate programs.

If Chapter 36, Wisconsin Statutes is clear (and I believe it is) that faculty and administrators are duty-bound to carry out regent policy, whether they agree with that policy or not, then how can the board and System administration ignore those who do not, even if they are tenured?

Faculty and Political Realities

I never have understood the insensitivity of some members of the faculty to the power the legislature has over the UW System. The legislature not only approves the System's biennial budget and sends it to the governor for signature, but can amend Chapter 36, Wisconsin Statutes to the detriment of the System.

Legislative mandates arise out of pressure from members of the legislature to correct what they perceive to be flaws in the System. Some legislative action is prompted by pressure from constituents. When legislative pressure was directed at the UW System, it was not unusual for the legislature to first offer the System an opportunity to respond in defense. It seemed incredible that members of the faculty were not willing to be serious about accepting that challenge. It was as if they were daring the legislature to take action.

Two examples illustrate the point:

The Ethics Code

Some members of the legislature were concerned about possible conflict of interest when faculty engaged in outside consulting, and that outside consulting might demand too much time, taking faculty away from their students. I recall that outside consulting was the only concern expressed to me by legislators during my confirmation hearing in 1984. System administrators and faculty failed to respond to legislative concern. They claimed there was no problem. Soon after, a bill was introduced in the Wisconsin legislature that would have required detailed reporting by the faculty of their outside consulting activities, identification of the company for which the consulting was done, the number of hours spent, and the amount of compensation received. An immediate howl was heard from the faculty. They argued that this requirement would make it difficult to attract private research funds and would make the UW System noncompetitive with peers.

I, along with some other regents, "went to bat" for the faculty and were successful in working out a substantially watered-down law. What happened? The Wisconsin Legislative Audit Bureau (LAB) found, to everyone's chagrin, that many members of the faculty did not comply. Now what? No action was taken against those who did not comply, although their actions reinforced the mindset of many legislators that the university could not be trusted. In the end, that perception cost the System in terms of credibility and, no doubt, dollars. The renewed desire among some legislators to require much more detailed reporting could have been predicted. My own view was that the regents should not get involved again and should let the legislature settle the matter.

Transferring Credits from One Institution to Another within the System

Legislators, parents, and students complained that credits earned in one System institution were not being recognized uniformly by other System institutions. It was not easy to explain. We were, after all, one System. The various faculties argued that governance gave them the right to determine admission standards, and, therefore, only they should judge the value of credits earned in other System institutions. This resulted in a lack of uniformity and confusion on the part of students.

In some states where this issue had been raised, legislatures had mandated that all credits earned in one institution be transferred for full value to any other institution within the same system. We warned campus administrators that unless faculty would deal with this issue, the legislature would. Faculty did not want to respond. Their position was that each institution would continue to establish its own admission criteria — period — and that the regents ought to protect the UW System from such bad legislation and preserve the status quo. In order to ward off a legislative mandate, regents faced political reality and took action because the faculty would not. The result was a uniform transfer policy designed by the board.

Faculty Objection to Raising Admission Standards

This is an example of faculty not taking action in areas they insist they govern, yet, because no action is taken, they leave a vacuum for others to fill. It was obvious that the regents were serious about the need to raise System minimum admission standards. The faculty would not move. The regents did, and to this day faculty complain that the board interfered in an area reserved exclusively for them. Yet all agree that since the admission standards were raised, retention rates have improved — an achievement that has improved the quality of the student body.

Discrimination Against Women and Minorities in the Granting of Tenure

The board was aware of allegations and lawsuits leveled at the System based on discrimination against minorities and women in the awarding of tenure. In order to understand where the problem was, we asked for data showing the number of women and minorities in the national Ph.D. pool. and compared it with new hires by System institutions. This data, as well as the reports discussed in open and closed sessions, raised further concern about possible discrimination in awarding tenure.

On September 8, 1991, in a "Special Report," the *Wisconsin State Journal* reprinted statistics received from UW-Madison, which showed that in 1980, women held 10.9% of the tenured faculty positions at UW-Madison. By 1990, 10 years later, 14.9% of the tenured faculty were women. The caption on the data read: "Small gains for women at UW-Madison."[4] The reporter concluded, "Those improvements mask a more troubling pattern of female faculty members departing the UW in waves. Since 1981 the UW has hired 1,281 female faculty members, according to the UW System report. But during the same time, 966 women have left the UW System."

The *Milwaukee Journal* reported on September 4, 1991, "Deep-rooted sex bias prevents many women faculty at the University of Wisconsin from climbing the academic ladder, according to the state chapter of the National Organization of Women."[5] In an editorial, dated September 13, 1991, Madison's *Capital Times* called for reform in the tenure path. In an editorial dated September 15, 1991, the *Wisconsin State Journal* called for:

- tenure equity and a standardization of tenure-granting procedures in all UW-Madison departments and schools,

- stopping the tenure clock when a faculty member takes maternity leave, and

- the support of pending legislation that would allow regents to grant tenure where discrimination was shown to exist.

Adding to regent concerns was the report on October 31, 1991, that Ceil Pillsbury, a former assistant professor at UW-Milwaukee's School of Business, was planning to file a federal lawsuit alleging that she was illegally denied tenure because of sex discrimination.[6] As of this writing, the U.S. Department of Labor has ordered that Ceil Pillsbury be reinstated with tenure.

In March 1992, the LAB published its report on UW-Milwaukee's affirmative action record.[7] In the transmittal letter to the Joint Legislative Audit Committee, the state auditor wrote, "UW-Milwaukee has been unsuccessful in establishing and managing effective procedures to investigate and resolve complaints of harassment and discrimination on campus." It concluded that some serious complaints had not been investigated. For example, a female faculty member filed a complaint. No action was taken. She won her federal lawsuit against the university and was awarded $291,200. While campus rules required that investigations be done within 90 days, the average was 198 days. Even though female and minority faculty members left the university at rates greater than males and non-minorities, there had been no attempt to determine the reasons and statistics available at the university had not been assembled. The LAB recommended that the System inaugurate a regular schedule of monitoring to ensure campus compliance with regent policies.

I met with the UW-Madison faculty executive committee on this issue in early 1991. (The faculty is governed by a faculty senate, composed of delegates from various departments and schools. The executive committee of the faculty senate is the faculty committee.) During the meeting I asked what was being done to implement regent policies on gender equity, namely, the hiring of women faculty. To my surprise and shock, I was told that the committee was preparing a resolution to bring to the faculty senate that would endorse the concept of gender equity. I said that such a resolution was irrelevant, since the System already had such a policy from the board. What was needed was implementation — action — not more words.

What makes the situation even worse is how discriminatory lawsuits have been resolved. In Wisconsin, cases involving public higher education are handled by the attorney general. If a suit is lost, money damages are paid by Wisconsin tax payers. The faculty or the department that engaged in the discriminatory behavior are not held accountable in any way. Neither System administration nor the board of regents was willing to take action beyond producing and receiving reports and urging departments to "get their act together." No disciplinary action was recommended or taken.

In March 1992 the governor signed into law a bill that gave the board authority to grant tenure when it found that tenure was denied because of impermissible reasons, such as discrimination based on race or gender.

Stonewalling Regent Decisions

Many will argue that the use of the word "stonewalling" is too strong and unfair, because what is really taking place is an honest difference of opinion. We shall see. When there is disagreement with regent policy and there is no desire to carry it out, it is simply not carried out. Stonewalling differs from the response that invokes concepts of shared governance to explain inaction. Stonewallers recognize the existence of the policy, but talk it to death while doing nothing to implement it. It is another way of preserving the status quo. Stonewalling has the trappings of a highly intellectual discussion, but the discussion's purpose is to ignore the policy. And since there is no precedent for disciplining those who ignore regent policy, there is no great disincentive not to stonewall.

The response of some faculty to Design for Diversity, the regents' multifaceted plan to diversify the student body and the faculty, is a classic case study of stonewalling. The stonewallers developed a tortured argument that such plans threatened academic quality. Assume, for the moment, that their argument was valid. They, nonetheless, disregarded entirely the fact that the regents, by law, had the authority to enact such policies, and by law, the faculty was obligated to carry those policies out. They seemed unable to reconcile themselves to the fact that the debate was over and action should begin. The continuation of the debate over the merits was a way to obstruct action or compliance. This behavior should not have been tolerated. In Chapter VIII, I will propose some ways the board might deal with noncompliance with regent policy.

What follows is stonewalling as it was applied to Design for Diversity:

Allegation: The Wisconsin Association of Scholars attacked policies they believed were inspired by the "Politically Correct" (PC) agenda of radical-liberal faculty and administrators. Those who disagreed with the policies would suffer at the hands of "thought police."

Response: Wasn't it absurd for tenured faculty, who had lifetime appointments as well as the specific protection of the Wisconsin Administrative Code[8] regarding one's views, to allege that there was a system of thought police that prevented them from disagreeing with board policy? However, disagreement and inaction are not the same.

Allegation: These policies endangered educational quality because they established quotas and mandated the hiring of faculty based on gender, ethnicity, or race rather than academic qualifications.

Response: A fair reading of Design for Diversity made it clear that there were goals, not quotas. One must understand the context of these goals. It was a fact that university tenured faculties had been and remained white and male-dominated. The policies underscored the principle that universities cannot thrive in a vacuum; they must reflect the changing demographics of the world at large. To imply that diversity and academic excellence were somehow mutually exclusive was a gratuitous insult to the minorities and women who made up more than 50% of our nation's population.

Allegation: Minority faculty were overpaid.

Response: Not only are individual departments given tremendous authority to set faculty compensation, but faculty have always argued that they must be paid competitively with the market. Why should minority faculty have been treated differently, if indeed they were? The same market factors that influence differences in faculty pay between surgeons and historians, for example, can also influence pay for minority faculty.

Allegation: Design for Diversity mandated ethnic studies. This requirement diluted quality of the curriculum.

Response: No evidence was provided to support this allegation. Ethnic studies were never viewed by the regents as a cure-all, but a small step meant to help students learn that the whole world does not consist of white Europeans, assumed by some to be superior to other cultures. If we are to live in peace with one another, we ought to learn something about each other. No one has suggested that we do this to the exclusion of learning about European culture. Education in a university is not a novel idea.

Status Quo Problem: What's really going on? It may help to better understand the deep-rooted problem by quoting from others.[9] Professor Gary Sandefur, UW-Madison: "There is still a good-old-boy's network in most disciplines ..." Ohio State University's Associate Provost Barbara Newman: "There's a common assumption that the person of Hispanic or black cultural background will somehow be inferior, and that in order to recruit blacks or Hispanics to the faculty you're going to have to give up something that you call quality. I don't accept it." Former UW-Madison Chancellor Donna E. Shalala: "I argue that we can't have first-class universities without diverse student bodies and staffs. We've got to convince faculty members that what is at stake is the quality of the university. ..."[10] My concerns were that negative allegations were nothing more or less than attempts to dismantle affirmative action.

Not Invented Here

The "NIH" syndrome, which does not stand for the National Institutes of Health but for "not invented here," is a standing joke among regents to explain why faculty do not carry out regent policy. In other words, even though the idea may have merit, it did not originate on the campus with the faculty and, therefore, is suspect.

A case in point is the Student Conduct Code, UWS 17, Wisconsin Administrative Code. The UW-Madison chancellor, in an attempt to deal with discrimination among students, appointed a committee to develop a revision to an existing administrative code that would include hurtful language as well as physical abuse. The regents wanted a uniform code and were opposed to having each campus develop its own set of revisions. It was decided to have three constitutional scholars from the Law School write the revision that would be sponsored by the regents. The chair of the UW-Madison committee contended that "their" code was better. When the Court for the Eastern District of Wisconsin ruled that the regents' code did not meet the constitutional test protecting free speech, the UW-Madison committee told the regents that the "Madison code" would have fared better in the courts. Reason: NIH. The constitutional scholars disagreed.

Faculty View of Their Role in Running the University

How does one explain the positions faculty leaders take to obstruct implementation of regent policy? One faculty member described it to me this way: The faculty believe they run the university. Regents have the responsibility to provide the money so that the faculty can do their jobs; after that, the regents must essentially stay out of the faculty's way. That rewrites Chapter 36, Wisconsin Statutes! But that view exists, and regents must be willing to confront it. It governs the behavior of many members of the faculty, and can constitute a major obstacle to change initiated by the regents.

We Misunderstood or You Misunderstood

When the established deadline for achieving regent goals had expired, and the goal had not been met — "We misunderstood." When one of the campuses exceeded their enrollment target it was claimed that campus administrators did not know that graduate students were included in the target. "We misunderstood."

Perhaps most damaging to the System's credibility was the manner in which the issue of instructional positions was resolved. System administration, in explaining why additional instructional positions, authorized by the legislature, had not all been used for instruction purposes, contended that there had been a misunderstanding on the part of the legislature.[11] "You misunderstood." As could be expected, that did not sit well with members of the legislature. How did this come about? The history is worth detailing.

Among my earliest recollections of board business was that of showing that "time to degree" was beyond the expected eight semesters. While we were told that students held jobs to pay for school and took reduced credit loads, we were also told that there was a shortage in the availability of class sections. This made it difficult to complete prerequisite courses in a timely manner. The solutions suggested were to create more class sections by adding instructional positions and reducing enrollment. We asked for data.

In a March 15, 1985, memo to the legislative Joint Committee on Finance, Budget Planner Kathleen Sell reported results of a survey of campuses titled, "Length of Terms to Degree." Her findings showed that in 1978, UW-Madison's average number of semesters to completion of a bachelor's degree was 8.5, whereas in 1984 it was 10.3. At UW-Milwaukee, the number increased from 8.7 to 11.2 in that same period. Other UW institutions reported similar data. She concluded that the "increase in terms (semesters) to degree is caused by insufficient instructional staff and a number of other factors including economic factors which cause students to work more hours and take fewer credits; increasing attendance by returning adults and evening students, who are ... part-time" and requirements for degrees of more than 120 credits. She stated that additional instructional positions "will enable us to address the most immediate bottlenecks in staffing and course sequencing which is the critical need for our request." There can be no doubt in anyone's mind that she was addressing the needs of undergraduate students, not graduate students. We began the process of securing the additional instructional positions from the governor.

In the document *Planning the Future*, adopted by the regents in December 1986, the shortage of class sections was highlighted as one of the "cracks in the foundation of educational quality."[12] The governor had been convinced there was a need. He included 480 additional faculty positions in his 1987-89 System budget. On May 13, 1987, Wisconsin's Department of Administration (DOA) Secretary James Klauser wrote to the co-chairs of the Joint Committee on Finance: "The centerpiece of the Governor's budget for the UW System is the addition of 480 faculty positions. The additional positions will address the main problem facing students today, the availability of sufficient classroom sections."

On May 18, 1987, as president of the board, I wrote to Assembly Speaker Tom Loftus, "There is no question that additional positions are needed in order to offer additional class sections." I copied the governor, the regents, and the System president.

The legislative Joint Committee on Finance did not accept the recommendation of the governor. In an unusual appeal, Shaw wrote to the Wisconsin Senate and Assembly leadership on May 28, 1987:

> My second major concern is the clear need for an adequate number of faculty positions to respond to problems of educational quality caused by shortages of classes, inappropriate class sizes and major student backlog problems in high demand courses. The committee (Joint Committee on Finance) recommends funding 200 new faculty positions, about half the number proposed by the governor. It is important for you to understand that the Committee's action, while quite helpful, will not permit the kind of progress necessary to add the number of class sections to meet student needs or to shorten the time required to receive a degree.

After much negotiation, 328 new positions were authorized in the budget.

In April 1991, the LAB issued a scathing report on how the additional positions had been actually used by the System. The first page of the summary concluded:

> *Campuses Created Fewer Course Sections Than Expected.* The University reported to the Legislature in March 1989 that the 328 new staff were teaching 990 additional course sections in high demand disciplines. ... However, the report to the Legislature neglected to point out that, from Fall 1988 to Fall 1989, existing instructional staff reduced course sections offered by 688. ... The net increase in course sections offered between Fall 1986 and Fall 1989 was only 302, 30 percent of the increase of the 990 reported to the Legislature.[13]

To make matters worse, two campuses had a net section decrease, despite additional positions. And in some disciplines, which had been represented as facing serious access problems, the number of courses actually dropped despite the addition of positions. The LAB report noted that the System had responded that many access problems had been alleviated through other means: reducing enrollment, changing the drop/add policy, and other management initiatives.

The most damaging LAB conclusion of all was that *"Student Access Problems May Have Been Overstated."* The report flaunted the documentation as being incomplete and even erroneous. "These documentation problems contributed, we believe, to the University apparently receiving more instructional positions than were needed to adequately address student access problems. Because fewer staff and course sections were needed to alleviate student access problems, university officials shifted existing staff to other instructional activities, such as curriculum development and course preparation. ... However, given past budgeting and documentation problems, we question whether the University can justify the need to reduce enrollments further."

Adding fuel to the fire, a May 6, 1991, "Supplementary Analysis" prepared by regent staff at the request of Regent President Thomas Lyon, stated in summary, "Nevertheless, it is possible that the allocation decision regarding teaching resources may have had a significant effect in either helping or hindering the elimination of course bottlenecks. *Because information on students closed out of courses is not collected at every UW institution, it is not possible to determine whether the net number of sections created between 1986 and 1989 did in fact remove most or all of the course bottlenecks, especially at the undergraduate level* (emphasis added). The analysis also pointed out that there had been a shift in teaching resources from undergraduate to graduate sections. This was contrary to the stated needs for additional undergraduate class sections.

In response to the LAB report (April 17, 1991), Shaw argued that the report was "too narrow and [did] not support many of [its own] findings." In a word, the LAB misunderstood the significance of the various System initiatives to improve quality by placing so much emphasis on the number of class sections, rather than on the improvement of student/instructional staff ratios, enrollment reductions, smaller average section size, etc.

In reviewing the materials, it is clear to me that the purpose of the original request for more instructional positions was to deal with the "bottleneck," which contributed to the time to degree. I was puzzled by System's response and said so at the time. I did not believe that the LAB misunderstood at all. The response of legislative leadership, as reported to me by Lyon, was that of anger, which added to the System's lack of credibility.

Playing Intra-System Politics with Regent Policy

Paul Schilling, who served as my vice president, observed: "The most important meeting is the one that takes place between System administration and chancellors. That's where the real decisions are made." True?

A few examples may provide an answer. All of the examples were described by me in a closed session (October 1988) of the board. Some are in a memo to Paul Schilling dated September 15, 1988. I had expressed my concern about the mode of operation when chancellors did not seem to agree with board policy. To appease the chancellors, System administration did not ask the board to reconsider the policy, but would either reinterpret the policy or go so far as to say that either we or they had misunderstood. Then they asked the board to support System's position in order to avoid embarrassment for System officers. Now the examples. There are three, and each demonstrates obstacles to change.

1. *Mission statements and centers of excellence*. The history of the mission statement revisions and centers of excellence is a prime example of how an easily understood, straightforward regent policy can be turned inside out by internal System politics.

The discussion paper the regents received in April 1986 announced that, "A clearer delineation of institutional priorities and institutional focus is desirable. This might take the form of identifying institutional areas or centers of excellence" on each campus. Every institution could not be everything to everyone. Regents wanted campuses to focus their missions by establishing priorities, taking into account funding constraints. That exercise was to *precede* the rewriting of their mission statements.

Planning the Future, the regent's strategic plan, was adopted in December 1986. SG9, "Mission, Program Array and Program Review and Evaluation" (p.A7) required that academic programs have an adequate resource base and that "each institution was directed to undertake an analysis of current missions for the purpose of [1] identifying and establishing appropriate areas or centers of excellence which will become the foci for institutional decision making for future program development; [2] identifying potential modification to missions which result from this analysis; and [3] submitting ... proposed changes in the mission statement by January 1, 1988."

Nowhere in the discussions or the resolution was there any hint that the purpose of identifying these "foci," or centers of excellence, was to become the basis for new funding proposals. As a matter of fact, it was the lack of funds that was behind the directive for each campus to prioritize. This approach was a bold statement by the regents, based on the reality of funding sources.

It was soon clear that regent policy was being changed without the board's approval. As I travelled the state, I learned that System administrators were saying that centers of excellence were to be funding initiatives, much like grant proposals. Schilling and I met with Shaw in February 1987 to express our concern that if centers of excellence were tied to funding rather than to prioritizing of missions, we would not have accomplished the purpose of the resolution. Campuses must do the prioritizing with or without extra funding. That was the whole point of the resolution.

Despite this, the campus mission statements came to the board for approval *without* the identified centers of excellence. I wrote to Shaw on September 25, 1987, expressing my concern that the centers of excellence report would not be ready until Fall 1988 and that I had been told explicitly by the governor's office that specific mission statements were expected before that time. I asked to have the deadline moved ahead.

Before receiving a response to my request, the System informed the Regent Education Committee (September 29, 1987) that "... we can initiate funding of centers by 1989-90." This was completely contrary to the meeting Schilling and I had had with Shaw in February and the clear language of the regent resolution.

On October 14, 1987, I received the answer to my request to move the deadline ahead in a letter from Shaw objecting to shortening the time to completion of the mission statements. "[I]t is a complex task requiring the careful and *willing* participation of the campuses" (emphasis added). Why willing? What happened to regent authority?

By November 1987, System administration was talking to campuses about matching funds for centers of excellence. Identifying centers of excellence was no longer a prioritization exercise leading up to development of an institutional mission statement, but the exact opposite — they would now be simply "related to the institutional mission" (letter from Eugene Trani to Vice Chancellors, November 4, 1987).

Shaw wrote me on November 18, 1987, to make sure I was "on board." He pointed out that previous guidelines "indicate that funding will be sought for centers of excellence — 1/3 funded by the campus and 2/3 new funding." My records do not indicate that the board ever considered or took action on this proposal.

On December 1, 1987, Shaw wrote: "First, let me strongly state that the campuses are moving ahead to identify Centers of Excellence regardless of the ultimate budget allocation and are setting priorities among programs within their plans for revitalized mission statements." The funding of Centers of Excellence was a question of strategy and he did not think "a public reversal of [his] position would be productive." Left open was the question of what would happen to these so-called Centers of Excellence if they were not funded. That concern had been expressed to System administration as early as February 1987. On December 21, 1987, I wrote Shaw, "Regent Schilling and I have expressed concern to you previously that centers of excellence have been linked with funding, whereas they are intended to focus the priority setting that is needed at every campus."

When the mission statements came to the board on February 4, 1988, Regent Ody Fish, chair of the Committee on the Future, concurred with my observation that Regent Resolution SG9 directed that institutions *first* identify their priorities and then incorporate them in the mission statements, which had not been done. He added that Resolution SG9 sought to have those academic activities that were the particular focus of each institution incorporated in the mission statement. At the meeting on the following day, Regent Ruth Clusen expressed concern that half of the project was missing — centers of excellence. Until that was done, she did not believe the board could get an accurate assessment of the special missions of the institutions (UW Board meeting, February 5, 1988, p.16).

On July 29, 1988, the board received 47 proposed centers of excellence, selected in competition with campuses who had submitted proposals to System Academic Affairs. Shaw would request state funding of six million dollars for the centers. One campus had no recommended center of excellence! Given that the mandated exercise of mission development required that centers of excellence be identified *first*, what would they do? It was obvious that centers of excellence no longer were the "foci" or priorities of the campus mission, but a gimmick to get more funding.

At the Education Committee meeting of September 8, 1988, by a vote of 13-3, the funding request was struck from the resolution. In the discussion that preceded the vote, there was concern that centers of excellence, as proposed by the System, could not possibly be the "foci" of institutional missions since such world-class programs as UW-Madison's Computer Science Department, UW-Oshkosh's Learning Disabilities program, or UW-Whitewater's Production Management program had not been included in their institutional mission statements, and one campus had no proposed centers of excellence! There was confusion whether the original 47 (expanded to 49) were true campus priorities. It was a mistake to say that they were and then ask the legislature to fund them, thus giving the legislature the power to set priorities for each campus. Further, an institution's "foci" ought to be part of its base budget. Nowhere in the original discussions of centers of excellence and missions was funding perceived as a condition precedent to establishing the "foci" of the institutions. One chancellor told the regents that his list was his campus' highest priority, regardless of funding. His seven programs were those he wanted his campus to be known for. He admitted that while his campus would reallocate 1/3 of the requested funds, it would not do so for the 2/3. This said, it was clear that these programs were *not* the highest priority for his campus. That was not surprising since other chancellors had told me they did not consider centers of excellence to be the "foci" for their campuses, but rather "program and revenue enhancements," and if they did not receive funding, they would be dropped. Shaw agreed with the chancellors that these 49 centers of excellence might or might not be the highest priorities of a given campus.

The resolution submitted by System administration left the impression that the 49 centers of excellence were the foci of the campuses. Since the original regent intent had been turned upside down, I moved to amend the resolution to make it clear that these programs were not necessarily the foci for institutional decision-making. Challenged by other regents that this was a substantive change in the motion, I withdrew my motion, which meant that these 49 centers of excellence would, indeed, "become the foci for institutional decision making," even though it was clearly not the case. I then moved to amend the resolution to strike the words "eligible for special funding requests." The amendment passed by a wide margin (UW Board of Regents meeting, September 9, 1988). I voted against the final resolution because it was not responsive to SG9, which established the idea that campuses should prioritize. What we had before us were not the "foci" of the campuses. The amended resolution passed. There was no request for funds. The original intent to have campuses prioritize their programs had been trashed.

2. *Schools of Business.* The regent resolution on schools of business was clearly understood by everyone. It, too, became a victim of intra-System politics. We wanted the UW-Madison School of Business to become one of the top 10 in the nation. In order to do that, an additional three million dollars were needed annually, 1/3 to be raised privately, 1/3 from additional state revenues, and 1/3 through campus reallocation from Madison's base budget. Instead of the 1/3 reallocation, the System provided a plan to raise tuition for the MBA program by $500,000, which was not reallocation as everyone understood and was short by 50% of the amount the campus was to provide through re-allocation.

3. *Enrollment Management.* There were two strategies in the first enrollment management initiative: a 7,000 systemwide reduction in enrollment over a four-year period; and a cap on programs that were overcrowded, so that students could make it through their major in an orderly fashion. The 7,000 enrollment reduction was never achieved. Six months later, I learned that UW-Madison administrators had not told department heads that they could cap enrollment if needed. Those department heads who had heard about it were told by the dean of Letters and Science that he forbade it. I called this to System administration's attention. Apparently nothing was done because I was told by a faculty member that his department could simply not handle the student load. I feared for our credibility. Having refused to use the self-help measures that we had, how could we now complain about class sizes or class section availabilities?

The Endless Search for the Elusive Consensus

Academic administrators are anxious to explain that "universities are not businesses." I never heard it argued that the university ought to be motivated by profit-making, as is the private sector. Nevertheless, universities can learn a great deal about management practices from the private sector. For clarification, I have embraced what has become more current usage by critics of the university: While a university is not a business, it ought to be run like a business, making decisions in a more timely manner so that they are responsive to the changing needs of the "customers," who are the students and taxpayers. It should be willing to adopt new ways of performing old tasks. There has been a general understanding in the private sector that management must not only set the goals for the enterprise, but implement them by assigning responsibility and controlling results through regular follow-up (Chapter IV). It is the goal-setting element in the equation that is under discussion in this section.

In the private sector, there is a sense of urgency in establishing and implementing goals. The fact that this urgency does not often exist in the university setting is an obstacle to change. However, there is, in the culture of the academy, the need to search for consensus in defining goals. That is based on the theory of collegiality. Administrators often have come from faculty ranks and are colleagues of the faculty. Colleagues do not give each other orders. They certainly do not order other colleagues to do that which they do not want to do. In the article referred to in Chapter IV, written by several former chairs of the UW-Madison Committee, we were told that: "Faculty governance, like shared governance in the larger view, ... assumes that the successful operation and improvement of the university ... are a common interest shared by faculty and administrators, as well as by students and society at large. It follows from this assumption that rational investigation and discussion will ordinarily lead to agreement on most issues. ... Governance operates by considering each problem independently and seeking the optimal solution to it through a series of bodies and review processes."[14] When this view is accepted, as it usually is by university administrators, it leads to an endless search for a consensus. People who have nothing to gain or lose by disagreeing can hold up consensus for what seems an eternity to some.

The process used to reach consensus is in itself a further delay. The all-too-familiar steps are:

1. The System president appoints a systemwide committee, consisting of faculty, administrators, academic staff, and, perhaps students, and gives the committee its assignment.

2. The committee meets to outline its procedures.

3. The committee holds statewide hearings, at which it will hear diverse views.

4. The committee writes an interim report, which often reaches no conclusion. In order to accommodate diverse views, and to keep in mind

the goal of consensus, it is not unusual for the committee to offer recommendations that do not move the System very far, if at all.

5. The System president reviews the interim report and may make recommendations to the appropriate board of regents standing committee.

6. The board of regents committee may hold further hearings.

7. The appropriate units in the UW System rework the interim report, which goes back to the regent committee. Often the report does not assign responsibility or contain a timetable for completion. When timetables are provided, they may be set quite far into the future.

8. This may cause the report to go back to System administration to be reworked.

9. Finally, a resolution will go to the board for action.

It would not be unusual for the process to take over a year. A faculty member once observed — the more one knows about a problem, the more complicated it becomes! Or is it in the very nature of academe to favor tentative conclusions, pending further research? While this may be the best approach to take while doing scholarly research, it does not bode well for decision making when it comes to managing the System and instituting timely changes.

There Is Little or No Incentive to Carry Out Regent Policy

Design for Diversity, the multifaceted approach to increase racial and ethnic diversity, was adopted by the regents only after extensive public hearings. Annual reports indicated that some campuses had failed to put into place the most minimum steps to implement the policy. Outside of public criticism by some regents, the chancellors of those campuses were not "punished" in any way even though the inaction did threaten to penalize the programs. For example, System administration did not suggest that those who did not comply should not receive merit pay increases. As a matter of fact, all were recommended for merit raises by the System president.

In the case of implementing enrollment management policies, which the regents established in order to improve the quality of the campuses, those campus administrators that failed to meet the regent targets received essentially the same treatment as those that did. For the first time in 1990, following my suggestion, Shaw incorporated in his evaluation of chancellors his appraisal of how they had carried out regent policy. All were recommended for merit raises. One regent put it rather well: "It seems that all of our chancellors are the best!"

Assumptions without Facts

Earlier we talked about faculty "stonewalling." Regents also engage in "stonewalling" tactics. During the debate over Design for Diversity we asked why there was so little diversity in the faculty. A regent alleged that the pool of women and minority Ph.D.s was too small and needed to be made larger. "As the water in the harbor rises, so do all the boats," the quote from President Kennedy was recited. So we studied the pool of Ph.D. graduates vs. hires. It was easy to conclude that in many instances, the size of the pool had no influence on hiring practices. Even though the pool had gotten larger in some disciplines, this was not reflected in departmental hires. In other instances, even though the pool was not growing, faculty had taken seriously the regents' charge and were bringing women and minorities on to their faculties. It was clear that it was a matter of will, not the size of the pool.

Why Apply Principle When It's Easier Not to?

Regents can also obstruct change by ignoring well-established policies they have already adopted. An example is the Reserve Officers Training Corps (ROTC) issue.

Board policy on discrimination against students because of their sexual orientation is crystal clear. It is not to be tolerated on the campuses. It is also contrary to state law.[15] On the other hand, ROTC policy is also crystal clear. Known gays and lesbians may take ROTC courses, but they cannot receive federal scholarships or be commissioned in the armed forces upon graduation. No one has argued that these acts of denial are not discrimination. Yet ROTC remains on campuses in the System and the discrimination continues. As a matter of fact, that act of discrimination is so blatant that when students enroll in ROTC, they are asked specifically whether they are gay or lesbian. While the board passed a resolution which said this practice was not acceptable and constituted discrimination, it would not discontinue the program, even on those campuses where teaching military tactics is not required by law.

The rationale used by some regents is interesting. They argue that there is a benefit to society to have some military officers trained in our universities, rather than have them all trained in military schools. It is also argued that those who receive federal scholarships will be disadvantaged if ROTC were to be discontinued. I asked whether the same argument would be advanced if ROTC discriminated against blacks. No answer. For some issues, regents will take the position that a little prejudice is OK. "Little" is applied to groups with which one is uncomfortable! To be consistent with regent policy and to show good faith with the students, the board should, at the very least, eliminate ROTC from every campus except UW-Madison, which is the only land grant campus in Wisconsin.

We Should Not Be Involved in Social Engineering

Another way to obstruct change or reverse policy with which one does not agree is to give the policy a "bad name." Take Design for Diversity, for example. Depending on one's frame of mind, Design for Diversity can be characterized as a bold, innovative, long-overdue initiative. Past experience has taught us that its goals would not be achieved by themselves, but need to be encouraged, even demanded.

On the other hand, I have shown how some faculty members will throw up a variety of "straw men" — claims that there will be an erosion of academic quality, quotas will be established, minority faculty will be overpaid, etc. Recently, some regents proclaimed that we are an open society and there is no need for "social engineering," in spite of all the statistical evidence of discrimination in hiring.

Lack of Flexibility and Disincentives to Be Efficient

Many hours of regent discussions were taken up with the issue of flexibility. "If we only had more flexibility, we could solve the problems of inadequate compensation for faculty, academic staff, and administrators. We could construct buildings in a more timely fashion. We could better maintain our buildings. Our labs and libraries would be in better shape. We would even be more efficient." I agree. The state is in the way here.

The major obstacle created by the state is its unwillingness to give the UW System the flexibility it needs to manage. The University of Michigan was created by the constitution of that state, rather than by legislation, as is the case in Wisconsin. As a result, the University of Michigan has equal standing with all other constitutional bodies. While it receives funds from the state, those funds are given in a lump sum. Internal control of those funds, including shifting funds between line items, is in the hands of the governing body of the university. The university is also able to establish its own personnel costs. Not so in Wisconsin. The UW System was created by the legislature enacting Chapter 36, Wisconsin Statutes. It is an agency of the state, which can, and often does, control line items of the budget: the number of positions, tuition, salaries of chief administrators, percentage pay raises for faculty and staff, budgets for libraries, and building schedules.

What's more, the UW System has been "punished" by the state for being efficient. When UW Hospital and Clinics accumulated a surplus, which its governing body believed it needed, it was simply taken by the state and put into the general fund. Another example: UW System institutions built up a surplus in their auxiliary funds for residence halls. The fund was to be used to do repairs and replace furnishing in an orderly fashion while maintaining level payments for student room and board. This approach had been approved by the board of regents. The LAB concluded that the surplus was too large, and $22 million were lopped off of the System's budget! The hundreds of pounds of System documents that detailed the needs for the surplus were ignored and student costs have since gone up. Then, in 1985, Section 36.46 was added to Chapter 36, Wisconsin Statutes. It limits the board's ability to accumulate auxiliary reserves by providing that such reserves may not be generated from student fees without the approval of the state secretary of administration and the Joint Committee on Finance of the legislature.

The state sometimes seems to take the position that the way to achieve efficiency in the administration of the System is to squeeze the budget and then let the university administrators figure out how to "make do" with less. There is a limit to what an administrator can do, no matter how talented. For example, funds the state provides for maintenance of buildings continue to be less than adequate. The buildings will reflect the neglect. One could argue that there is enough "water" in the System, so money can be found for maintenance in other places. That may or may not be true. The consequences for the quality of maintenance are clear if there is no other place to find the funds.

There is little incentive to be efficient, since there is no reward for doing so. Funds not expended in the biennium for which they are budgeted are forfeited. Funds for equipment not spent in the year for which they are budgeted lapse. Everyone knows that the buildings of the universities in the System are relatively empty in the summer. The population of the country is aging. Some students might prefer going to school in the summer so that they could graduate sooner. Then why isn't there more activity on the campuses in the summer? There is no incentive. If the universities were to go into high gear and generate extra revenue greater than the expenses, the state would take it out of the next budget.

VI.

Learning from Past Initiatives

Conclusion #6: Regents can learn from past experience how to overcome the obstacles to change.

I have discussed the need for the UW System to change, provided a short guide to this huge and complicated system of public higher education, pointed out the significance of the mental attitudes that regent appointees bring to the board, discussed the regents' role in governance, and enumerated the major obstacles to change that I encountered. Obstacles like those can be overcome. How that was done during my years on the board provides the subject matter for this chapter.

Given the proper mix of leadership and resolve, obstacles to change can be overcome. The leadership and resolve manifested themselves in various ways. Sometimes the System president led the way; sometimes it was the board; sometimes the plans for change evolved through consultation between the two.

While this discussion is focused on System administration and the board of regents, it is important to recognize that changes also take place at the campus level. Strong campus leadership can bring about profound change for individual institutions. When the UW System, through the board of regents, proposed changes, however, they affected every campus in the System.

Generally speaking, the board adopted policies that called for change under two circumstances:

1. The regents determined that certain initiatives must be taken at the System level in order to avoid confusion and ensure uniformity. We shall examine seven examples.

2. The regents concluded that those to whom they had delegated authority had not acted in a meaningful or timely manner. We shall examine eight examples.

Some will not agree with the board's previous actions as shown below. These examples are provided for illustrative purposes only. They not only show that change can be made despite obstacles, but they demonstrate why shared governance as a type of partnership usually does not work in practice.

Regent Actions for Uniform Policies

Following are seven examples of changes made because the regents believed that they were best handled at the System level.

Completing Merger

This is an example of change occurring because the board ordered it, and the System president carried it out.

When I first came onto the UW Board of Regents in 1984, I was told by members of the faculty and administrators at UW-Madison that the merger of 1971 (described earlier) was a mistake. This seemed odd, considering the fact that merger legislation had been passed 13 years before. Would the debate never end?

There were several factors that finally convinced the board that action was needed to stop the debate about the merits of merger and get on with the work of governance:

1. In 1984-85, while the first faculty catch-up pay plan was being debated in the legislature, it was obvious to everyone involved that system administration was not in control. Disregarding the system and board proposal, individual campus chancellors came to Madison to negotiate separate catch-up plans for their campuses. I was told by leading members of the legislature that they were fed up with these chancellors and thought they should be discharged. Some regents shared this view, but the system president was not willing to take any action.

2. A report of the Legislative Audit Bureau, completed years after merger legislation had been enacted, concluded that merger had not been completed and that the regents were not carrying out their responsibility.

3. It was well known that there was a personal tension between the chancellor of the major doctoral campus and the System president that undermined systemwide cooperation.

4. System officers complained to board members that campus administrators set up roadblocks to regent policies.

During the interviews of candidates for System president, following Robert O'Neil's resignation in 1985, the board made it clear that it wanted merger completed. It was to be understood that all chancellors reported to the System president and were duty-bound to carry out and support regent policies. Going off on their own would no longer be tolerated. Candidate Kenneth Shaw was asked what he would do if chancellors refused to "march to the same drummer." He replied, "I will break their drum sticks!" Shaw was hired and did complete merger. He had the full support of the board. At this writing, one can still hear a faint voice or two, grumbling about merger. But the voices become dimmer with each passing year.

Planning the Future

Strategic plans for the UW System can be adopted only by the board. Faculty would find it impossible to agree on a strategic plan formulated for the entire System. How would faculty members representing different campuses ever decide on how to balance emphasis between campuses, decide on course duplication between campuses, or establish an overall enrollment target for the System, just to name a few examples. The responsibility for assuring this balance belongs to the board of regents.

The process of formulating and adopting the strategic plan, Planning the Future, is another key example of what happens when the board leads the way and makes a major commitment of time, and the System president assumes a proper leadership role and pushes the project to completion. The process that produced Planning the Future may be as important as the plan itself, because it forced the board to deal with a number of systemwide issues, most of which were controversial and had been avoided in the past. This was a new experience for the board. Special meetings were convened for the sole purpose of developing this strategic plan and adopting policy statements that would implement it. When it was done the board came away with a real sense of empowerment. We knew that we could deal with important and controversial issues and implement change. Of equal importance, we were able to show the campuses that major changes were possible when System administration and the board worked together.

Planning the Future was also significant because of its substance. Not only did the subject matter of the report dominate the regent agenda for the entire year during its formulation, but it has done so since its passage. I predict that it will dominate the regent agenda for some time to come. It is for these reasons that I detail the history of the development of this strategic plan.

It all began with a growing concern that educational quality was being effected by a lack of leadership from System administration and from the board. I recall chatting informally with Regent Paul Schilling, who had been on the board for five years by that time. Schilling remarked, "Everyone is setting our agenda except us." I agreed, and we continued such discussions with Executive Vice President Katharine Lyall. Schilling and I were determined that the board was going to accept its appropriate role in leading the System. "Quality" should be the primary issue for the agenda. It had long been the tradition in Wisconsin that access rather than quality had priority. There was the naive notion that since quality was high, it would take care of itself because the state would provide funds in proportion to growth in enrollment. That had not been the case. Wisconsin citizens came to understand that resident high school graduates could enroll in a UW institution almost as a matter of right, no matter how ill-prepared they were. "Let them in and flunk them out" was regarded as a politically acceptable operational mode, while not letting them in was seen as not politically acceptable. Quality was being threatened in the following ways:

1. Political pressure to maintain an open admission policy resulted in low admission standards and low retention rates.

2. Demographers, on whom UW officials relied, were consistently wrong. They predicted that with diminishing numbers of high school graduates, enrollment in the UW System would decline. Instead, enrollment continued to rise. The forecasts failed to take into consideration that an increasingly larger percentage of Wisconsin high school graduates were enrolling in System institutions, larger than the national average.

3. Financially, the UW System was in trouble. Despite increasing enrollment, state revenues were declining in real dollars. In terms of public appropriations per student, Wisconsin's rank dropped nationally from 4th in 1972-73 to 31st in 1983-84 — $600 per student below the national average — a shortfall of about $60 million per year.[1] As we shall see in Chapter VII, the shortfall on a per student basis became even greater in the ensuing years.

4. Compensation of faculty was below that of peer institutions.

5. Faculty/student ratios were deemed to be unsatisfactory and getting worse.

6. Students were finding it increasingly difficult to get into classes in order to complete requirements of their majors, extending the time to graduation beyond eight semesters.

7. Laboratories, computer centers, and libraries were not keeping up with the high standards expected.

8. UW System admission standards were low. The K-12 system was attempting to raise graduation requirements, but felt dragged down by the UW System. For example, the graduation requirements at West High School in Madison were higher than the admission standards of UW-Madison.

On April 1, 1985, I wrote to System President O'Neil and expressed my concern that the legislature "may be getting too deeply involved in the functioning of the board." I also listed 11 items of concern, including retention, regent authority and a review of delegated authority, admission standards, program duplication issues, credit transfer within the System, and administrative pay levels. I sent a copy to the regent president.

Before his departure for the University of Virginia, the board asked O'Neil to summarize in writing the issues he thought the board might face in the future. In his July 12, 1985, response, he reviewed the board's authority as outlined in Chapter 36, Wisconsin Statutes and pointed out what he saw as the constraints on that authority. They included total number of positions available, limits on the use of non-pay plan funds to increase salaries for reasons other than equity and reclassification, executive pay plan constraints, and "disincentives for economies and savings through reallocation or program elimination." In response to the allegation that the System did not have a long-range plan, he said it was "technically correct" in the sense that there was no single volume containing such a plan, but that the "elements of a long-range plan do for the most part exist in current documents and materials." He concluded by outlining what he thought such a long-range plan should contain.

I wrote O'Neil on July 19, 1985, "I hope we can find appropriate vehicles to deal with the broad range of issues. If we do not, others will surely do it for us." "Others" referred to legislators. I sent a copy of the letter to the regent president and System executive vice president. The materials O'Neil referred to did not have the weight of regent policy with a coherent theme, which is what long-range plans should contain. My concerns were verified by the findings of the LAB, which completed its evaluation of the UW System Administration on November 10, 1986.[2] In his letter of transmittal to the Joint Legislative Audit Committee, Dale Cattanach, state auditor and head of the LAB wrote, "... System administration has been only partially successful in meeting the legislative objectives of merger because it has not provided effective leadership and control in managing the University." The LAB found that student enrollment, academic programs, and the allocation of funds had not been properly managed, that there had been no long-range plan regarding enrollment, and that enrollment had exceeded budgeted levels by 2,712 students annually from 1979-80 through 1985-86. It found, further, that the allocation of funds to the campuses was not consistent with the development of needed new programs or the elimination of lower priority programs. The need for a strategic long-range plan was clear. I learned later that UW System Executive Vice President Katharine Lyall, who had been appointed acting System president after O'Neil left, persuaded Regent President Ben Lawton to appoint a special regent committee to develop a strategic plan for the 1990s. Lyall deserves full credit for getting the process started.

It was at the November 1985 meeting of the board at which Lawton announced the appointment of a special eight-member regent committee to develop a strategic plan for the future of the UW System. I was not included, even though I had written to O'Neil and Lawton more than a year before. In addition, I was chair of the Business and Finance Committee, a member of the regent executive committee, and had served on the UW Hospital and

Clinics Council of Trustees. Regent Herbert Grover objected immediately to the small number of regents on the committee. He pointed out that this was a most important regent activity and that all regents should be allowed to serve. His idea was adopted. All regents served.

The charge to the committee was to complete work by December 1986. In order to do this, the special committee scheduled meetings on Friday afternoons following the conclusion of the monthly regent meetings. In addition to the regents, UW-Madison Chancellor Irving Shain and UW-Stout Chancellor Robert Swanson served on the committee along with UW System Executive Vice President Katharine Lyall.

Kenneth A. Shaw became System president in February 1986. Shortly thereafter, he showed me a list of the major subjects he hoped to see covered. He lost little time in getting out front.

The final document, *Planning the Future*, was adopted on December 5, 1986, by a unanimous vote of the board.

What about those obstacles? How did the creation of a strategic plan help us overcome them?

The committee dealt with the gross errors made in forecasting enrollment. It had been predicted in 1979 that enrollment would reach 137,289 by 1986, whereas the actual enrollment in 1985 was 165,548, an error of 20%. There had been no proportional increase in state funding support.[3] Regents were genuinely concerned that quality would be threatened if these trends were left unchallenged. According to *Planning the Future*'s introduction, "The major objective of the study was to find ways to ensure the continued quality of education in the UW System." This official call for quality over access guided the regents from that point forward.

In order to deal with the issue of quality, the new agenda would include a study of and adoption of policies pertaining to:

> ... institutional and system missions, program array, admissions policy, access, appropriate future enrollment levels, economic development, cooperation with the Vocational, Technical and Adult Education System, tuition and fee levels, transferability of credit within the system, appropriate State tax funding levels, [General Purpose Revenue or GPR], opportunities for minorities, women, disadvantaged and the handicapped, utilization of physical facilities, and management accountability, flexibilities and constraints.[4]

All of these subjects were considered to be elements of quality, and, therefore, were properly within the jurisdiction of the regents.

Public hearings were held to provide an opportunity for faculty, staff, students, and the public to be heard on every issue. Through the two chancellor members of the committee, the other chancellors in the System had input to the regents. The committee was given excellent background work papers prepared by the System administration. There was not always agreement among the regents or between the regents and the chancellors, faculty, and others about how to resolve the issues. The debate was vigorous. We knew that we were engaged in an historically important task; we alone had the responsibility and authority to act and did. We were told that this strategic plan had been hailed as a national model.

What caused this turnaround in the way the regents viewed their responsibility? Several factors were at work. First, regents were willing to meet an additional afternoon each month to confront the issues and plan for the future. Second, President Shaw embraced the concept at once and provided strong leadership through his staff. The working papers were excellent and helped us think through policy alternatives. Regent Fish, who chaired the special committee, summarized the debate and forced decisions. In a word, strong leadership both at the System and regent levels, working together, transformed the regents into a board willing to deal with complicated and often controversial issues.

I am convinced that the remarkable transformation that took place on the board was a result of working together for a year, wrestling with these complex issues, and coming to a conclusion. It set the stage for further board action. Board members now knew that they could make a difference if they chose to do so. System administrators knew that their leadership was also essential if changes were to be made.

Design for Diversity

The regent policy, Design for Diversity, followed Planning the Future, and is another example of how obstacles can be overcome. This document set forth goals that the regents hoped to accomplish.[5] By "diversity" the regents meant efforts to enhance multicultural diversity among the students and faculty as well as gender equity among the faculty, so that campuses would better reflect the demography of our nation. Diverse groups included people of color, gender, differing ethnic and national backgrounds, and sexual orientation. As to all of those groups, discrimination was not to be tolerated and inclusion was to be vigorously promoted.

This was not the first effort that the board of regents had exerted in this regard. Diane Hatton Bailiff, UW-Madison, in her 1991 Ph.D., thesis dealt with the history of this subject in great detail.[6]

However, for purposes of this discussion, which has to do with overcoming obstacles to change, it is important to point out that Design for Diversity was a substantially different initiative than those previously adopted by the board as explained by Bailiff. For the first time, in dealing with this subject, recognition was given to two well-accepted management principles: Everyone's business is no one's business, and people do what you inspect, not what you expect. Also included were the three previously discussed necessary elements to any management decision: establish the goal, implement it, and control the outcome. Design for Diversity differed from previous regent initiatives in the following important ways:

1. The statewide hearings resulted in the regents having a broad sense of ownership of the concepts articulated in the plan.

2.   The plan established goals *and* a timetable for accomplishment.

3. The plan fixed responsibility for implementation.

4. The plan set up a system of accountability.

5. The plan called for a special assistant to the president with sole responsibility to implement the plan, work with campuses, and report to the board on a regular basis.

6. The plan required an annual report from the president of the System, outlining his appraisal of how chancellors had carried out this regent policy.

This did not happen by accident. I was the board president at the time. Before going to the regents, it was clear to me and to Shaw that substantial groundwork had to be laid before anything could be done. We wanted to make sure that there was a broad sense of ownership. To accomplish this, regent hearings were scheduled on several campuses. In addition, hearings were held in Madison and Milwaukee's predominantly black neighborhoods, and at the Lac De Flambeau Indian Reservation, where, we were told, regents had never visited. While the testimony was often bitter and accusatory, it was nonetheless, very helpful. Regents who attended were able to understand the feelings of frustration expressed about a system that did not seem responsive to the needs of these people. I chaired the hearings in Madison. I was told by those attending that we knew what was wrong, we ought to stop studying the issue, and take bold, corrective action. No regent could attend these hearings without coming away with the conviction that action, not more words or resolutions, was needed, and that our credibility with these constituents was in deep trouble.

Shaw and I discussed an outline of the proposed plan that would go to the board. According to the Bailiff dissertation, a regent committee had previously proposed to O'Neil that there ought to be a person reporting to him who had sole responsibility for carrying out regent resolutions on minority education and hiring. But he believed that the creation of such a position would demean those whom the regents were attempting to help. Instead, he thought a person in System's Office of Academic Affairs ought to be given the responsibility along with other responsibilities. Unaware of this history, Schilling and I insisted that there ought to be a person who would report directly to the president of the System. Furthermore, this special assistant to the president would report to the board on progress made by each campus and detail areas that needed improvement. That commitment would send a clear signal to everyone that we considered this a serious matter. It would also establish a pattern for chancellors to follow. The hearings showed us that on the doctoral campuses there was little opportunity for coordination and a general lack of training and supervision among those charged with the responsibility of counseling minority and other disadvantaged students.

Despite having seen that setting goals, implementation, and evaluation were essential ingredients in the diversity policy, I am always puzzled to find in the regent agenda resolutions calling for action *without fixing responsibility or establishing a timetable for completion*. The lessons learned apparently have to be learned over and over again. Regents must insist that any proposal for action contain the essential elements described above.

UWS 17 — Student Non-Academic Disciplinary Procedures

There were at least two interesting aspects to the revision of this section of the Wisconsin Administrative Code. Not only did it attempt to deal for the first time with what was referred to as the quality of the campus environment, but it also provided an example that some changes initiated by the board of regents must first receive legislative approval. Such approval would be necessary for any proposed revision of Chapter 36, Wisconsin Statutes or the Wisconsin Administrative Code, of which student disciplinary procedures are a part.

There were in the Wisconsin Administrative Code two general categories that dealt with student discipline: academic[7] and non-academic discipline.[8] Of interest here is non-academic discipline, which dealt with physical violence of one student toward another or the destruction of university property, and provided for disciplinary measures including expulsion. The enforcement of the code is at the campus level. Section UWS 17.06[1][a][b] prohibited physical abuse, the threat of physical abuse, or physical intimidation "... because of that person's race, sex, religion, color, creed, disability, sexual orientation, national origin, ancestry or age."

There had been some ugly incidents on the campuses involving verbal assault. In one instance, a fraternity had sponsored a mock slave auction and in another there had been a "Fiji night," in which the lawn in front of the fraternity was decorated with demeaning cartoons of Fiji Islanders. Consistent with the thrust of Design for Diversity, UW System Administration and some regents felt that a review of the student conduct code was in order since it did not deal with verbal assault. It was argued that the campus environment was a key factor in giving meaning to policies that were directed toward recruiting minorities and women. We believed that everyone should play on a level field. How could students be expected to devote their time to study if they were being verbally assaulted, harassed, and demeaned because of their race, creed, gender, etc.?

The UW System Administration proposed an amendment to the code that would deal with verbal assault and racial epithets. The proscribed behavior was limited to "race." I argued that if such a contemplated change were to take place, the proposal was too narrow, and the language should be more inclusive, along the lines of Wisconsin Statutes, which included gender, sexual orientation, ethnicity, and national origin. A redraft was submitted that included this broader language.

Debate began. Initially, I was uncomfortable with the proposed limitation of speech. This seemed to me to be tinkering with the First Amendment of the United States Constitution. When I had attended public schools in Madison, I had been subjected to ethnic slurs — "Christ killer," "dirty Jew," "kike," etc. As a defense mechanism, we learned either to say out loud to our tormenters (or think it silently if they were much larger physically than we were), "Sticks and stones will break my bones, but names will never hurt me," a commonly heard chant among children. Of course, the names hurt deeply. Was the wound inflicted less than that of a stone? In addition to the name-calling, I was excluded from some high school social clubs because I was Jewish. At the UW-Madison, I was president of the Jewish student organization and joined with some non-Jewish student organizations to combat discrimination in university-approved housing to which campus administrators seemed to have a blind eye. Why shouldn't university students understand the "real world" in which they would live and develop a "thick skin"? I was deeply troubled, however, by the thought that more than 40 years after I had graduated from the UW-Madison, there was evidence of vile and sometimes violent student prejudicial behavior.

While I was opposed to limiting abusive language, I was also convinced that certain types of language could actually interfere with the educational process. I persuaded myself that we ought to give the idea the benefit of the doubt. The faculty senate of UW-Madison had written a revision to the code and urged the regents to adopt it. Schilling and I agreed that any revision of the code would have to apply uniformly to every campus as does the code itself. Since the First Amendment, and subsequent Supreme Court cases, which interpreted the meaning of the amendment, was a complicated legal issue, and we were not getting expert constitutional legal advise, I suggested that we confer with faculty members of the Law School. We should have a panel consisting of a strict constructionist, a liberal constructionist, and a moderate. This panel should bring us a proposed revision with which they could *all* agree would meet the constitutional test. That would, at least, put the legal issue to rest. Little did I know that the ensuing arguments made against the proposal on constitutional grounds would come from non-lawyers. Everyone is an expert!

A Law School faculty committee was appointed by the regents. A draft was presented to the board. It proposed to amend section UWS 17 of the code to include certain types of verbal assault. Its key elements were:

> The University may discipline a student in non-academic matters in the following situations: For the racist or discriminatory comments, epithets or other expressive behavior directed at an individual ..., if such comments, epithets, other expressive behavior or physical conduct intentionally:
>
> 1. Demeans the race, sex, religion, color, creed, disability, sexual orientation, national origin, ancestry or age of the individual or individuals; and
>
> 2. Creates an intimidating, hostile or demeaning environment for education, university-related work, or other university-authorized activity.

The intent required would be determined after considering "all relevant circumstances." Some examples of prohibited behavior were listed. In order to find a violation, there had to be a finding of intent and the demeaning of the person for the reasons stated, all of which created an "intimidating, hostile, or demeaning" educational environment.[9]

Hearings were held and the debate began in earnest. The hearings not only caused me to change my mind, but convinced me to become one of the leading advocates for the code revision. Students described in detail the intimidating, harassing campus environment they encountered. I became convinced that it was a sham to hide behind the free speech arguments, which we heard over and over, while at the same time proclaiming that we were concerned with the quality of the campus environment in which students were expected to learn and study. All students had the right to a level playing field, and the governing board, namely the regents, had an obligation to do what it could to provide that level playing field. I argued that if the university was nothing more than an extension of the "street," with its bigotry and intolerance, than the university had lost a real opportunity to contribute to the betterment of our society. I found that unacceptable.

Some argued that we were going too far, while others argued that we were not going far enough and the proposed revision was nothing more than a symbol. Those who opposed the revision — regents, the American Civil Liberties Union (ACLU), a legislator, faculty, and others — argued that the proposal would violate the "free speech" clause of the First Amendment to the U.S. Constitution. I, along with others, took the opposite view — limitation of so-called "free speech" already existed in many areas and this was a proper subject for code revision. The ACLU countered that all of the examples of the limitations on "free speech," such as sexual harassment in the work place, slander, and protection of union organizational activities in the work place, were irrelevant. It threatened to sue the board if it adopted the code revision.

After extensive hearings, the proposed language was adopted unanimously by the board on August 9, 1988. Before the vote was taken, I called several regents. I believe I changed their minds. I did not want to leave it to chance. The revision was then taken to the legislature for approval. On July 12, 1989, an administrative rule hearing was held by the Wisconsin Assembly Colleges and Universities Committee and the Senate Education Committee. I testified with System administration and chancellors. There was opposing testimony from the ACLU, a legislator, and the mayor of Madison, among others. The joint committee approved the proposed rule change; it went into effect in August 1989.

On March 20, 1990, the *UW-Milwaukee Post, Inc.* (a student newspaper), and others filed a lawsuit in the United States District Court Eastern District of Wisconsin, naming the UW System Board of Regents as defendant (Case No.:90-C-328). The plaintiffs asked the court to enter a declaratory judgment that section UWS 17.06[2], which dealt with verbal abuse, violated the right of free speech guaranteed by the First Amendment to the U.S. Constitution and Article I, Section 3 of the Wisconsin Constitution and violated the plaintiff's right to due process and equal protection under the laws guaranteed by the Fourteenth Amendment of the U.S. Constitution and Article I, Section 1 of the Wisconsin Constitution. The court was provided with examples of how campuses had enforced the rule.

On October 11, 1991, Judge Robert W. Warren granted the plaintiff's summary judgment and found that the rule "... on its face violates the overbreadth doctrine and is unduly vague ...," permanently enjoined the board and its agents and employees from enforcing the rule, vacated all disciplinary action taken under the rule, and expunged from the files any records related to such action. We were told that campuses were applying the rule too broadly. The board of regents decided not to appeal the judgment.

Constitutional scholars of the Law School at UW-Madison offered to revise the rule so that it would be more limited in scope and would mandate the UW System Administration to oversee the enforcement at the campus level. It passed the board 12 to 5 on June 9, 1989. The makeup of the board was changing. On September 11, 1992, upon reconsideration, the board voted to repeal the revised code with a vote of 10 to 6, a decision with which I strongly disagree. That decision sent the wrong message. I will revisit this subject in Chapter VIII which deals with the future of the campus environment.

Board Action to Reduce System's Budget Proposal

It is not always possible for the board and the System administration to agree. For example, for the last budget I voted on (1991-93), there was a major difference of opinion between regents and the System administration as to the size of the budget that should be presented to the governor. The accepted practice in the past had been that after System administration had developed its biennial budget, it briefed the regents, and the budget was adopted without change. Not so in this case. No compromise seemed possible. The board prevailed over System administration. That had not happened before during my term on the board. This must have sent a shock wave through the System administration offices.

In presenting the 1991-93 budget, the System incorporated an idea I suggested, namely, that it should indicate options it would take in the event that the amount requested was not obtained when the state adopted its final budget. What caused the disagreement was the System administration's budget request that went to the board. The System budget request asked for 20% of the projected increase in total state tax revenue. I thought that was wholly unrealistic and said so at the briefing. Historically, we had received 11-12% of state tax revenues; it was most unlikely that the System would suddenly receive almost twice that amount of any increased state revenues. While I was willing to be an advocate for what the System needed to maintain quality, I did not want to jeopardize the entire budget by presenting what I considered to be a wholly unrealistic request. In addition, the request called for a very substantial increase in student tuition — greater than anticipated inflation, which I opposed. The fallback position of the System included eliminating areas that belonged in the core mission, which I found unacceptable. I telephoned other regents and learned that they had expressed the same concerns at the briefings. I reiterated those concerns to both the System and regent presidents. System administration made no substantial changes when it sent its final proposal to the board.

I phoned Paul Schilling, who had served as vice president when I was president of the board. We shared the same views regarding the size of the total budget proposal as well as the requested increase in tuition. He said that he had talked to other regents, who were of the same opinion. It was left that he and I would each review line items to be omitted in order to reduce the overall budget that the board would send to the governor. This would include a reduction in state-requested funds and tuition increases. Among the items we agreed should be eliminated were those that were basic to the mission and should have been covered in the base budget, such as undergraduate education initiatives. I had communicated these and other concerns to President Shaw and Regent President Tom Lyon in memos dated October 2 and 31, 1990.

The line items Schilling and I identified had two components: funds requested from the state, or General Purpose Revenue (GPR), and tuition. We agreed that at the board meeting he would move to eliminate the identified line items from the request to the state, which I would second. I would then introduce a "friendly" amendment to reduce tuition accordingly, which he would accept. We identified more than $20 million. Before the board meeting I asked one of the System officers whether President Shaw knew that a proposal to reduce the budget was going to be introduced. I was told that he thought it would be between $5 and $10 million. He, obviously, was out of sync with the regents. The amendments passed. An additional amendment was introduced to reduce the budget by another $20 million and lost by one vote, because a regent, who would have supported the amendment, misunderstood it and voted against it. I suppose System administrators viewed this action as undercutting them. But true advocacy does not mean rubber-stamping every System administration decision. And the System administration was warned well in advance that the regents were not going to approve the budget as presented.

Mission Statements

Chapter 36, Wisconsin Statutes assigns to the UW Board of Regents the responsibility of establishing mission statements for each System institution.[10] First drafts were submitted by the campuses and were rejected by the regents because they were too broad and did not adequately distinguish one campus from another. While I served on the board, we rewrote the mission statements for the System and each campus.

To the extent that mission statements accurately reflect the emphasis attributed to each campus by the board of regents, they have significant value. To the extent that they do not, they are essentially worthless and even dangerous, because they may send the wrong message to the faculty and campus administrators concerning the goals of the campus.

Strengthening Extension

Bringing the knowledge of the university to the citizens of the state has been referred to as the "Wisconsin Idea." In writing about the Wisconsin Idea, Vernon Carstensen quoted from a legislative committee that declared in 1858 that the people of the state:

> have an unquestioned right to demand that ... [the University] shall primarily be adapted to popular needs, that its course of instruction shall be arranged to meet as fully as possible, the wants of the greatest number of our citizens. The farmers, mechanics, miners, merchants, and teachers of Wisconsin ... have a

right to ask that the bequest of the government shall aid them in securing to themselves and their posterity, such educational advantages as shall fit them for their pursuits in life, and which by an infusion of intelligence and power, shall elevate those pursuits to a dignity commensurate with their value.[11]

The tradition for Extension as an essential part of the mission of the university is clear. Indeed, in a land-grant university such as UW-Madison, teaching, research, and service are inextricably tied together and are at the very heart of the university. The faculty, therefore, must be engaged in the "creation, assimilation and dissemination of knowledge."[12] Earlier, I referred to the Morrill Act of 1862, which gave land grants to each state for purposes of establishing universities. In addition to requiring the teaching of military tactics, the Morrill Act expanded the role of the university to encompass three major purposes:

1. To broaden the horizons of learning and scholarly exploration to include all fields of human and scientific endeavor, including "agriculture and the mechanic arts."

2. To provide higher education to the common people, rather than only to the upper-class elite.

3. To make the knowledge and resources of the university available to people of all ages, in their fields, factories and homes, and to apply these resources and research to the problems of society — the extension concept.

UW Extension, an integral part of the System's mission, is mandated by Chapter 36, Wisconsin Statutes. It begins by describing the mission of the University of Wisconsin System. Section 36.01[1] provides that it is in the "public interest" to establish a system of higher education:

"... which stresses undergraduate teaching as its main priority; which offers selected professional graduate and research programs ... ; which fosters diversity of educational opportunity; *which promotes service to the public* ..." (emphasis added).

36.01[2] states: "The mission of the system is to develop human resources, to discover and disseminate knowledge, *to extend knowledge and its application beyond the boundaries of its campuses* ..." (emphasis added).

Section 36.05[1][7] defines Extension: "Extension means the community outreach, public service and extension services of the system."

In some states, extension services, as well as the budget, are integrated completely into the campus and academic departments. There is no separate institution. In Wisconsin, however, extension services from 1965 to 1982 were a separate organization that had its own chancellor, administrative staff, and some faculty.

Before I came onto the board in 1984, there were discussions and hearings about the best way to have the UW System carry out its outreach or extension mission. Some argued that extension should be fully integrated into academic departments on the campuses, along with the Extension budget. UW Extension would then be dissolved. This argument was advanced by several campus administrators, department heads, and faculty members.

In the late 1970s, prior to integration of programming, Extension was running a deficit of nearly $2 million. The legislature mandated that the UW System review Extension's fee structure, federal funding, and reallocation process. A Special Regent Study Committee on Extension was formed in 1980 to "more fully examine Extension's programs, budgets, and inter-institutional relationships and to make recommendations to enhance the efficiency and operation of Extension in the UW System." Hearings were held between September 1980 and December 1981.[13]

At the regent meeting of April 9, 1982, recommendations of the regent committee were adopted.[14] The main provisions:

- The University of Wisconsin-Extension would "continue as an institution of the University of Wisconsin System with the chief administrator's title continuing to be that of chancellor."

- The System administration would "monitor ... the extension programs offered by the institutions ... and review annual program plans and budgets ... and budget submissions. System administration will not assume operational responsibility, but will mediate any unresolved inter-institutional disputes."

- The chancellor of Extension would be assigned the responsibility of "program coordination and statewide planning" of Extension functions.

- The UW System and campuses would continue to integrate "existing UW-Extension faculty with faculties of the other institutions" in the System.

- Inter-institutional committees would continue "to review existing inter-institutional agreements."

- Allocation of funds from UW-Extension to the campuses would be done only pursuant to agreements reached between the chancellor of Extension and the chancellor of the institutions and "such allocations [would] permanently retain their budgetary identity as funds in support of extension programs."

- Extension would establish "three separate and homogeneous units — [a] general extension and special mission programs; [b] cooperative extension and special mission programs; and [c] educational communications," each to have a dean or director.

Nowhere in the report was there a hint that Extension would give up control of its budget.

I was told shortly after my term began in May 1984 that the resolution on the Extension was badly written so that it was not clear what was expected. We received an update from System President O'Neil on May 3, 1985. It was not until February 13, 1985, almost three years after the regent resolution (1982), that the UW-Madison Faculty Senate and the Extension Faculty Senate came to an agreement on the integration of the Extension faculty and academic and classified staff. The same was true of UW-Milwaukee.[15]

In addition to what seemed an inordinate amount of time to integrate the Extension faculty, regents became concerned that there was a movement by some of the campuses to take all Extension programs and budgets into existing academic departments and to eliminate Extension. There were some of us who believed that this would destroy the outreach mission. Furthermore, there was evidence that many academic departments had no real interest in providing the service. As far as we could determine, tenure was rarely awarded because of outreach work done by the tenure track faculty in the doctoral campuses. The notable exception was the School of Agriculture at UW-Madison. Being a member of the state bar, I was required to take continuing education courses in order to maintain my license. Even before becoming a member of the board of regents, I could not understand why the School of Law at UW-Madison, the only law school in the UW System, did not provide this required education. Instead, the overwhelming number of courses were offered through the state bar association, and the courses were taught by other lawyers. How strange, I thought, that the students were the teachers. As a matter of fact, the dean of the law school served on the advisory committee of the state bar. It was clear that the law school faculty had little interest in continuing education, an essential component of outreach. Under these circumstances, why would anyone want to abandon Extension and turn the money over to the academic departments?

Of course, the Extension budget was a "plum" coveted by many. There were private hall conversations between those of us who were concerned. Extension had a national reputation for excellence. We did not want to be a party to fixing something that was not broken!

Regents Grover, Schilling, Lyon, and I met and planned how to overcome what we feared was an assault on Extension by some campuses and faculty. We were convinced that the extension must remain an independently managed operation in charge of its budget.

In 1988, the board held hearings to determine the current status of Extension vis a vis the campuses. We learned that no one had received tenure as a result of their outstanding Extension work, and there was little coordination between campus academic departments where outreach was concerned. For example, UW-Madison's School of Engineering and UW-Milwaukee's School of Engineering did not coordinate their course offerings in continuing education.

At the hearing held January 8, 1988, the chancellor of Extension, Patrick C. Boyle, was asked to provide the regents with recommendations that would ensure the continued excellence of Extension, take advantage of the campus academic departments, and provide for statewide planning and coordination in order to avoid unnecessary duplication and enhance program delivery.[16] His recommendations were incorporated in Regent Resolution II.4.c on May 6, 1989. They further clarified the 1982 resolution, which the board reaffirmed, and dealt with the concerns of the regents. The revised policy prescribed:

1. Establishment of structures to enhance statewide planning, coordination and communication among related disciplines and program areas of the UW institutions, between the UW-Extension Cooperative and General Extension divisions, between county and campus-based faculty and staff, and between UW-Extension and the other UW institutions.

2. Establishment of joint appointments to allow integrated extension faculty and staff to participate in UW-Extension institutional governance and in statewide extension program planning and development (later defined as collaborative appointments).

3. Establishment of a role for UW-Extension in personnel decisions for integrated faculty and staff holding Cooperative and General Extension appointments in the UW institutions.

4. Consistent use of the term "extension" to identify UW institutional extension units, faculty and staff, and programs within the statewide extension function.

5. Incorporation of UW institutional extension programs currently conducted outside the inter-institutional agreements within the program planning and coordination of UW-Extension.

The resolution called upon the president of the UW System to charge the chancellor of Extension "in consultation with the other UW institutional chancellors to develop and implement the resolution as soon as feasible" and to report to the UW System president by December 1, 1988.

The regents' resolution further strengthened Extension. With Extension controlling the funds, outreach was assured. If the academic departments would not provide the service, then Extension would not pay those faculty members who were expected to carry on outreach. It was also understood that Extension would play a role in personnel matters, including tenure, heretofore not articulated as regent policy.

At present, UW Extension controls its budget and determines how it will be allocated to the various campus departments. The Extension budget totaled $107.8 million for the fiscal year 1990-91.[17] It was larger than the total budget of any campus within the System, except for UW-Madison, which had a budget of $1.08 billion, and UW-Milwaukee, which had a budget of $200.4 million. Of the total Extension budget, $44.7 million was provided by the state of Wisconsin. The balance came from federal grants and contracts, gifts, operational receipts, and fees.

Regent Actions When Others Failed to Act

Following are eight examples of change in which the regents determined that those to whom they had delegated authority had not acted in a meaningful or timely fashion, .

Improving the Quality of Undergraduate Education

Maintaining and improving the quality of undergraduate education was clearly among the most important mandates before the regents. Chapter 36.01, Wisconsin Statutes requires the UW System "provide a system of higher education ... which stresses undergraduate teaching as its *main priority* ..." (emphasis added).

In 1990, the board began to examine the quality of undergraduate education. It was a subject being discussed nationally, and it had begun to receive more of the board's attention. Most writers agreed that undergraduate education was in need of improvement. Regents were aware of this debate. We received *The Chronicle of Higher Education*, as well as the publications of the Association of Governing Boards, the trade association of college and university governing boards, whose pages were full of articles from around the country related to undergraduate education.

Chapter 36.01, Wisconsin Statutes provided that undergraduate teaching was to be the "main priority." Chapter 36.09[4], Wisconsin Statutes assigned to the faculty primary responsibility for academic affairs, "subject to the responsibilities and powers of the board, the president and the chancellor ..." There was no way, therefore, of dealing with the quality of undergraduate education without asking about the weight it received in the tenure-granting process and in post-tenure review and promotion procedures. Faculty, campus and System administrators preferred not to make the inevitable linkage, but to talk around the subject. Tenure was seen by them as the "holy of holies" — certainly not to be looked at in any detail by the regents. It was traditional that candidates for tenure came from the departments to deans and divisional committees to the chancellor, on to the president of the System and finally to the board, where the list was "rubber stamped." It was assumed that all of those recommended for tenure were worthy of this lifetime appointment — no questions asked. The same was true of post-tenure review and merit raises.

Some of us began to suspect that Wisconsin was not immune to the concerns being raised nationally. Regents received phone calls from parents of students who were unhappy with the fact that their children were being taught by teaching assistants on the doctoral campuses. Some teaching assistants could not be understood because of their lack of oral English skills. In addition, regents generally concluded that in the doctoral campuses, research and publications — not undergraduate education — were the major factors considered in awarding tenure and in post-tenure review.

In my early years on the board, I did not detect any resolve on the part of most regents to deal with the way tenure was awarded or to examine the processes for post-tenure review and how those processes affected the quality of undergraduate teaching. They seemed satisfied to continue the "rubber stamp" approach.

In preparation for this book, I reviewed the history of the board's deliberations regarding the issue of undergraduate education. I was struck by the fact that the UW System Administration seemed reluctant to respond to the issues being raised nationally and that faculty resented the board's involvement.

Official pronouncements, on the one hand, indicated that undergraduate instruction was of prime importance, which was consistent with Chapter 36.01, Wisconsin Statutes. On the other hand, the board, which was responsible for the overall quality of System institutions and for carrying out statutory mandates, essentially left the "main priority" to campus administrators and faculty without asking any important questions or engaging in any meaningful review. As a matter of fact, when those outside the System — parents, the general public, or lawmakers — raised questions about the quality of undergraduate education, most regents became defensive and clung to the status quo. In private conversations, some regents expressed concern that this issue was being ignored.

The board had adopted some broad policy statements and then left it to the faculty to carry them out. Regent Policy Document 74-13, adopted October 4, 1974, states: "Merit determination for faculty should be based on positive contributions by the faculty member to teaching, research, public service, *and/or* the support functions inherent in the institution's mission. Assessment of teaching faculty shall include consideration of student evaluations" (emphasis added). But mixed signals were also being sent. In a document titled "Report on Systemwide Initiatives in Undergraduate Education," dated September 26, 1990, sent from the acting vice president for academic affairs to the regents, in the section labeled "Completed Efforts," the board's policy is quoted as, "The Board of Regents *encourages* each institution to consider teaching as a major component of faculty employment ..." (emphasis added). The use of the word "encourages" is not consistent with the statutory mandate cited above. In the same document,

Ernest Boyer, the well-known authority on educational policy, is quoted as saying that "at every research university, teaching should be valued as highly as research and good teaching should be an equally important criterion for tenure and promotion." However, he notes, most faculty members are often torn between obligations to undergraduate teaching and top research and publication upon which promotion and tenure depend. Under those circumstances, words such as "encourage" and "should" seem entirely too weak, especially in view of Wisconsin Statutes.

In the introduction to *The Undergraduate Imperative: Building on Excellence*, prepared by UW System Administration and presented to the board of regents in December 1991, the role of undergraduate education is restated:

> *At the core* of the University of Wisconsin System is undergraduate education. Chapter 36.01, Wisconsin Statutes states that the public is best served by a system of higher education 'which stresses undergraduate teaching as its main priority.' National concern about the quality of undergraduate education has led to a review of commitment, accomplishments, challenges, and initiatives in undergraduate education[18] (emphasis added).

Why was it necessary to repeat in 1991 the clear language of Wisconsin Statutes, which had been in effect for 18 years? Obviously, there was a problem. The board and System administration were responding to national concerns as well as to what they perceived to be an issue for our System, and realized that changes had to take place. Wisconsin had not been exempt from these concerns about undergraduate education that were being expressed nationally.

An example of this problem comes from a conversation I had with some UW-Madison faculty leaders, who told me that if they were expected to teach undergraduates, they would have to be paid for doing so. Obviously they did not subscribe to the idea that undergraduate instruction is "at the core" of the university's mission, nor would they agree with the mandates of Chapter 36, Wisconsin Statutes that undergraduate education is the institution's "main priority." Other faculty members denied that there was a problem.

I don't know when the board began to change. Perhaps it started with a letter I received from Regent Grover, state superintendent of public instruction, who was the chair of the Regent Education Committee. The letter was dated August 31, 1990. He wrote: "This issue of the quality of undergraduate education is one of growing concern. Regents cannot ignore the consensus that colleges and universities have to do a better job in providing quality undergraduate education." He enclosed an article from *The Chronicle of Higher Education*, dated July 25, 1990, reporting the annual meeting of the Education Commission of the States.[19] According to the article, John I. Goodlad, professor of education, University of Washington, made two points: improve teacher-education programs and place a higher value on good teaching. At the same meeting, Governor Garrey E. Caruthers, New Mexico, outgoing chair of the commission and former faculty member of New Mexico State University, said, "If top faculty don't teach freshmen and sophomores, how in the world are they going to get enthusiasm for the discipline? If colleges continue to emphasize research and service, the taxpayer, one of these days, is going to ask, 'Why are we paying these people?'" Frank Newman, president of the commission, said that higher education leaders should not dismiss the complaints as mere college-bashing. "This is the year that higher education is coming on the griddle. What we want is a higher-education system that is more focused on teaching and learning, not less focused on research," he was quoted as saying. Perhaps our problem was that faculty did not read the *Chronicle*.

The American Association of State Colleges and Universities reported on August 31, 1990, that a survey based on information received from state system heads in all 50 states, Puerto Rico and the District of Columbia identified the top issues facing higher education in the United States:

- Improving undergraduate education.
- Increasing minority student achievement.
- Addressing concerns over accountability and effectiveness.
- Supporting research and economic development.
- Reviewing institutional roles and missions.
- the need for new faculty and competitive salaries.
- Reforming teacher education programs.

On August 27, 1990, I wrote to Regent President Lyon, noting that the subject of undergraduate education was not listed on the future agendas of the Regent Education Committee: "This is probably one of the most important issues before us and needs to be addressed in a timely manner."

On the same day, I responded to a copy of a memo he had sent to System President Shaw on the same subject, and related an earlier conversation with Shaw in which I urged him to prepare an "Issues for the 90s" paper on undergraduate education, as part of the series of papers System had been providing the regents. Undergraduate education had not been included. In the memo, I suggested that quality of undergraduate education hinged on three elements: the quality of the students, the quality of the instruction, and the quality of the facilities. "It would be helpful if our discussions were so organized." I sent a copy to Shaw, the acting vice president for academic affairs, and regents Grover and Erroll Davis to make sure that they were in the loop. At the September 7, 1990, meeting of the board, the Education

Committee was told that System administration would be providing informational reports on undergraduate education, beginning in October, including a review of what had been done, what was being done, and what needed to be done. The item was *now* on the agenda.

Shaw announced at the September 1990 meeting that improvement of undergraduate education would be a major goal for the ensuing year, and, per my request, the regents would receive a series of reports and proposals on that subject. I asked again to have quality of instruction, facilities, and students addressed. I also wanted some "how to" information; how to develop incentives for teaching; how to ensure that those teaching were good teachers; how to develop honors programs; and how to have access and quality.

On September 18, 1990, I wrote to Regent Grover, chair of the Education Committee, "Quality Undergraduate Education: I believe we have made the issue so complicated that we are left with generalities that are meaningless. First, we need to identify those variables that make a difference, such as quality instruction, quality students, and quality facilities. Second, we need a plan on how to get there. Third, we need a system for determining if we have achieved our goals. I have written you previously about the first step. I don't see much movement in making this identification."

System administration was slow to respond. At the October 1990 meeting, the board was given a report that listed previous systemwide initiatives as well as some general reading. The issues I had asked to receive information about were not included. I suggested again that the quality of undergraduate education should be evaluated in light of three variables: quality of instruction, students, and facilities. It was agreed that UW System Administration should address four issues around undergraduate education in the UW System institutions: "where we are now, where we want to go, how we plan to get there, and how we will know when we have arrived."

The national debate continued. On September 12, 1990, the title of the lead story in *The Chronicle of Higher Education* was: "Toward the 21st Century: Some Research Universities Contemplate Sweeping Changes, Ranging from Management and Tenure to Teaching Methods."[20] For background to the issues, the article referred to an essay by Kenneth D. Benne, professor emeritus of philosophy, Boston University. He concluded that Johns Hopkins instituted early on the German model, whose primary focus was research and scholarship. This was quickly followed by Harvard, Cornell, Michigan, and Columbia, which made graduate studies, research, and scholarship their reasons for being. Benne observed that at these institutions undergraduate education "was an appendage to the basic structure of the university."[21] In response to expressed dissatisfaction of undergraduate students with their education (as reported in 1987 by the Carnegie Foundation in its report *The Undergraduate Experience in America*) and pressure by governing boards, there had been institutional soul-search-ing nationwide. It was reported that a survey of the 56 members of the Association of American Universities found that a majority were taking steps to improve undergraduate education.[22] Cornell, Stanford, Michigan, Indiana, Northwestern, and Iowa State were advocating reforms ranging from new criteria for promotion and tenure to creating more effective teaching methods. Some faculty members at the University of Michigan suggested creation of an undergraduate college designed for freshmen and sophomores. Courses would be taught by senior faculty members. There was a general concern to seek ways to achieve a better balance between research and teaching. How about Wisconsin?

In September 1990, the UW System Board of Regents' staff, at the request of the board, prepared a report on the use of teaching assistants at the doctoral institutions as of October 1989.[23] The report concluded that 20% of students in entry-level courses at UW-Madison and 15% at UW-Milwaukee were being taught exclusively by graduate teaching assistants. About 48% of enrollment at this level at UW-Madison and 46% at UW-Milwaukee was in courses taught in part by a graduate teaching assistant and in part by a faculty or academic staff member. It was also reported that at UW-Madison, there was no campuswide procedure for assessing teaching assistant candidates' spoken English proficiency, whereas at UW-Milwaukee campus wide procedures and standards were adopted in 1986 that required all international teaching assistant candidates to take a standardized test of spoken English. Those who achieved below a cut-off in the test score were required to take an oral English course at their own expense, a cost of $300. Training at UW-Madison was at the college or departmental level, and was a mixture of voluntary and required programs. At UW-Milwaukee, training was required and, to a large extent, standardized. The evaluation of teaching assistants at both institutions and in all departments was based on student evaluation. Some, but not all, departments also used faculty evaluations. This came as a surprise to the regents. The report concluded by posing a series of policy questions for the board to consider, including whether the quality of instruction suffered because of the use of teaching assistants, whether they were being used too much, and whether there should be campuswide standards for training, supervision, and evaluation.

When the regents probed further into the report, it was explained by administrators and faculty that it was in the very nature of large, research universities that faculty/student contact could not be as intensive as on smaller campuses. The research demands are greater on the faculty and to demand larger undergraduate teaching loads would diminish the quality of research. Not only that, but it would make the doctoral campuses in the System non-competitive with peer institutions. In addition, in order to attract graduate students, there had to be employment opportunities for them. Awarding them a teaching assistantship was essential. On the other hand, students gained because of the availability of a greater array of courses, and they had an opportunity in the higher-level courses to interact with faculty who were on the cutting edge of their disciplines. Those students who wanted smaller classes and closer contact with faculty had a wide variety of choices within the UW System. The regents were not satisfied with the explanation. It still left open the issues raised in the report. Why couldn't we do better in training and supervising teaching assistants? What was the teaching load of the faculty? Was it large enough? Why were unqualified teaching assistants allowed to teach? What were the incentives for faculty to teach undergraduates? What were the disincentives? The regents were not operating in a vacuum. The arguments we heard were also being made during the national debate that was taking place. Others disagreed, and found no incompatibility between faculty in major research universities teaching undergraduates and engaging in research.

That same month, regents were given a summary of *College: The Undergraduate Experience in America*, written by Ernest L. Boyer and published in 1987.[24] The book was based on a three-year study of undergraduate education in the US. The study included two-week sight visits to 29 campuses representing the full spectrum of institutional types. Boyer observed that while our system of higher education is "the envy of the world," the undergraduate college is a "troubled institution" with deep divisions over priorities and interests that "diminish the intellectual and social quality of the undergraduate experience." Faculty members are torn between obligations to undergraduate teaching and to research and publication, upon which promotion and tenure depend. Among his recommendations:

> At every research university, teaching should be valued as highly as research and good teaching should be an equally important criterion for tenure and promotion. For most of the nation's colleges and universities, where large numbers of undergraduates are enrolled, priority should be given to teaching, not research.
>
> Further, research universities using the title Distinguished Research Professor should also establish the rank of Distinguished Teaching Professor, with special status and pay incentives.

In November 1990, after receiving reports from System administration describing current initiatives on undergraduate teaching from the System and institutional perspective, Regent Grover, chair of the Education Committee, consulted with Regent Davis and me. He then wrote to System President Shaw asking that future reports be organized around the criteria I had suggested months before — quality of instruction and the instructional environment, the quality of students, and the quality of facilities. He requested specific information about each of the three criteria. In a follow-up letter to Shaw (November 28, 1990), I asked that for each item, System indicate where we were, where we should be, how we were going to get there, and the expected time frame. A follow-up inquiry was made at the December 1990 regent meeting. There was no clear response by the System to the Grover letter, nor was there any indication that there would be. At that meeting, Regent President Lyon said that 90% of the comments about undergraduate education had been directed at the doctoral campuses. I assumed he was referring to the regent staff report and the complaints the regents had received about teaching assistants teaching undergraduates, their lack of English proficiency skills, and lack of supervision by the faculty, as well as the basis for awarding tenure, which did not give adequate weight to teaching. We had been given the general impression that at the non-doctoral campuses, teaching received much greater weight than in the doctoral campuses, where research received the greatest weight. (During the hearings on the revisions of the mission statements, some of us were under the impression that the non-doctoral campuses wanted to put greater weight on research.) Further, class sizes were larger on the doctoral campuses than at the non-doctoral institutions.

I asked the System to review retention (graduation) rates and the implications of retention on public policy. I had already told Shaw that there was an obvious disparity between admissions standards and graduation standards. I also asked that the four questions initially raised in September be addressed in February: where are we, where do we want to go, how will we get there, and how will we know when we have arrived?

On December 13, 1990, I wrote to Grover, "I detect a lack of enthusiasm for this exercise." I was referring to the System's lack of response to the Grover letter. My suspicion was confirmed in the response Grover finally received from the Shaw on January 24, 1991. Shaw reasoned that budgetary constraints and staff commitments must be taken into account, that some of the data requested was not collected. He raised the cost/benefit issue for gathering the information, and concluded by restating that a final report would go to the regents in February 1991, with no indication of what the report would contain. So much for the statutorily mandated "main priority," I thought.

In January 1991, System administration provided the board with what had originally been planned as the final February 1991 paper, which was to outline specific proposals. Instead, the board received a paper titled, "Continual Evaluation/Continual Improvement: Undergraduate Education in the University of Wisconsin System." It reported that "[t]hroughout the 1980's, best sellers, association reports, scholarly journals, government publications, and news magazines have discussed education, have usually been critical of the status quo, and have made numerous suggestions for change." Included were a number of articles which summarized national issues and related them to Wisconsin. Of special interest were comments about the reward system. System finally admitted that while the formal structures of regent policy required teaching evaluations to be included in awarding tenure and promotion, "faculty members may be reacting to another set of written or unwritten expectations. At the two doctoral institutions, research and publication [and the adjunct necessity to bring in external funding] has *always* been the primary requirement for tenure, promotion and salary increases" (emphasis added). This was the first time this had been acknowledged by the System administration. The paper included some discussion of the reward structure, training future teachers, general education requirements, the undergraduate major, maximizing student-faculty contact, facilities, undergraduate employment, retention and graduation rates, and assessment. For each there was a summary of national concerns, a Wisconsin perspective, some suggested solutions and consequences. Finally a series of public hearings were proposed. We were finally making progress!

At the February 1991 meeting, the board adopted a resolution calling for public hearings to "culminate in a package of policy recommendations to improve the quality of undergraduate education."[25] Executive Vice President Lyall announced public hearings and Regent President Lyon announced the formation of five regent working groups:

1. Rewards, incentives, and policies for undergraduate teaching.

2. Undergraduate programs.

3. Contact between students, faculty, and instructors.

4. Transition between high school and the university and between university and the work force.

5. Relationship between undergraduate education and K-12 teacher preparation, and between undergraduate education and the VTAE.

In announcing the hearings and appointments to the working groups, Lyon said that while the UW System "institutions provide[d] a quality undergraduate education," there was increased national concern about the baccalaureate years, and "we would be remiss if we did not examine our own system in a structured and rigorous way." (I served on the working group on "Rewards, Incentives, and Policies for Undergraduate Teaching" along with Regents Lee Sherman Dreyfus, Obert Vattendahl, and Schilling, who was the chair.)

In the meantime, national discussions about the status of teaching among faculty, the issue other regents and I raised originally, continued. Respected institutions around the country were addressing the problem in constructive ways. Stanford University announced a major program to emphasize undergraduate education. James Wilkinson, director of Harvard's Danforth Center for Teaching and Learning, was quoted as saying, "The program must overhaul the whole reputation of teaching. Being branded a good teacher now is almost a stigma. Indeed, the adage remains prevalent: Those who can do research; and those who can't teach."[26] The president of Stanford recommended that the definition of scholarship be broadened to include work related to teaching. He noted that because of the shift from teaching to research, junior professors who are outstanding teachers "fail at the tenure line too often," and said that Stanford would address this problem.[27] It was an issue the UW System talked about but did not have any specific proposals to consider.

Fannie Le Moine, associate vice chancellor for academic affairs, UW-Madison, is reported to have said in March of 1991, "if we are truly to give undergraduate education a high priority, the faculty must believe that teaching, especially teaching undergraduates, will be recognized and rewarded in the annual merit review."[28] We argued that the same criteria should apply in the initial awarding of tenure.

The board held hearings in April 1991 at UW-Fox Valley, UW-Eau Claire, UW-Stevens Point, UW-Madison, and UW-Milwaukee. The hearing at Madison attracted 28 speakers — chancellors, faculty, teaching assistants, campus administrators, students, and alumni. We began at 10 a.m. and went late into the afternoon. The same was true at the other hearings. The testimony we heard included a variety of views — teaching assistants needed more communication skills, class sizes were too big, faculty needed to learn teaching theory, and regents should not mandate anything. Questions we had about setting the standards, enhancing the status of undergraduate education in every department, and weighing teaching in the awarding of tenure, were unanswered. We were assured by one speaker from the Madison campus that teaching was one of the three criteria used in awarding tenure, although several speakers for the UW-Madison and UW-Milwaukee said that research was and should continue to be the paramount consideration in the awarding of tenure.[29]

The Madison campus policy provided that "[a] candidate [for tenure] ... must present evidence of excellent performance in either teaching or research and satisfactory performance in the other category and public service." I asked for examples of tenure being granted to candidates with excellent performance in teaching or outreach. None were supplied. Some faculty testified that tenure was not based on teaching but on research.

It was reported that at UW-Milwaukee, the weight given to teaching varied among colleges, schools and departments. And variance by department was not uncommon for the non-doctoral campuses. A few campuses set a minimum weight to be given for teaching.

At the June 6, 1991, meeting of the board, which was my last meeting, board members presented the preliminary findings of the working groups and reviewed areas for policy consideration.

I reported that the working group on "Rewards, Incentives, and Policies for Undergraduate Teaching" had agreed to focus on post-tenure review of faculty teaching performance, incentives for teaching, including weighing of teaching effectiveness in appointment, retention, promotion, tenure and merit decisions, the identification of programs and resources to support teaching improvement, and the qualification, training, supervision, and English language proficiency of teaching assistants. After the hearings, there was evidence presented indicating that these were areas that needed further exploration. I announced that the next meeting of the working group would include several faculty members who had been active at the System level as well as on their own campuses in efforts to improve undergraduate education. After that, the working group would meet to identify policy implications and report to the board.

At the September 1991 meeting of the board, this working group, as well as the others, reported its recommendations to the board, which the board unanimously adopted.[30] The proposals presented by the working groups called for action to be undertaken by the UW System Administration and the UW System institutions. The resolution reads in part "that Acting President Lyall consult with the institutions to review these issues and proposals, develop reasonable strategies for improving undergraduate education in these and any other areas, and report back to the Education Committee at the December 1991 meeting."

It is worth noting what the board resolution encompassed, since it was the most comprehensive set of initiatives on the subject adopted by the board in years.

The working group on "Rewards, Incentives, and Policies for Undergraduate Teaching" reported to the September 1991 board meeting that it had met on four occasions, beginning in May and concluding in July; had considered testimony from the public hearings as well as current literature on teaching issues; had exchanged views with UW System faculty members as well as members of the Undergraduate Teaching Improvement Council, and had concluded:

> The working group has identified three issues that it believes warrant *the Board's attention and action by UW System Administration and UW institutions* (emphasis added):
>
> 1. the post-tenure review of faculty teaching performance;
>
> 2. incentives for teaching, including the appropriate evaluation and weighing of teaching effectiveness in appointment, retention, pro-

motion, tenure, and merit decisions; and the identification of programs and resources to support teaching improvement;

3. the qualifications, training, supervision, and English language proficiency of teaching assistants.

The working group on "Undergraduate Academic Programs" proposals included:

1. institutional general education requirements;

2. credit requirements in the major, including time-to-degree and program review;

3. institutional academic program array, and fiscal implications of program review;

4. balanced perspective;

5. institutional academic honors programs.

The working group on "Contact Between Students and Faculty and Instructors" dealt with:

1. quality, consistency and coordination of academic advising programs for students at UWS institutions;

2. enhancement and promotion of quality contact opportunities between students and faculty at UWS institutions.

The working group on "Issues in Undergraduate Transitions" identified:

1. orientation to the university;

2. tailoring services to different constituent groups;

3. activities outside the classroom;

4. career planning and counseling.

The working group on "Issues in Relationships Between Undergraduate Education and K-12/VTAE" identified these issues:

1. communication and payment for cooperating teachers;

2. System capacity to alleviate specific teacher and school physical therapist shortages, and to expand and accelerate the recruitment and retention of minority faculty and students in teacher education programs;

3. coordination of the relationship between the National Council for Accreditation of Teacher Education (NCATE) and the DPI program approval process;

4. creation of integrated course work in mathematics, science and social studies;

5. dissemination of articulation agreements between the UW System and VTAE; and credit transfer for Tech-Prep curriculum for high school students.

At its December 1991 meeting, the board adopted *The Undergraduate Imperative, Building on Excellence*, presented by Acting Vice President Lyall, along with a schedule of reports and dates they were due. A fair reading of *The Undergraduate Imperative, Building on Excellence* and the documentation of September 1991 should convince anyone that there has been a major change in the position of both the board of regents and System administration regarding willingness to deal with issues related to undergraduate education that had previously been ignored. None of the issues identified for action by the working groups, including the granting of tenure and post-tenure review as they related to undergraduate teaching, was left out of the December action. The blueprint was clearly in place for major steps to be taken regarding the role of undergraduate teaching in awarding tenure and in post-tenure review. The importance of this action plan, if implemented, cannot be overestimated.

Will it be implemented? When?

Post-Tenure Review

The issues surrounding post-tenure review, and the reluctance of faculty, campus and System administrators to deal with those issues, were not substantially different from those around the granting of tenure. Was there an understandable, consistent standard? Was it articulated? Were there evaluation procedures in place? If so, what weight was given to undergraduate teaching and outreach?

While I served on the board, we asked the System about post-tenure review practices and procedures. We were told at the December 1989 board meeting that all was well. I was convinced that the System administrators were uncomfortable having the regents delve into the granting of tenure and post-tenure review procedures. And frankly, some regents also showed little interest in dealing with the issues.

Since it was established that teaching of undergraduates was at the core of our System's mission, according to Chapter 36, Wisconsin Statutes, I asked (September 1990 meeting of the board) the System to indicate to what extent faculty were being rewarded for instruction vs. research, how to put incentives on instruction by those most qualified, and how to assure that those who were teaching were good teachers.

Earlier in this chapter, I discussed the board's extensive investigation— beginning in the mid 1970s of the quality of our undergraduate programs. Undergraduate education and post-tenure review were tied to each other. On February 27, 1991, the board received a report from the acting vice president for academic affairs on the subject of post-tenure review. It described how the awarding of a Ph.D. degree began a rigorous process of selection that continued on through the granting of tenure. It described the evaluation process of probationary faculty, how tenured faculty were evaluated, what was done with non-performers, and how other universities dealt with post-tenure review. Nowhere was there any mention of the weight given to undergraduate teaching, except that it was considered along with research and outreach. The weight given to each varied from campus to campus and department to department. There did not seem to be a great interest on the part of the board in dealing with the issue. Page 11 of the report says, "Resources are limited for additional efforts in the areas of faculty evaluation and development." Further, the report made the point that post-tenure review was meant to enhance faculty development, and that, "[f]unds now available for support of faculty development are not adequate to the purpose. Each year, only about 450 faculty members, 6% of System faculties, chosen from many applicants, have been able to participate in Undergraduate Teaching Improvement grants, conferences, and teaching fellows programs." Some of us were upset, since this was not an adequate response to the clear language of Chapter 36.01, Wisconsin Statutes, which speaks of undergraduate teaching as the "main priority." Somewhere, the priorities had gotten out of sync with legislative intent. No one ever suggested that the System did not do quality research because of inadequate funds. I asked if there were examples of dismissal "for cause" because of inadequate undergraduate teaching performance. None were provided.

On March 13, 1991, I wrote to Regent President Lyon after reading the report.

> I believe we both have a sense of unease about the process. Since tenure is a life time commitment, more or less, mostly more, post tenure review becomes crucially important. The elements, to the extent they exist, are not understood. What is the basis for the review? Who does the review? What is the result of an unsatisfactory review beyond some possible financial punishment. How does that make things better?
>
> What should be avoided is a review that becomes a self review. The criteria are of significant importance because they should be consistent with the mission, the obligation of the faculty regarding instruction, research and outreach. While I have great respect for the faculty, we must also be accountable beyond the assurance of the faculty 'trust us.'
>
> I am not sure we know enough about the process to sign off.

On March 18, 1991, I received a memo from Regent President Lyon on the subject of post-tenure review.

It is my view that the administration and faculty are using the merit review process as a means of sidestepping the issue. I believe we need to know how thorough the merit review process is, how well files are maintained, and what significant changes in performance can be documented through this process. We also have a significant problem on the Madison campus with the divisional tenure review process. I have good reason to believe, at this level beyond the departmental scrutiny, undergraduate teaching and Extension are being penalized.

I wrote him on March 21 that I agreed, and expressed my concern that there be people at the hearing in Madison who could discuss this subject with us.

At the hearings in March and April 1991, campus administrators were asked directly how research, instruction, and outreach were weighted in the granting of tenure and in post-tenure review. Other than an assurance that they were taken into account, nothing more specific was provided. Regents began to express openly their concern that if the tenure system did not properly emphasize undergraduate instruction and outreach, those two aspects of the mission would suffer. They were concerned that teaching assistants were given responsibility to teach, while they did not possess the English skills or teaching skills to do so. If that was the attitude during the probationary period, how could it be expected to get better later on?

In the September 1991 report of the regent working group on "Rewards, Incentives, and Policies for Undergraduate Education," four issues were identified that would warrant the board's attention and action by the System administration and the System institutions:

1. Ensure regular and systematic evaluation of the teaching performance of tenured faculty.

2. Establish incentives for good teaching, *including evaluation and weighing of teaching effectiveness in appointment, retention, promotion, tenure, and merit decisions* (emphasis added).

3. Provide training, supervision, and English language proficiency for teaching assistants.

4. Ensure the existence of policies and procedures to address consistently ineffective performance of faculty.

At that same meeting, System Acting President Katharine Lyall made a major break with the past when she included among her priorities for the year development of a post-tenure review system for faculty. "Tenure is not, and has never been intended to be, a protection from regular review of faculty work or a means to insulate individuals from contributing fully to the collective responsibility of a department for quality teaching, research, and public service." She opened the door to regent involvement in an area hitherto seen as "meddling." It was a new and refreshingly bold step, and the regents responded. According to the minutes of the meeting, Lyall's position was:

> [The] ... tenure process should be reviewed in order to ensure that fair and impartial procedures are being provided for all candidates regardless of race or gender, that there are clear and equitable tenure expectations and voting rules across departments within an institution, and that there is timely processing of appeals and complaints, stemming from the tenure process. ... While this currently is done through peer reviews, accreditation procedures, student evaluations and other methods, [Lyall] considered it appropriate to develop a systemwide policy requiring professional reviews of each faculty member's work at reasonable intervals, coupled with retraining and professional development opportunities. "Innovative types of appointments also might be explored, which would enable faculty to adjust their contracted services among teaching, research, and service activities as they pass through their careers or phase into retirement. It (tenure) has never been intended to be a protection from regular review of faculty work or a means to insulate individuals from contributing fairly to the collective responsibility of departments for quality teaching, research, and public service.[31]

What a magnificent challenge to the board and the entire System! Will they act?

On December 5, 1991, Lyall presented "The Undergraduate Imperative: Building on Excellence" to the board of regents. Post-tenure review was identified as one of the issues.[32] Regents were informed that System Administration was developing a proposal for the institutional review in February 1992 followed by a policy recommendation to be presented to the board in May 1992.

Wisconsin Week reported on April 1, 1992, that the UW System was going to propose a policy on post-tenure review to the regents, "Tenured Faculty Review and Development."[33] Its purpose was to help faculty develop throughout their careers. Each campus would be required to develop a policy that "includes criteria for reviewing tenured faculty's activities at least once every five years, plans for who is responsible for conducting the reviews, and methods for rewarding outstanding performance and remedying problem areas."

In an interview with System President Lyall (Lyall became System president on April 1, 1992) in the April 15, 1992, issue of the same publication, she is reported to have said that post-tenure review is critical to the credibility of the university. "I think it is very important both to assure ourselves that we treat all of our faculty fairly and so we can assure our external audiences that faculty are reviewed regularly and that they are being treated as people in the rest of the economy are."[34] In that same publication, it was reported that the UW-Madison Faculty Senate voted overwhelmingly to *oppose* the System proposal. The resolution read, in part:

> ... [W]e believe that current review policies provide adequate quality assurance and accountability, although we acknowledge that the implementation of the policies can always be improved. In contrast, the proposed new mechanisms for post-tenure review would be costly, time consuming, and inefficient, and would yield little of added benefit. Instead of promoting excellence, the proposed mechanism would detract from the university's teaching, research, service, and outreach functions, and its ability to attract and retain distinguished faculty. Enhanced faculty development programs would almost certainly require additional funding for faculty development grants and an improved sabbatical system.[35]

I was not surprised by the response of the Madison faculty. I was taken aback, however, by the tone of the rejection as well as its timing. What was troubling was that the faculty was still out of touch with some important issues and seemed oblivious as to what was going on at the national, System and board levels:

1. The relevance of tenure was being discussed nationally. Because of the protection already afforded in the Wisconsin Administrative Code, it was becoming more difficult to explain to the "outside world" why faculty needed what amounted to a lifetime appointment on the one hand, but on the other refused to have the governing body of the System be assured that performance was adequately reviewed, that professional development was taking place, and that the missions and other regent policies were being carried.

2. How would the faculty response "play in Peoria"— with the citizens of the state, the political leaders, and the regents? Would it be surprising if the legislature intervened and enacted legislation forcing the issue? It has happened before.

3. The faculty was not only out of touch with the national debate, but, apparently, was unaware of the regent hearings — concerns expressed by regents at those hearings and at regent meetings, even though the faculty is represented at all regent hearings and meetings. Nor did the faculty seem aware of or choose to ignore the December 5, 1991, document prepared by System administration, "The Undergraduate Imperative: Building on Excellence" which specifically targeted post-tenure review as an issue to be dealt with.

4. More surprising was the fact that the UW-Madison Faculty Senate, by
    its vote of rejection, ignored the 1989 findings of its own report that
    were consistent with the board's report "Future Directions, The Uni-
    versity in the 21st Century." The report says:

> Tenured faculty who wish to redirect their efforts to teaching or
> outreach are discouraged from making significant readjustments
> in their careers because of concern that their efforts will not be
> recognized or rewarded. ... Tenured faculty should review the
> direction of their teaching, research, and service in a broader
> context every five years. ... This review should be tied to an
> examination by the departmental executive committee of how the
> tenured faculty member is contributing to the tripartite mission
> of the department and should provide the tenured faculty mem-
> ber an opportunity to redirect his or her energy to entirely new
> areas of endeavor. For example, a tenured professor might wish
> to concentrate upon undergraduate teaching or outreach or an
> entirely new area of research for a specified period and to have
> his or her performance reviewed in the annual merit exercise with
> that concentration kept in mind.[36]

I cannot understand why the faculty found it so difficult to acknowledge
that everything was not perfect, there was room for improvement, and that
they would take the initiative and comply, rather than reject the idea even
before it was proposed to the regents. How had they been harmed? Their
resolution did not explain their objections. In my view, the resolution made
no sense either substantively or from a governance point of view. It asked
for a confrontation, which served no purpose. And as the System president
stated, it raised real credibility questions for the citizens of the state.

The regents held hearings on the Lyall proposal, "Tenured Faculty
Review and Development," at the May 1992 meeting.[37] It referred, specifically, to UW-Madison's "Future Directions," and clearly stated that, "[w]hile
most current procedures and practices to ensure faculty quality are on the
whole effective, they need formalizing and expanding." The proposal set out
guidelines and stated that the faculty, through their governance procedures,
would propose an institutional policy for faculty review and development.
The proposal pointed out that the regents and public must be "assured that
the university takes seriously its responsibility to maximize the talents of its
faculty."

Lyall's guidelines provided that every faculty member's activities be
reviewed every five years, in accordance with the "mission of the department, college, and institution." The policy would include "effective criteria
against which to measure progress and accomplishments of faculty during
this review and a description of the methods for conducting the evaluation."
The evaluation would include both peer and student evaluations, "and *give*

appropriate emphasis to activities in support of undergraduate education" (emphasis added). The policy would also include "[m]eans by which the merit process and faculty review and development process would be linked and used to facilitate, enhance, and reward outstanding performance," as well as "[p]rocedures defining means for remedying problems in cases where deficiencies are revealed." A written record of each faculty review would have a designated location in the personnel file and a "[d]escription of the accountability measures the institution [would] use to ensure full implementation of the institutional plan." The plan would be implemented by the fall semester 1993-94.

According to an article in *Wisconsin Week* (May 13, 1992), those faculty members who appeared in opposition to the "Guidelines" argued that this would erode academic freedom. Others complained that the Guidelines would create unnecessary bureaucracy.[38] According to an article in the *Wisconsin State Journal* (May 1, 1992), Lyall responded, "Our constituents need to be assured that our faculty are reviewed regularly and fairly. We must be able to assure the public, which will actually serve to strengthen the tenure system."[39] Regent George Steil countered that, "Tenure is a valuable right, but its continuance depends upon the public's perception of it."

According to the *Wisconsin Week* article, Regent President Lyon stated, "I don't think this signals any change in freedom for academics. What it is about is accountability — to the public, to the faculty and to the consumers of education in this state." Lyall agreed, as reported in the May 1 *Wisconsin State Journal* article, "Just as there is rigorous examination of performance before tenure is granted, we cannot afford to be inattentive to continuous improvement after tenure is awarded." Regent Ruth Clusen was quoted as saying that legislators were reluctant to hike faculty pay because they believed "[f]aculty members don't work very hard and once they get tenure they never have to do anything again. This is a chance to blow that myth."[40]

Resolution 1.1.a, "Guidelines for Tenured Faculty Review and Development," was adopted by the regents by a vote of 14-1. As reported in the May 13, 1992, *Wisconsin Week*, the lone dissenter explained that there ought to be a fiscal note attached to provide funds to put the resolution into effect. Lyall explained that by not filling vacant positions through quality reinvestment, campuses could divert funds.

Enrollment Management

Enrollment management had its beginnings in Planning the Future. But, the board could not implement the plan on its own. It would take Governor Earl's agreement to avoid potential political repercussions.

Planning the Future stated that as a matter of regent policy, "[w]hen faced with a choice between maintaining educational quality or providing free market access for students, the regents place priority on quality." It called for an "enrollment management" policy beginning 1987-1988. Coordinated with increased state funding and tuition policy, the goal was to achieve "... national average levels of support per student." In order to achieve this goal, we had four choices: funding for the System would have to be increased by $88 million per year; tuition would have to go up $640 per year (an increase of 36%); enrollment would have to drop by 2,000 students; or a combination of the three.[41]

State funding was paying about two-thirds of resident undergraduate instructional costs, and tuition paid the balance. (In Chapter II, I described how the budget and tuition fit together.) If enrollment increased faster than state funding, the total available on a per-student-basis would decline, unless tuition were to make up the entire difference. The regents had no desire to implement such tuition increases, nor did they believe that would have been politically acceptable or that there was substantially more money available from the state. The only choice, therefore, in order to preserve the quality of the institutions, was to reduce enrollment in accordance with the policy described. The reduction would take place by raising admission standards, which will be discussed later in this chapter.

Previous boards and System administrations had operated under the assumption that it was politically unthinkable to talk about reducing enrollment. As a result, enrollment had been allowed to continue to grow regardless of available funding. Knowing that we were plowing new ground by calling for enrollment limits, which would also mean raising admission standards, various proposals were discussed. Some thought that enrollment should be reduced by 10,000. The board finally agreed to accept Shaw's proposal that a reduction in the student body of 7,000, or about 5% over the next four years, would be proposed. While the regents agreed with the plan, it was obvious that we needed the Governor's agreement in order to implement it. We wanted to avoid being "punished" at budget time.

In an unprecedented upset, Tommy Thompson (R) defeated incumbent Democratic Governor Anthony S. Earl in November 1986. On the morning following the election, I told System President Shaw that it was urgent that he arrange a meeting with Governor-elect Thompson so that we could discuss the enrollment management plan and seek his approval. Thompson, James Klauser (Secretary of Administration designate), Shaw, Regent Vice President Schilling, and I met for breakfast three days later. We discussed the need to reduce enrollment because of our assessment of potential state funding. We told them that while we understood the state's inability to provide funds commensurate with previous enrollment increases, we were concerned about maintaining the quality of the System. We explained the 7,000 figure. To our surprise and delight, Thompson said that as far as he was concerned, we could go to 8,000, and if it were necessary to do more, he wanted to be notified before we announced. He later confirmed this in writing to Shaw. We were now able to go ahead with implementation of enrollment management.

Enrollment management had two goals:

- To reduce the total number of students in the System by setting a maximum enrollment for each campus. If a campus exceeded its enrollment goal, the tuition dollars from the number of students over the goal would revert to System administration.

  The purpose was to better serve those students who could "make it" by responding to funding realities. Enrollment would be reduced by raising admission standards, which would also improve retention rates.

- To make it possible for students to complete their majors in an orderly fashion, we gave the campuses the authority to limit enrollment by major and course.

Goals were not met because implementation processes and controls were not in place. The final reduction was 5,709.[42] We did not meet the enrollment reduction target of the System of 7,000. Why not? A conversation I had with a faculty member after enrollment management was adopted was revealing. I asked how the plan was working in his department. He said he didn't know about the "plan" and the department was overwhelmed with enrollment. I asked him why they didn't control it. He said that the dean would not allow it. I could not believe that he had never heard of the regent initiative and wondered how widespread that was. I contacted Shaw and urged him to send a memo to every department chair and dean explaining the policy, since it was apparent that some campus administrator had "dropped the ball." I don't know whether he ever sent a memo.

As the annual reports came out showing that targets were not being met, other regents and I expressed our concern, privately and publicly. We knew that we would have to pay the price for not doing what we said we needed to do and had the authority to do. No one can prove that it came to pass, but I have concluded from conversations I had with members of the governor's staff that an enrollment reduction of 5,709 over four years, when we had the authority to implement an 8,000 reduction, cost the System in terms of credibility, a price that could not be calculated in dollars. This is a case where the regents believed they had overcome a previous obstacle to changing the enrollment policy, only to find out later that their policy had only been partially carried out. It was a classic example of what happens when a goal is not properly implemented and controlled.

Enrollment Management II was adopted for the period 1991 to 1994, with a planned reduction of 4,045 full time equivalent students (FTEs).[43] For the first year, Fall 1991, the target for the System was 130,070 FTEs, whereas the actual was 132,106. The target was exceeded by 2,036, which means that in order to achieve the 1994 fall target, enrollment will have to be reduced by

6,081 FTEs, an unlikely scenario based on previous experience. Another instance where regent policy was not implemented.

Raising Admission Standards

There was no question in anyone's mind that the only way to reduce enrollment was to raise admission standards. Policy was that the board would set a minimum admission standard for the System below which no campus could go. Campuses could, and some did, adopt admission standards higher than the minimum. The debate around this issue was not so much about substance but about turf. Chancellors and faculty argued that campuses should be allowed to deal with the issue, not the regents. Yet, they did nothing. The debate ended when it was brought to the regent's attention that graduation requirements at Madison West High School were higher than the standards for admission at UW-Madison. While chancellors and faculty argued that admission standards were their responsibility, they had not discharged that responsibility. The regents decided it was time to fill the vacuum.

The board did just that with Planning the Future. This document contained a policy statement that raised the minimum admission standards effective Fall 1991. In addition, at the urging of Regent Grover, and over the opposition of the chancellors, the American College Testing Service (ACT) test was required of all entering resident freshmen beginning in Fall 1989. Those results would not be used as an admission criteria, but would assist in placement, or be used when a student was on the borderline for admission. The report stated:

> By setting 1991 admission standards above the 1988 high school graduation standards, the university intends to send a message to all parents and potential university students that it expects entering freshmen to be fully prepared to begin university study. This expectation will influence the education and performance of the state's young people in the secondary schools and should, in the long run, assure for these youths greater opportunity and success in the collegiate experience.[44]

And for the first time, it was stated publicly that the university's admission standards affected high school graduation requirements. This is important for the regents to keep in mind as they revisit admission standards in the future.

Even though the policy was adopted in 1986, I and other members of the board were berated by faculty as late as 1990 for changing admission standards when it was the faculty's business. I always responded the same way: "Had the faculty acted, the regents would not have. When the faculty fails to act, the regents have the authority and the responsibility to do so." It's a lesson I hope the regents, faculty, and administrators have learned.

The board adopted a more stringent admission policy in December 1986, and included the opportunity for admission offices to make admission exceptions.[45] While campuses were free to make exceptions to the admission standards and admit students below the minimum standards, it was expected that they would provide the support necessary so that those students would succeed. That was a major departure from previous attitudes, which, in practice, meant, "Let them in and flunk them out." I believe that if a campus is not willing to accept responsibility for students at risk, it is irresponsible to admit such students. Some of our campuses have not fulfilled this obligation, as shown in their retention rates.

Proficiency Testing

What happens when the board comes down on one side of an issue and System administration and campus administrators come down on the other side? That was the case in the debate over proficiency testing. This example illustrates how the board can through compromise, overcome very substantial obstacles put in its path by both the System administration and campus administrators.

The Education Committee of the board had discussed mathematics and English skills of undergraduates. It was a subject being widely discussed and written about. Faculty members complained that some graduate students could not write a coherent English sentence. "How did they ever make it this far?" they asked in frustration. Of course, some of their colleagues had "passed" those students along! Students who needed remedial math and English were being admitted to System institutions, and faculty members complained that they were being asked to teach the equivalent of high school math. The Education Committee asked System administration to research ways of dealing with these concerns. UW-Milwaukee had been requiring students to pass a math and English proficiency test at the end of the sophomore year as a condition to entering the junior year. Those who failed were required to take remedial courses. The campus had reported success with the program.

From the very beginning of the discussion, System Academic Affairs advanced the view that while proficiency testing was an option, it was a bad idea, since there were no tests that would apply with equal validity to all of the campuses within the System. In addition, this approach would pit one university against the other, because one campus' results would be compared with those of other campuses and would be used to judge the overall quality of each institution. We heard testimony from faculty members who objected to such a test since they did not want to "teach to the test." Furthermore, they contended such tests were not reliable. Other faculty members agreed that the regents should implement proficiency tests for English and math.

System administration advocated a "value-added" proposal. This struck the Education Committee as being too general, too inconclusive, and not likely to be implemented within a reasonable time. The committee asked for ideas on how proficiency testing might be inaugurated. At the December 5, 1990, board meeting, a proposal for verbal and quantitative proficiency skills assessment and development of 14 levels and standards of proficiency was discussed. Regents asked why external, readily understood benchmarks could not be formulated for the System as a whole — a basic "taxpayer friendly" competency test for the System. Regent Davis expressed the view that while one systemwide test might present risks, those risks were outweighed by the need for some uniform view of assessment that people outside the System could use to make rational, informed judgments about the institutions.

Since proficiency testing would test against a minimum standard, the regents did not believe the results would pit one campus against another, and to the extent it did, it would be a benefit. The argument of not wanting to "teach to the test" failed to convince the regents, since faculty members were using tests on a routine basis. That was the way of the world. The materials they covered in class were expected to have a relationship to the tests given. As to the unavailability of a reliable test, the regents learned that a proficiency test was available through American College Testing Service and could be tailored to the needs of the System.

While the committee and the System could not agree, there was a majority of the board who wanted to institute proficiency testing for English and math soon. System administration realized they had lost the argument. In the end, Regent Grover and I worked out a compromise that was accepted by Shaw. A pilot project was to be established in Fall 1992. The results would be studied by the System and the board to determine whether or not the test should be mandated for all students at the conclusion of the sophomore year.

Transferring Credits within the System

Each campus department had its own criteria as to how transferred credits would be handled. The regents were receiving pressure to standardize the transfer of credits from one System institution to another. Each institution could have worked this out, but refused to do so. The regents were concerned that the Wisconsin legislature, as had been done in other states, would mandate how credits earned in one System institution would be transferred to another System institution.

The board held hearings on the matter and concluded that it needed to move in order to forestall legislative action. Without saying so, the faculty took the position the board should do nothing and fight off any legislative movement — a position the board regarded as unrealistic. A systemwide committee was appointed. The compromise reached, which the board endorsed, was that *any* credit earned at a UW institution would count toward the general education requirements of the institution to which the student was transferring. At the same time, the admitting institution would be free to judge the quality of the credits transferred as they would apply to the requirements of the major.

UW System's Relationships with the VTAE

In Chapter II, I explained the differences in the missions and governance of the UW System and the VTAE. I also detailed statutory mandates for non-duplication of programs, and described the four joint committees that were charged with the responsibility of dealing with issues of credit and non-credit course duplication and the transferability of credits earned in the VTAE system to the UW System. During my term on the board, none of these issues were resolved. The professionals who served on these joint committees seemed to agree to disagree. Some of us saw it as nothing more than turf battles due to the absence of lay leadership to oversee what was going on as well as the lack of authority of the committees.

One of the joint System and VTAE committees, Joint Administrative Committee on Continuing Education (JACCE), was charged with dealing with program conflicts between the two systems. JACCE suffered from the same weaknesses as the others. It had no real authority. In March 1989, UW System Vice President Eugene Trani proposed to the board of regents that JACCE's authority be expanded to give it final authority to resolve conflicts.[46]

The proposal was adopted by the regents at the April 7, 1989, meeting.[47] However, its two basic weaknesses still existed. First, JACCE would have co-chairs, one appointed by the UW System president and one by the state director of the VTAE. What would happen in the case of a tie vote? Second, the implementation would depend on the approval of the state board of the VTAE and its certification that the district boards *all* agreed to abide by the JACCE decisions. The issue of credit transfers and duplication of mission remained unresolved.

I was president of the board and served on the VTAE board. Both boards were discussing credit transfer between institutions. The *UW System Undergraduate Transfer Policy-Revised*, approved by the board of regents on May 11, 1984, provided that UW System institutions accept credits earned in the college-parallel programs at the technical colleges in Madison, Milwaukee, and Rhinelander. Up to 72 credits earned in those college-parallel programs could be transferred to a UW System institution as "general education" or elective course credit. In terms of applying those credits toward a major in a UW System institution, each System campus was free to evaluate the VTAE credits.[48] The other 13 VTAE institutions had no college-parallel programs, but they did offer general education and/or liberal arts courses. Some directors considered those courses to be of equal quality to those offered in the UW Centers. I was told that in many of these VTAE courses, the same textbooks were used as in the UW Centers. Regent policy held that general education and/or liberal arts credits earned in non-college parallel programs at vocational-technical schools could not be transferred for credit to UW System institutions.

In essence, VTAE institutions (other than Madison, Milwaukee, and Rhinelander) were on their own to work out agreements with individual UW System campuses with the approval of the UW System Vice President of Academic Affairs. Individual campus departments were free to treat VTAE credits earned as they saw 'it. VTAE district directors complained that the campuses were arbitrary in how they accepted credits earned in VTAE institutions, and since there was no uniformity, VTAE students could not know in advance what value their credits would have in the UW System. For example, VTAE math was given little or no value in some UW institutions and greater value in others. Some VTAE directors argued that they should move toward community college status so that their students would receive the same treatment accorded to UW Center students. Some district directors felt that the UW System policy was demeaning to their institutions. Others complained that UW Extension was duplicating VTAE programs.

Our campuses were using enrollment management as a tool to protect themselves from VTAE transfers. They argued that under the enrollment management plan adopted in 1986, UW institutions were forced to reduce enrollment on the one hand and deal with the increased retention due to higher admission standards on the other, and so had to be even more selective in their admission policies than before. Students who could not meet the admission standards of UW institutions could meet the lower standards of the VTAE, which had an open enrollment policy. That would be unfair to UW System students. Furthermore, VTAE institutions were charging less in tuition than UW institutions. And UW System faculty argued that the admitting institution, *not* the transferring institution, should determine the qualifications of entering students, which included making a judgment about the quality of the credits earned elsewhere.

The Wisconsin Association of Independent Colleges and Universities studied the quality of students that transferred from the VTAE to Wisconsin private colleges and concluded that "VTAE transfer students tended to progress in their educational programs as satisfactorily as other degree-seeking students. ..."[49] I asked Shaw (April 13, 1987) whether we had done a similar study. I don't recall seeing one. I referred to the regent's *Future* report that called for a joint task force regarding UW and VTAE course duplication, and indicated that both the president of the VTAE board and I had agreed that we should initiate such a joint effort "at the earliest possible time." The VTAE strategic plan (January 1987) called for an expansion of "... transfer of credit opportunities with the UW System through the use of options, such as articulation agreements. ..."[50]

One of the VTAE's solutions was to explore assimilation of the UW Centers and VTAE into a Junior College system. By May of 1987, the VTAE director's Executive Committee wrote the VTAE board suggesting that the relationship between the UW Center system and the VTAE system be formally reviewed by the recently appointed governor's commission on the VTAE system. The letter referred to this as "The only issue that ... can be termed controversial ..." — and it certainly was! Testifying before the commission, VTAE State Director Robert Sorensen called for a merger of the UW Centers and the regional technical schools. This would get to the problem of credit transfers. He said, "They should be put together in a community college system. The transfer of credits is a major problem."[51]

In a letter dated May 20, 1987, I asked that the matter be put on the agenda of the Regent Education Committee's June meeting. "We cannot sit by and have no position on this matter." Governor Thompson was quoted as saying, "I do not want to turn them [VTAE schools] into junior colleges. ..."[52] On May 21, 1987, Sorensen wrote me saying that he had been misquoted in his testimony. He explained that he had responded to a question about what he would do if he had the freedom to restructure the system. He had described an ideal restructuring —"... that is, if I were to drop-in from Mars and [be] asked to give the ideal structure for a post-secondary two-year system and then leave with no other political caveats attached to it. ..." He added that "... there [was] not a great deal of interest in that kind of restructuring. ..." On June 23, 1987, following a VTAE board retreat, I wrote Shaw that credit transfer was a major issue, and suggested that some board members of each system meet and attempt to get beyond the turf battles.

The governor's commission showed little interest in the merging of the two systems. In the meantime, the issue of credit transfers remained unresolved. We were told that Shaw and Sorenson were "working it out." On June 2, 1987, the chancellor of the UW Centers wrote the board opposing the merger idea. On July 13, 1988, Trani (UW System Vice President for Academic Affairs) sent the regents a copy of section 36.31, Wisconsin Statutes, which limited the authority of VTAE institutions regarding college parallel programs. It provided that such programs could not be offered beyond those offered in 1972-73 "... without the approval ..." of the board of regents. That did not settle the issue.

Shaw and Sorenson appointed a task force, For Review of Non-Credit Programs, in the two systems. The task force was co-chaired by Regent Lyon and Regent Paul Hassett, the VTAE president. The task force held hearings. The final report, dated July 15, 1988, concluded that:

- "Neither the local nor the regional JACCE committees were perceived as being an effective means of resolving non-credit disputes between the two systems." The report recommended a change in the structure so that JACCE would become a decision-making body rather than merely advisory.

- Program duplication could not be avoided by internal review alone. The report suggested having an outside consultant.

- The task force called for a study committee to address "overlap between credit and non-credit programming."

- Most telling was this comment in the report: "The inability to agree on a differentiation in mission and content between the two systems is recognized. If this had been possible, it would have provided direction in program decisions in order to avoid duplication between the two systems."

On August 9, 1988, I wrote to my successor in office, Regent President Paul R. Schilling, suggesting that he charge the Education Committee with the responsibility of addressing the issue. On July 20, 1988, the director of Milwaukee Area Technical College once again proposed a merger of the VTAE institutions and UW System Centers.[53] Sorenson was reported to have said (July 29, 1988) that while he and Shaw were making progress in facilitating the transfer of vocational school credits to UW System institutions, there was a major disagreement regarding general education courses such as mathematics and social sciences.[54] Hassett and Lyon acknowledge that VTAE ambitions to develop college-parallel courses would be "a big bag of problems."[55] On July 9, 1988, Shaw confirmed to the board of regents that he and Sorensen could not agree on the transfer of general education credits which duplicated the offerings of the UW Centers. I said publicly that he, Shaw, was wasting his time, since the state VTAE board did not have the authority to bind the districts, while the board of regents could bind the UW institutions. Both Lyon and Hassett agreed. Because the issue was heating up, I expressed concern that the legislature "will take the initiative without any input from us." I did not think the public or the legislature would understand the differences nor tolerate the inability of the two systems to resolve them. Legislators, with whom I spoke, confirmed my perception. They had already received complaints from their constituents. In addition, they were puzzled why three of the VTAE institutions (Milwaukee, Madison, and Rhinelander) should be given special treatment for their college-parallel programs while other VTAE districts felt shut out and demeaned.

In October 1988, Shaw presented his "Position Statement on UWS/VTAE Relationships." In the paper he restated existing policy and recommended no changes other than strengthening the authority of JACCE. He did not support the task force's recommendation regarding an outside consultant.

On March 29, 1989, I wrote Shaw and enclosed a copy of an interview with 21st Assembly District Representative Richard A. Grobschmidt.[56] Grobschmidt was asked, "How do we resolve the transfer of credit issue from the VTAE/Technical College System to the UW System?" His answer was, "First, we can encourage the development of articulation agreements between institutions, as we did with the UW-VTAE Nursing Education Study Committee. Second, we can *statutorily* prohibit the current policy of the UW Board of Regents which denies or limits credit transfer from the VTAE. Third, we can change the focus of the Joint Administrative Committee on Academic Programs [JACAP] from one of focusing on duplication to one of promoting the coordination of the systems. I can assure you, if this is not done voluntarily from within the systems, *the Legislature will require it by statute*" (emphasis added).

Regent Frank L. Nikolay, a former state representative, wrote Representative Grobschmidt on April 3, 1989:

> I was one of the sponsors of the legislation that created the present VTAE System. I can assure you that we never intended it to be a junior college system nor for the respective campuses to become "colleges." We expected the Districts to train students for employment and not give them a liberal arts education. ... We already have one junior college system in the State with the Centers. ... The vocational schools ought to stick to their original objective of training young people and adults for immediate employment.

These ongoing inter-institutional arguments did not fall on legislative deaf ears. As could have been predicted, at the May 5, 1989, meeting of the regents, it was reported that a legislative bill was being drafted that would have 30 co-sponsors. It would direct the board of regents and the VTAE board to jointly designate courses other than college-parallel courses that would be transferable for credit between the two systems. In addition, a VTAE student with an associate degree (earned after two years) admitted to a UW System institution would receive a minimum of 12 credits toward fulfilling a degree requirement. The governor, according to the bill, would appoint a joint UW/VTAE task force to study methods of improving transferability of credit. And the bill would modify the VTAE mission by eliminating the word "terminal" from its mission of awarding terminal associate degrees.

At the same meeting, Regent President Schilling reported on his meeting with the VTAE board, in which he repeated regent and campus concerns regarding credit transfers. They included enrollment reduction initiatives, efforts of the regents to increase admission standards, and the varying tuition rates and resulting issues of equity. Regent Delmar DeLong, president of the VTAE Board, responded that the issues should not be determined by the legislature, but that a problem exists and must be faced by both boards. He pointed out that the training at the VTAE institutions at that time involved much more in the way of communication skills, mathematics, and general education components of an associate degree than had been the case in the past. The issue was how should such credits earned be treated in the future if students wished to pursue a baccalaureate degree. While the VTAE board was unanimous in its opposition to having its institutions become community colleges, some portion of the general education courses that were not part of the three VTAE institutions with college-parallel programs was equivalent in subject matter, rigor, and quality to some UW System courses, and should be determined through assessment tools. The regents must understand that employees pursue a baccalaureate degree in order to qualify for a promotion or meet the requirements of changing jobs. Nurses who wanted to pursue a baccalaureate degree had to attend private institutions to get credit for the two-year courses they had taken in the VTAE system. As far as enrollment management, the UW System had to take into account all transferring institutions. The public, as represented by the legislature, "... did not believe the two publicly funded systems of post-secondary education were fulfilling taxpayer's wishes that credit from certain kinds of courses be transferable."

In his comments, Shaw pointed out the dilemma of the credit transfer issue: differences in mission and providing service to students of the state. The UW campuses, he reported, did not embrace the idea because it could lead to 16 college-parallel courses; the citizens would be doubly taxed, because there would be 16 VTAE institutions turned into community colleges in addition to the 13 UW Centers. Shaw thought this could be solved by agreements that no more than 15 general education credits would be transferred and that no additional college-parallel programs would be initiated.

I was concerned that the ability of a campus to establish its own admission standards, commensurate with regent policy, would be eroded if mandatory credit transfers became regent policy. Yet something had to be done to ward off legislative intrusion. VTAE President DeLong agreed that each campus should set its own standards as before. All VTAE was asking for was that the credits earned by its students be treated in the same manner as credits earned elsewhere.

Other regents expressed concern that the state VTAE board could not bind the districts. This was only partially true. While the state VTAE board could not discontinue a program at the district level, it could cut off state funds, and no new programs or modifications could be implemented by a district without state board approval. Furthermore, the state board had persuasive power if it chose to exercise it by speaking out publicly. The problem was that it rarely did.

Regent Ness Flores sounded the warning that unless the two publicly funded institutions did not come to some agreement, there would be legislative intervention. Lyon agreed and urged that the two board presidents and the UW System President and the state VTAE director meet "as soon as possible" in order to develop a strategy to convince legislators that the two systems intended to resolve these issues.

At the June 1989 meeting of the board, Regent President Schilling reported that he and VTAE President DeLong, UW System President Shaw, and Interim VTAE Director Glenn Davison had a tentative agreement on a *Statement of Principles,* which was adopted by the VTAE board at its May meeting.[57]

The statement provided the following:

1. The VTAE and UW systems agree not to expand their missions.

2. The VTAE system would offer only those general education courses needed for students to complete their associate degree programs, normally not to exceed 15 credits.

3. While the three college-parallel programs would continue, no other college-parallel programs would be initiated.

4. "The board of regents [would] revise the UW System undergraduate transfer policy to permit UW System institutions to accept up to fifteen general education credits from a successfully completed non-college-parallel associate degree program at a VTAE system institution. Where the quality and consistency of that course work is judged to be comparable to the course work of the receiving institution, the credit[s] would transfer. In cases where UW System institutions find VTAE System course work not acceptable for transfer, VTAE System students will have an opportunity to earn credit by examination as outlined in the UW System Undergraduate Transfer Policy."

5. Both Systems agree that all students who apply to either will receive an "... advising statement that describes the purposes, programs, and opportunities related to both vocational-technical and university education. Such a statement will encourage students who have a goal of a baccalaureate degree to enroll in a university or VTAE college parallel program, while technical-education oriented students will be encouraged to enroll in a VTAE System institution."

6. The principles were to be implemented by December 31, 1989.

7. Both systems, through their governance processes, would implement the principles by December 31, 1989.

The resolution passed the board of regents with two members voting "no." In his statement to the regents, Regent Delmar DeLong, president of the VTAE board, summarized the statement he had made to that board at its May meeting:

> One of the concerns the UW System had was whether or not we had a commitment to our mission. I stated to the VTAE Board that if anyone had any question at this time about what the mission of the VTAE System is, they should speak now or forever hold their peace. One part of our commitment is that we do not want to come into the general education component, except to the extent required by a need for vocational courses. We presently have three campuses which have college-parallel courses, at Milwaukee, Madison and Nicolet [Rhinelander]. The [VTAE] Board is on record by adopting these principles that we will not seek to expand that mission into any other district in the state. We do not believe that is our mission. Our mission is vocational/technical education and the [VTAE] Board is unanimous in that regard. ... If they wish to obtain baccalaureate degrees [initially], the way to do that is to start at one of the UW System campuses. If they want to pursue a vocational associate degree, they go to the VTAE System. This [policy] is to affect only those people who have obtained an associate degree and, for one reason or another, after they have been in the work place, need to go back to an educational institution, including the UW, to pick up extra courses to further their career path.

The two dissenting regents expressed fear that this was tantamount to a "foot in the door." Regent President Schilling responded that never before had the VTAE Board stated that there would be only three college-parallel programs, that no other programs with a large component of general education credits would be initiated, and that the VTAE districts would not become community colleges. Prior to this action, the door had been closed artificially. Now students could present their credentials for review.

This was a major breakthrough in the relationship of the state's two post-secondary public educational systems. I am convinced that without the leadership of Regent President Schilling, Regent Vice President Lyon, and VTAE President DeLong, nothing would have changed and the legislative action would have continued. At the June meeting, after the regent adoption of the principles, State Representative Peter Barca said that he now saw no need to advance his proposed bill on VTAE general education credit transfer to the UW System.

As the regents look to the future, they would be well-advised to heed the words of DeLong that there were those in the VTAE System who doubted that the UW System would implement the *Statement of Principles* in good faith. As with all regent action, adoption of principles is only the first step. Implementation is of equal importance.

Leave of Absence Policy

Another example of policy out of control was the leave of absence policy. The board decided to intercede. A leave of absence is defined as a "temporary separation of a faculty member from the University during which the faculty member is not paid."[58] The regent leave of absence policy covered employees who were elected to political office or who served as appointed officials. It came to the board's attention that there were faculty members on leave for periods exceeding 10 years. Neither the board nor the System president had been notified, nor had they given permission contrary to the provisions of the policy.

On November 10, 1989, the board adopted a revised leave of absence policy, which required that a leave of absence cannot be open-ended but must be for a specified period of time.

The initial leave could not exceed two years or the term of an elected or appointed government office, not to exceed four years. Any extension beyond that "must receive specific approval of the board and must be for a fixed period of time." Failure of the university employee to return after the conclusion of the leave would constitute a resignation from the university. An annual report of those on leave was required by the regents.[59]

Effective with the 1991-92 academic year, the faculty rules of UW-Madison further restricted the policy. They required that under normal circumstances, a leave of absence would be granted for a maximum of one year, subject to renewal.[60]

VII.

Regents Must Make a Realistic Assessment of Financial Resources

Conclusion #7: To preserve quality, a realistic assessment of financial resources will lead to the conclusion that substantially larger amounts of funding are not available.

Thus far, I have provided background material for decision-making by the UW Board of Regents, and described the inner workings of the UW System so that political leaders, the media, and the public can better understand it. The "Short Guide" (Chapter II) described the size and complexity of the System. I identified the major obstacles to change and listed some examples of how those obstacles had been overcome. I dwelt on governance issues because I believe they are at the heart of problem-solving. While regents have statutory authority to govern, they must feel the obligation to do so and act accordingly.

Now it is time to look to the future, and that means looking at change. The UW System is no different than most organizations when it comes to change. Change makes people uncomfortable and so they resist.

Early on, I talked about the struggle between those who wanted to maintain the status quo and those who sought change with the intention of preserving quality. We know that departments don't willingly downsize or go out of business; no campus will willingly close or consolidate its programs with other campuses; faculty won't willingly increase their teaching loads at the expense of outside consulting or research; faculty don't want regents involved in tenure and post-tenure review decisions.

Regents are also tempted to play the status quo game. They usually accepted System budgets as presented. Budget presentations generally concluded that there was a shortage of funds. In response, regents and System administrators sought more funds either from the state or the students. That was easier than dealing with all of the other variables, and thus the status quo was preserved. I noted two exceptions: Regents reduced the System's 1991-1993 budget proposal during the last budget deliberations in which I participated; and Acting President Lyall introduced a plan to reallocate from the next base budget by reducing positions. Both bode well for the future because they are a break from the past and show a realistic assessment of funding possibilities.

The Challenge

Any serious observer of higher education knows that both private and public American colleges and universities are faced with challenges that require change. The UW System is no exception. Its woes are due not only to waning tax revenues but to the shifting priorities of state government.

"Budget cuts hurting state universities" was the February 18, 1992, headline of an article by The Associated Press.[1] Nineteen states had cut allocations to state universities for 1992, cuts emanating from the recession. *Time* magazine (February 3, 1992) carried a story with the headline, "Big Chill on Campus. After decades of growth, U.S. colleges are facing a financial squeeze that threatens the quality and breadth of higher education."[2] The article describes deficits, mid-year tuition hikes, reduction in faculty, canceled course sections, and supply shortages. A similar report appeared in the *Milwaukee Journal* on February 18, 1992. *The Chronicle of Higher Education*, the *Wall Street Journal* for higher education administrators, faculty, and staff, reported in its February 12, 1992, issue, "Mid-Year Budget Cuts Reported by Public Colleges in 22 States." A page 1 story in the March 24, 1992, edition of *The Palm Beach Post* reported "Regents discuss closing branches." According to the *Post* report, the Florida legislature proposed a $45 million cut in their System's budget as part of its "reality" budget. In response, a chief administrative officer was quoted as saying, "I feel like the emperor with no clothes. We're naked. There's nothing else to take unless you want to take our heart."

The Green Bay Gazette reported on March 17, 1992, that Yale University expected a $15 million deficit and an 11% decrease in the number of its arts and science professors in 1992. Columbia University's deficit could reach $30 million by 1994. Stanford University needed to reduce its budget by $43 million, and the 20-campus California State University system laid off 1,000 faculty members and reduced class sections by 5,000, or about 9%. *USA Today*, on March 17, 1992, reported "State college cuts limit enrollment." The State University of New York's 34 campuses faced budget cuts of $143.5 million. "You can't withstand cuts like this and not be considering very seriously alternatives, even closing of campuses," according to Chancellor D. Bruce Johnstone. The California State University system asked for approval of a 40% hike in student fees. Commenting on the budget cut in Florida, board of regents spokesperson Pat Reardon said budget cuts have "shown up in ... layoffs, cutbacks in library acquisitions, and reduced summer school enrollments." There has been a freeze on overall enrollments in Florida, and Virginia has set enrollment caps.

Former UW System President Shaw, chancellor of Syracuse University since July 1991, did not escape the problem of downsizing by leaving Wisconsin. He wrote to Syracuse alumni on February 17, 1992, announcing his plan to restructure the university in an attempt to deal with a projected four-year budget deficit of $38 million. "We will be stronger and the highest levels of academic quality will be ensured because the University is dedicating the resources and support services necessary to maintain excellence."

Closer to home, the University of Minnesota at Waseca held commencement and then permanently closed its doors in 1992, "a casualty of a new era of fiscal restraint in higher education."[3] The community of 8,500 was vocal in its protests, but the president of the University of Minnesota System explained that this was part of a $60 million reallocation plan. The plan will shift priorities, cut, and consolidate programs and operations. Closing the Waseca campus would save the system $5.4 million. Ironically, plans have been discussed to convert the campus to a federal prison. The proposed solutions to the fiscal problems are the same — downsize to maintain quality. As a matter of fact, the UW System Board of Regents has ordered an additional 4% reduction in enrollment by 1995, on top of an earlier mandate to cut enrollment by 5%.

There are those in Wisconsin who contend there is no need to be concerned because the UW System is doing "just fine." The UW-Madison is among the leading public research universities in the world. According to the 1992-93 *Chronicle of Higher Education Almanac*, UW-Madison ranked sixth in the nation in student enrollment, 13th in library holdings, sixth in fundraising, and fourth in the number of doctoral degrees granted.[4] The UW-Madison Hospital and Clinics is among the top-ranked in the nation, and fund-raising from the private sector is at an all-time high.

While all of the above is true, there is a major threat to the quality of the institutions that make up the System— lack of funds. Wisconsin has not been exempt from the problems that have been confronting campuses nationwide. Fortunately, in Spring 1992, Katharine C. Lyall, then acting System president, recognized the problems and acted. It became clear that the University of Wisconsin System was not going to receive additional state funds and, as a matter of fact, might receive reduced funding. In former days, there would have been a great deal of hand wringing and speeches that the politicians did not care, and the board of regents would have passed a resolution calling upon the state to provide more funds. Instead, on February 6, 1992, Lyall proposed a "Quality Reinvestment Plan" to the board of regents. Lyall's plan was expected to reduce faculty and staff positions and reallocate $26.5 million from the base budget over three years to the UW System's highest priority needs: compensation for faculty and staff, computer needs, electronic library resources, engineering technology, improved instructional materials, modern labs and equipment, and program assessment. Her plan addressed the fundamental issue of preserving quality in light of inadequate funding.[5] She said, "Quality must come first. When resources and needs do not match, resources will be reallocated from lower to higher priority needs." The plan was approved by the regents at the February 19, 1992,[6] meeting.

Instead of endorsing the plan as being a bold and realistic response to the reality of circumstances that confronted the System, there was criticism from within. UW-Milwaukee's chancellor reported that faculty on his campus didn't trust the plan. The president of the Association of University of Wisconsin Professionals accused Lyall of "doublespeak" for saying the plan would improve quality.[7] Having seen the proposal before the board met, Professor John A. Korgman, College of Engineering, UW-Platteville, wrote the regents (November 8, 1991) and described the plan as a "cannibalization of the Wisconsin University System."

After listening to these remarks, one regent, angered by the lack of internal support for necessary changes, characterized faculty opposition to the plan as an "... immature reaction by a group of intellectually superior people. If their reaction is suspicion, it puzzles me. This whole world is based on finite resources. We're in a recession and we don't have the resources to do everything we want to do."[8]

What, indeed, is going on? A struggle between those who would preserve the status quo and those who understand the need for change — between those who are afraid of change and those who are not.

Is the current recession the problem or does it simply exacerbate old problems which have not been adequately addressed? I subscribe to the latter view. The need to change existed before the current recession. While I served on the board the following major issues were identified. Some were addressed and others were not.

1. Faculty and academic staff salaries were not competitive with peer institutions. The shortfall was somewhere between $30-60 million.

2. University administrators were not being paid competitively.

3. Labs and classrooms were in dire need of repair and refurbishing. New construction was needed.

4. Maintenance budgets had not kept pace with needs.

5. The budget for supplies was too low.

6. The quality of undergraduate education was being questioned because of the lack of tenured faculty involvement in instruction, low retention rates, and low admission standards.

7. The quality of the campus environment for minority students was not adequate.

8. Some academic staff felt they were being treated as second-class citizens.

While I was determined to carry out the responsibilities assigned to the board of regents in Chapter 36, Wisconsin Statutes, I was disappointed that some regents thought that accepting this role was micromanaging and that it was the responsibility of the faculty and administrators to manage the UW system. In addition, some faculty members and administrators ignored Chapter 36, Wisconsin Statutes. Their contention was that the regents should have a minimal role in management. As far as I was concerned, those attitudes increased the challenge.

The recurring theme in this book is that in the effort to seek change, governance is the most important issue before the board. Chapter 36, Wisconsin Statutes puts the responsibility to govern squarely with the board. In order to carry out their responsibility to the System, the members of the board must understand that there will be challenges to their authority that present obstacles to change. I have addressed other issues all related to governance and the authority of the board: how regents are selected; conflicting views of governance; quality of the student body; campus environment and facilities; administrative and faculty issues surrounding tenure, and elements of access.

If it is true that the state will not increase the portion of total tax revenues appropriated to the System, what is to be done to address these problems? Should the needed funds only come from tuition? That is not politically viable. What other options are there? Are all elements of quality dependent on funding? The System will have to change or allow quality to be jeopardized. What will those changes be? What should they be? The attempt to balance quality, access and funding is not a new issue. In attempting to reach a balance, there will be conflict between the board and the institutions. Conflict requires compromise, and compromise leads to change.

The "good old days," if they ever existed, are gone. In order to maintain and improve quality, very difficult choices have to be made, and that means change. This challenge can be met, provided that the System and campus administrators, regents, faculty, staff, and politicians accept their roles and keep the goal of maintaining quality sharply in focus. Challenges can be turned into opportunities.

Regents are the only ones who can deal effectively with the issues of change in this System. If they don't, quality will suffer. The board made a commitment to the policy "... when faced with a choice between maintaining educational quality and decreasing access to its programs and resources, the University of Wisconsin System must choose to maintain quality. For if academic programs, research, and public service are not first-rate, access to the institutions will be of little value."[9] Therefore, the focus must be on quality. Assuming that this policy will remain in effect, it cannot be implemented unless there is an understanding of what is meant by access and quality. It is obvious that there is a limit to the number of students who can receive a quality education given a finite amount of funding. Knowing the proper balance is a challenge for the regents. Too often it is assumed that quality is dependent only on funding. That is not true. There are elements of quality that are independent of funding.

There Is No More Money

Before looking for solutions, the board must be realistic about funding possibilities and match those against needs. The System has announced that there is an annual shortage of funding somewhere between $30 million and $100 million. The response to this problem by regents and administrators traditionally has been to declare a revenue shortfall and look for additional dollars, either from the state or the students. Political leaders say that there are two other sources — reduced administrative costs and increased funds from the private sector. Setting aside for the moment which elements of quality are dependent on more funding and which are not, I will examine how realistic it is to expect these four areas (administrative costs, private sector, state funds, and tuition) to produce substantial amounts of additional funds. In keeping with my promise to put my conclusions up front, I conclude that they will not produce substantial additional funds and the board will have to look at other options. First, they must define the elements of access and quality, and look to solutions that do not require additional funding. This is the subject of Chapter VIII.

Financial Resources

Why do I believe that reduced administrative costs, private sector, the state, and tuition will not meet System needs? What follows is a closer look at each.

Reduce System and Campus Administrative Costs

Because of the huge size of the System, legislators and some regents believe that there is "water" in administrative budgets, both at the System and campus levels. They are not sure where it is, but they are convinced that administrators know where to find it. Therefore, if the budget is reduced, administrators will squeeze the "water" out, the System will become more efficient, savings will be used to increase faculty compensation or pay for other needs, and more state funding or tuition will not be needed. It is a very appealing idea.

During my term as president of the board of regents, after being briefed by a state official on the System's biennial budget that the governor planned to present to the legislature, I remarked that there was not nearly enough in the proposed budget to cover building maintenance, and that buildings would surely continue to deteriorate unless this issue was addressed. The response was that there was plenty of "water" in the System's budget, and if we would "get our act together" there would be sufficient funds for maintenance. Some regents appear to agree with that assessment. In his acceptance speech of June 5, 1992, Regent President George K. Steil, Sr., said, "We cannot afford any waste and we must have fiscal responsibility — not only in fact — but also in the perception of the taxpayers of this state." He urged System administrators to "set the example," and pointed to an article claiming that in the "1980's administrative budgets at public universities increased almost three times the rate of increase in instructional budgets." There are, in my opinion, two problems with that statement. First, I question whether this was an obtainable standard (i.e., no waste) and whether holding it out raised unrealistic expectations. Second, actual statistics for the UW System had been supplied by the regents a year earlier; the System compared very favorably with national averages. Occasional Research Brief 91/1: January 1991, "Trends in Staffing," shows that:

- "From 1975 to 1985, the overall full-time faculty and staff growth for the UW System was 9.8%, lower than the national growth rate of 13.8%. This occurred at the same time UW System student enrollments grew at twice the national rate."

- "The UW System had a lower than national growth rate in faculty/teaching staff at 3.8%, compared to 6.0% nationally over this ten-year period, despite the fact that enrollments grew at twice the national rate."

- "From 1981-89, total UW System Administration positions declined by -.16 FTE [.1%]. Since merger, total System Administration positions have declined by -4.8%."

As I stated, the claim of excessive administrative costs arose while I served on the board. I learned that the System was more efficient than other university systems. This did not mean, nor did anyone contend, that improvements could not be made. But, the discussion ought to be kept in context. In 1987 I asked for some comparisons, which I shared with my regent colleagues. Administrative costs as a percentage of total budget per campus varied from a low of 2.74% for Madison to a high of 6.11% for Superior. The overall average for all campuses, excluding Extension and the Centers, was 4.9%. The System's administrative costs were .53% of the total System budget. For the period 1984-85, the System spent about 18% less than peer institutions.[10] A 1983 study, compared the System with 22 public university system offices in the United States:

UW System Versus 22 Public University System Offices

Total Central Office Personnel	-20%
General Office budget	-33%
Central Office Professional per $100 million of System Expenditures	-51%
Central Office Professional per 1,000 FTE System Faculty	-46%
Central Office Professional per 10,000 Students	-56%

Elwin F. Cammack, associate vice president for analysis and information systems, wrote on March 6, 1987, that in 1984-85, total System administrative costs were 4.44% of total System expenditures, compared with the national average of 7.69%. For the period 1986-87, System administrative costs had dropped to 4.33% of the System budget.

Once again, this does not mean there is no room for cutting costs. Regents appointed a special committee to investigate and found some areas will be worth exploring. However, there is no reason to believe that cutting in those areas would make a substantial difference in the overall System administrative costs or budget.

Then how about campus administrative costs? Matt Pommer, feature writer for *The Capital Times*, suggested that consideration be given to consolidation of chancellors and, presumably, campus administrative staffs in those areas of the state where campuses are close to each other.[11] I agree.

If we could start from square 1, would we have campuses so close together in some parts of the state? While closing campuses *would* save administrative costs, it is important to keep in mind that of the total administrative costs systemwide, UW-Madison accounted for about 33% and UW-Milwaukee was about 10%, a total of 43%. This left 57% to be divided among the other 25 institutions. The other campuses had administrative costs ranging from $1.1 million to $3 million. In addition to administrative costs, other savings would result from closing or consolidating campuses. They are worth considering. On balance, the System has done a remarkable job. Later in this chapter, I will show that the state has funded the System substantially lower on a per-student-basis than the national average, tuition has remained lower than that of peer institutions, and administrative costs have been lower than the national average. It is unrealistic to assume that this can go on without eventually affecting important administrative and staff functions, including student services.

While every option should be looked at, the "payoff" in this area may be less than hoped for.

Raise More Money from the Private Sector

Private sector funds are controlled by the donor and are generally not given to pay for undergraduate instruction, student services, maintenance, supplies, or administrative costs. It is given for research, physical plant and equipment, and scholarships, not for the portion of undergraduate education paid by the state. In addition, private contributions may be pledged over a number of years, so the cash is not all available at once.

The board, at the meeting of October 9, 1992, heard a report from the Physical Planning and Development Committee. Martin Grenzebach, representing a consulting firm that had worked with seven of the Big Ten campuses said that only 15 to 20% of private fund-raising goes toward facility construction. Private donors take the view that such construction is the obligation of the state. The Physical Planning and Development Committee reported that it is "wary of drifting into a position that will require private funding for academic buildings.[12]

Substantially more money was being raised from the private sector for UW-Madison due to the efforts of Chancellor Donna Shalala. She had infused an incredible amount of energy into this effort. The goals are ten times higher than ever before and will be realized. For the period 1990-91, the UW-Madison ranked sixth in the nation in private fund-raising.[13] But what about other campuses around the state that may not have a large or wealthy group of alums?

Private funds are not always good news. I find it offensive that public universities would "sell" parts of themselves to the highest bidder in the private sector. Campus stadium billboards feature products; university bands play the theme of a product's commercial. There is always concern that the public universities will be "bought" by private interests and influence the research being done. The board must be vigilant in reviewing its policies on conflicts of interest. According to the dean of the School of Law, University of Texas, Austin, there is further concern that the growing reliance on the private sector for financial support creates within the university "haves and have-nots."

"The professional schools and natural sciences [and], to a lesser extent, the social sciences, may prosper as they receive the lion's share of the external resources; their missions closely mirror the personnel and research needs of the private sector and government. Meanwhile, the humanities, general libraries, and education schools wither. It is as if every state university is really two universities, one reasonably financed and the other starving for funds." He is concerned that reliance on private funds versus public funds would undercut the historical mission of public universities —

"the [university's] public responsibility to transmit cultural traditions across generations, to prepare future teachers, and to foster inquiry and learning for their own sake."[14] Private funds will not replace the need for public funds, nor should they.

Obtain More State Funds

After reviewing the history of state support for the System, it would be naive to expect that there will be increased funding beyond inflation. The reasons abound.

The following compares the level of combined local and state support for post-secondary education in Wisconsin (UW System and VTAE) for 1989-90 with the national average.[15]

	Wisconsin	National Average
Support per full-time equivalent student	$4,956.00	$5,667.00
Per capita expenditure	$170.29	$189.89
Expenditure per $1,000 of personal income	$11.39	$9.62

The appropriation per equivalent full-time student will determine the compensation level for faculty and staff, faculty-student ratio, number and quality of laboratories and libraries, number of class sections, number of computers available for student use, and complexity of student support services. Wisconsin ranked 31st in the nation in combined state and local appropriations per equivalent full-time student. But Wisconsin ranked 15th in the nation in combined state and local tax appropriation on a per capita basis, and 16th in the nation for combined state and local tax appropriations for higher education per $1,000 of personal income. That is because the demand for public higher education in Wisconsin, measured by the percentage of students enrolled in public institutions as compared with total population, was higher than the national average. Wisconsin ranked fifth in the nation.

On the one hand, demand in Wisconsin was high, but expenditures per full-time equivalent student were relatively low. At the same time the citizens of the state were spending more per capita and more per $1,000 of personal income than the national average. The only cure for this problem would be to raise taxes or shift state priorities, neither of which are likely to happen.

The dilemma that the state and public higher education faced can be further explained with the following data for 1990-91.[16] While Wisconsin ranked 12th in the nation in tax dollars collected, it ranked 18th in the nation in state tax dollars appropriated to higher education, and 44th in the nation as a percentage of tax dollars appropriated to higher education. This excludes appropriations to vocational/technical schools. Wisconsin appropriated 12.42% of its tax dollars to higher education. Its ranking of 44th simply indicates that it appropriated a greater percentage of tax dollars to other state agencies than the national average. On a per capita basis, however, Wisconsin ranked 10th in the nation in spending for higher education.[17]

State appropriations per full-time equivalent student in the System have been lower than the national average for a number of years. In a letter dated March 2, 1992, from Jennifer Presley, associate vice president, UW System Office of Policy Analysis and Research (OPAR), to Robert L. Reid, vice president for academic affairs, University of Southern Indiana, the gap was described. Appropriations to the System by the state of Wisconsin per full-time equivalent student had been *less* than the national average by the following amounts:

Fiscal Year 1986	$1,143
Fiscal Year 1987	$1,105
Fiscal Year 1988	$910
Fiscal Year 1989	$950
Fiscal Year 1990	$880

This amounted to a very substantial difference. For the period 1989-90, for example, the total number of FTE students in the UW System was 134,135.[18] A difference of $880 per FTE amounts to a total gap of $118 million per year, an amount far exceeding the claimed shortfall.

In a letter to the regents dated September 12, 1990, then Executive Vice President Lyall reviewed the same statistics for 1984-85, 1986-87, and 1987-88, which were essentially the same as those for 1989-90. She summarized the statistics as follows:

> Wisconsin is making a large tax effort for public higher education, but the state is simply trying to accommodate too many students relative to our resources in our public institutions. The large enrollments thus drive our support per student significantly below the national average and this shortfall shows up in accumulated infrastructure needs, faculty salaries that continually require catch-up, and many other basic areas. To see how significant this difference has become, just note that if our 135,000 FTE [full-time equivalent] students were funded at the national average level, the UW budget would be ... $109.89 million higher, enough to catch up all the deferred depreciation problems

throughout the System and to bring all faculty and staff salaries
to competitive market levels.

Why do these differences exist? It is not because the regents and System
administrators don't know how to convince the state to appropriate more
money to the System from General Purpose Revenues, or because the
System has lost its credibility.

I was an active participant in budget negotiations, and while there is no
doubt that there have been some credibility problems, I do not believe that
better presentations or more credibility would have made any difference.
The problem is that Wisconsin has relatively high enrollment in its public
universities. It is, relatively speaking, a poor state, and other priorities have
received an increased share of state revenues. There is an unwillingness to
raise taxes or reorder the State's priorities. This is important to understand
so that regents and the System don't spend their time chasing rainbows, but,
rather, deal with realistic options.

A review of the arguments and counter-arguments between the System,
the Joint Legislative Audit Committee, and the Legislative Audit Bureau
(LAB) in 1986-87, and the failure to resolve the issues presented, demonstrate why substantially increased state funds are not likely. In 1986, while I
served as president of the board, System President Shaw presented studies
concluding that the system had an annual shortfall of $88 million, or $600
per student. In order to make up this gap, System administration and the
board of regents proposed several alternatives:[19]

1. Increase GPR (state revenues) by $88 million.

2. Reduce enrollment by 22,000 students.

3. Increase annual tuition by $640.

4. Some combination of the above.

The first three options for closing the funding gap became known as the
"Shaw Triangle." The gap was determined by comparing System funding
per student with the U.S. Department of Education's Higher Education
General Information Survey (HEGIS). The conclusions received wide
publicity. Shaw and I travelled the state and explained the issues and
proposed solutions to all who would listen.

On December 2, 1986, Shaw requested that the Joint Committee on Audit
convene a panel of university, legislative, and executive staff to review the
methodology used for determining funding needs. His request was rejected
on December 11 in a letter by the chairs of the Joint Legislative Audit
Committee. The reason given was that "from our discussions with staff at
the DOA (Department of Administration), LFB (Legislative Fiscal Bureau)
and LAB, the priorities and timetable of each [of the] staff[s] are not
compatible with the joint review concept." In addition, it was stated that the

legislature preferred to have independent auditors, namely, the LAB, review the issue.

On December 13, 1986, Shaw wrote Dale Cattanach, Director of the LAB, expressing his disappointment. He explained again that the "benchmark" hoped for was not intended to be a "rigid funding formula," but that a benchmark was needed. He offered to cooperate fully with the bureau. A copy of the System's analysis was enclosed.

On December 22, in a letter to the chairs of the Joint Legislative Audit Committee, the LAB attacked the report for being selective in its data, claimed that Extension funds were omitted in making the calculation, and that Wisconsin enrolled considerably fewer high-cost graduate students when compared with the national average. The letter concluded by stating that no comparison was valid. "Calculating a reliable comparison to other states with which everyone can agree is inherently difficult, because all the flaws in the data may not be known and different methodologies can produce widely differing results." The letter continued, *"Therefore, rather than make significant policy and funding decisions based on disputable comparison, the Legislature may wish to consider other indicators of funding needs, such as the State's ability to fund the University, the types of programs the Legislature wishes to offer, and the level of access to the University System"* (emphasis added).

In response, Shaw argued that the use of a national database rounded out the differences. He included debt service for the UW System ($50.3 million), and the State Lab of Hygiene ($3.6 million), which other states had not. The UW System also included central administrative costs, whereas states such as Illinois, Texas, and Minnesota did not. In Illinois, administrative costs amounted to $20 million.

On January 21, 1987, after explaining the differences between the UW System analysis and that of the LAB to the Joint Audit Committee, Shaw concluded that the interests of the System and the legislature "don't always coincide" — quality higher education and greatest possible access on the one hand, and the need for a balanced budget on the other. That was precisely why he saw the need to work out the needs of the System cooperatively through state funding, tuition, and enrollment. While admitting the conflict, he saw his role as that "of demonstrating our needs forcefully and honestly and attempting to obtain those needed dollars to provide quality education to as many individuals as possible."

State support per resident undergraduate student has actually been dropping since 1978-79 when viewed in terms of constant dollars. Dollars are deflated by the Higher Education Price Index to determine constant dollars compared with 1978-79. In 1978-79, the state support per resident undergraduate student was $3,708, whereas in 1991-92, it was $3,327, in constant dollars, according to information supplied by the System to the Governor's Commission on Compensation.[20]

It is also important to understand that the state had shifted priorities over the years. In 1990-91, Wisconsin appropriated 11.4% of its General Purpose Revenues to the System. In 1972, just after merger, that amount was 16.3% of the state's budget. A drop of 4% amounted to a whopping $260 million per year, substantially more than the extra amount needed to fund the System adequately. The reduction in the percentage had been gradual, but steady over the years. The reason? The state had increased the percentage of GPR that it appropriated to School Aid and Medical Assistance. There was no evidence that this trend would change. As a matter of fact, total state GPR expenditures increased by 224% since Chapter 36, Wisconsin Statutes created the UW System, whereas the state's appropriation to the System increased by only 136% during the same period.

Based on other statistics, however, the state had been generous in its support of the System. The *Wisconsin Taxpayer Alliance* stated in its 1991 report that on a per capita basis, "As in public education, Wisconsin was 10th highest in higher education. Compared with the U.S. per capita average of $295, Wisconsin's amount was $393, or 33% more. Again, all the Great Lakes states except one has lower per capita expenditures."[21] The report showed that whereas Wisconsin appropriated 11.6% of its state and local expenditures on higher education for 1989-90, the national average was 8.8%.[22] A two-year study covering 1992 and 1993 concluded that Wisconsin ranked 15th in the nation in total appropriations to higher education and 14th in the nation in terms of the two-year change in state support for higher education. The national average two-year change, adjusted for inflation, was -7%, whereas Wisconsin showed 0% change for the same period. Wisconsin also compared favorably with states close by. Adjusted for inflation, the two-year change in support was:[23]

Minnesota	-10%
Illinois	- 8%
Michigan	-3%
Ohio	-13%
Indiana	-5%

One can mount statistics and hand out data endlessly to show that Wisconsin did not contribute enough to public higher education on the one hand, but is generous on the other. Cattanagh (LAB) stated it clearly. The issue will not be resolved based on which statistics are used. It is not a question of statistics but how much the state is willing to spend. No one was impressed with our comparisons. As a matter of fact, they relished tearing them apart. The real issue was not confronted. The percentage of the state's revenue that goes to public higher education will remain at about 11%. The economic fortunes of the state in general, and its agencies in particular, will determine how much greater or smaller the amount will be, but the percent will remain about the same. As a matter of fact, on October 1, 1992, all state agencies, including the System, were ordered to return to the state 1.5% of the state's appropriations. For the UW System that amounted to $10.2 million.[24] In commenting that this was not the fault of the System, President Lyall said, "The UW System has lived within its budget, but is being asked to lapse funds to cover excess spending in other parts of the state budget." This was the second time in the current fiscal year that the System was asked to cut spending from supplies and expenses, telephone, and federal indirect cost accounts, amounting to $7.7 million. These cuts increased student share of instructional cost from 35.3% to 36%. [25]

Raise Tuition

Tuition had been a favorite source for making up whatever was perceived as being a shortfall in state revenue. The raises had little to do with inflation. That had not only been true in Wisconsin but nationwide. On October 21, 1992, *The Chronicle of Higher Education* reported that tuition at public colleges was up 10% nationwide for 1992-93, which was three times the rate of inflation. This followed a 12% raise nationwide in 1991-92.[26] While some would look to these figures to justify raising tuition in Wisconsin, I find the figures depressing. I am convinced that such raises reduce financial access for students. "A lot of students have been driven from public colleges and universities," according to Stacey Leyton, president of the UW Student Association. "A lot of middle-income students are graduating from school $20,000 or $30,000 in debt." Against these tuition hikes, federal, state, and institutional financial aid rose less than 8% in 1991.[27] Tuition was 13.8% of the UW System's budget for 1984-85.[28] In 1981-82, students paid 26% of the total cost of undergraduate instruction, the rest being covered by state tax funds.[29] By 1990-91, tuition was 14.7% of the budget[30] and constituted 31.5% of the total cost of instruction.[31] Those most current overall averages were made up of undergraduate resident students paying approximately 1/3 of the instructional costs and the state paying 2/3 and out of state undergraduate students paying 105% of instructional costs. In 1981-82, the state of Wisconsin paid 42.76% of the System's budget, and only 34.92% in 1991-92,[32] the difference being borne by students in the form of increased tuition.

Is there a "fair" tuition policy? In my view, the only "fair" tuition policy is no tuition for anyone. An enlightened society ought to provide publicly financed education for its citizens. Admission should be based on one's potential ability to succeed, not on one's ability to pay or one's willingness to go into debt. Why should those with greater family incomes receive an education and graduate debt-free while those with smaller family incomes graduate with debt? How is that "fair?" What is fair about a policy that results in some families paying out 20% or more of their disposable income to send a child to college, and really sacrifice, while for others more fortunate, it hardly makes a dent in the family's style of living. And what is fair about a tuition policy that says the children of some families will have to juggle a work schedule with classes while in college and take longer to graduate, while the children of others do not have to work at all? That is precisely what results from any tuition policy, because those who can't afford to pay the tuition, fees, room and board, and books are not given a grant for the entire difference and have to borrow it. We will examine the shift that has taken place in federal policy away from grants toward loans, which puts an additional burden on students. Tuition is not charged in the K-12 System. It makes no sense to adopt a different policy for public higher education whether it be for the UW System or the VTAE system. If we are serious about the need to educate our children so that we may compete in a global economy, then we need to reexamine our priorities. It certainly costs less to give a young person a skill than to build a prison cell for that person to occupy. To the extent that we charge the user for the educational service, we have privatized the public institution. I totally disagree with those who say that to the extent the state does not fund instructional costs, the students should be forced to pay through higher tuition.

Unfortunately, the reality is that tuition is charged because the state and federal government have established different priorities and there is no well-organized protest against that. Tuition is a relatively easy way out. David Martin, associate vice president for government and business relations for the UW System, in arguing against a bill that would cap tuition, was quoted as saying that the bill "takes away flexibility" from the university. "Tuition is one of the few avenues the UW has to raise revenue when state funds fall short."[33] Milton Neshek, chair of the governor's commission on UW System compensation, was reported to have said on June 17, 1992, that the System had three main sources of revenue — taxes, reallocation, and tuition — and since the former two were "somewhat limited," an increase in tuition was the "most feasible" solution. Latching on to that "feasibility," the System announced that it wanted to increase tuition by 6.7% for Fall 1992, instead of the 4.5% originally intended.[34] It was adopted by the board. No mention was made that 6.7% was substantially more than inflation. Nor was there any meaningful discussion that related this increase to the current economic recession. On top of this, at the October 1992 board meeting, there was talk of raising tuition 10%, even though the recession continued and the economic state of the nation dominated the presidential campaign last year. I am further troubled by the failure of the regents to become more involved in the variable costs of operating a university system. As enrollment is reduced, so is tuition income. The immediate response seemed to be to raise tuition to make up for the shortfall rather than examine other alternatives, such as reducing personnel costs by consolidating programs and administrative positions and reviewing faculty teaching loads. At the time of this writing there are 134,000 FTE students in the System, and tuition averages $2,000 per year. A reduction of 5,000 students will reduce tuition income by $10 million. If the only option considered is to raise tuition among those who are left, then tuition will have to go up by about $77 per student, or over 3%. There *are* other alternatives which will be discussed in the next chapter.

How is tuition established? Tuition for the System is set after the regents submit a total budget to the governor. The legislature and the governor determine the overall expenditure level of the System. A specific amount of state funds are appropriated, which is less than the total expenditures authorized. The difference becomes tuition.

On March 7, 1992, in response to a proposed legislative budget cut, UW System Acting President Lyall was reported to have said that unless the legislature could be convinced not to make those cuts, the System would lobby lawmakers for a tuition surcharge in addition to the 4.5% increase already planned for the coming school year.[35] "We are hovering now on the brink of where we are starving our students educationally to keep the tuition at the bottom of the Big Ten. I wouldn't think we would be looking ... at double-digit increases."[36] Regent Ness Flores said, "We have to show them [legislature] this will mean an increase in tuition of X number of dollars per student, or point out the services that will have to be cut."[37]

Wisconsin's tradition of "low" tuition was considered, in the past, to be good public policy. It was responsive to the wish that tuition not be the gatekeeper to admission, a policy I support. That was changing as System administrators and regents proposed higher and higher tuition. Those who proposed and continue to propose higher tuition used a variety of well known arguments. Some argued that tuition was too low compared with "peer" institutions, the Big Ten, or median family incomes of entering freshmen. Others argued that tuition was a bargain in any event. Others said that if you're "using the service — you ought to pay for it."[38] At the board meeting held in July 1991, the debate focused on whether or not tuition should be raised by an average of 3.4% across the entire System.[39] One regent called the increase a "... tax on children." Taking exception to this, another regent responded that tuition is the "cost of matriculating."[40] The president of the statewide student organization, United Council, was quoted as saying, "It's always tough for me to come here and listen to the Board of Regents talk about what's a bargain. It's probably a bargain for them, but for the students it keeps getting more expensive." Since the debates continue, I believe it worthwhile to examine the arguments being made to raise tuition beyond inflation. I do not believe they are persuasive.

Is "Low" Tuition a Subsidy to the Rich?

It has been argued that low tuition constitutes a subsidy to the rich; it would be fairer for everyone if tuition was charged on a sliding scale tied to family income. Thomas P. Wallace, president of Illinois State University, wrote in *The Chronicle for Higher Education* that since state funds are not likely to increase, universities should raise tuition substantially, with a portion set aside to subsidize those who cannot afford the higher amounts.[41] The University of California system raised tuition $650 in Fall 1991, according to Wallace, and set aside 20% of the increase to be used for student grants. Students with adjusted family incomes of less than $30,000 would receive the entire $650, whereas those with adjusted family incomes exceeding $30,000 would receive decreasing amounts, according to income levels. He claimed that if Illinois State University had instituted such an increase, and if 25% had been used for grants to 29% of the undergraduates, the university's operating budget would have increased $9.4 million. W. Ann Reynolds, chancellor at the City University of New York, disagreed. In the April 29, 1992, issue of the same publication, she contended that Wallace failed to mention that because middle-class salaries have declined in the past decade, few would be able to pay the kinds of increases Wallace was talking about, and a greater number of students would need financial aid.

This is verified in a December 12, 1991, article in Madison's *The Capital Times*. An Associated Press story concluded, "The middle class is worse off financially now than it was in 1980." The Congressional Budget Office estimated that median income for families with children would be $37,300 in 1992, which would be $1,600 less than in 1980, with both figures being measured in 1992 dollars. Taking the recession into full account " ... the projections for middle class earnings next year are likely to drop further."[42] Reynolds contended that particular harm would be caused to minority students, "people on the economic margin ... part-time students ... single parents ...," and that we not forget why public universities were founded in the first place, beginning with the Morrill Act of 1862. The huge growth in universities following World War II was meant to give the widest range of the population the opportunities of public higher education, so that America would have the scientists and educated citizenry for world leadership. "Our university research in science, technology, medicine, and agriculture has transformed history." Wallace's proposal would change the nature of public universities so that they would become private or merely publicly assisted institutions with drastic drops in enrollment for immigrants, minorities, and the middle class. She quoted President Derek Bok, former president of Harvard, "If you think education is expensive, try ignorance."[43]

Parent income may be less relevant when we consider the demography of the student body. In writing about the campus of the future, *Time* magazine reported that today " ... only 20% of the nation's undergraduates are young people between 18 and 22 who are pursuing a parent-financed education. Two-fifths of all students today are part-timers, and more than a third are over 25."[44] The idea of tying tuition to family income was suggested while I served on the board. It was rejected because it would have required every student to submit the family's tax return, which would have substantially increased administrative costs.

Students Should Pay More than They Pay Now

Because UW System tuition is low compared to peer institutions, and median family incomes for entering freshmen at UW-Madison are higher than the national average and higher than other System institutions, shouldn't students pay more than they do now?

In testifying before the Governor's Commission on Faculty and Academic Compensation, on April 24, 1992, W. Lee Hansen, professor of economics at UW-Madison, argued that since the amount of tuition paid by Wisconsin citizens to UW institutions is less than that paid to peer institutions, and that since the majority of Wisconsin students attending UW-Madison come from families with median family incomes of $48,000, compared with the national average of $34,000 for 1990, tuition ought to be increased so that faculty could be paid more. He argued, further, that the earnings differential for college graduates relative to high school graduates is great enough so that this extra cost is justified, even when increased borrowing is necessary.

At the June 1992 meeting of the board of regents, it was reported that median family income of freshmen entering UW-Madison in Fall 1991 was $48,678, compared with $32,500 to $40,253 for the other UW System campuses.[45] Regent Erroll Davis reasoned that this was "evidence of a 'middle class subsidy.'" Davis said, "I have great difficulty understanding why someone making almost $50,000 hasn't been able to carve out $2,000 over 18 years' to pay tuition for their freshman daughter or son."[46] I will examine both arguments.

Following his election as president of the board on June 5, 1992, George K. Steil, Sr., said: "As desirable as it might be, we cannot remain the second-lowest in tuition in the Big Ten. If we do, we will find this System in the same predicament as California is at the present time, where they are advocating a 26% tuition increase in one year."[47] The reference to the Big Ten was, apparently, aimed at UW-Madison, which is the only member of the Big Ten. For the period 1990-91, tuition plus fees for resident undergraduates at UW-Madison were the second-lowest of the nine public Big Ten universities.[48] What Steil did not mention was the board resolution on this very subject, adopted at the November 1990 meeting, Resolution 1.2.b [revised], "Long Term Tuition Policy."[49] The original purpose of the policy was to bring tuition for undergraduate resident students in the System institutions to the "midpoint of their peer institutions." My notes indicate that the peer group for UW-Madison and UW-Milwaukee was to be the Big Ten. There was a major debate among board members as to the *timing* of the implementation of the policy. There were those of us who feared that additional increases in tuition would bring about decreased state funding or no commensurate increase in state funding, raising even further the percentage of instructional costs that resident undergraduates would pay. In addition, we worried that moving to the midpoint of the peer group should be phased in over a longer rather than a shorter period of time. Compromise language was added as a hedge: "This policy *assumes continued reasonable GPR contributions to the budget.* The board reserves the right to reconsider this policy in unusual circumstances to assure that both state and student contributions are fairly determined" (emphasis added). Those "unusual circumstances" were understood to include the lack of proportional state funding as well as general adverse economic conditions. Proportional state funding meant that for every dollar of resident undergraduate tuition increase, the state would contribute two dollars so that the current one-third/two-third relationship would remain intact.

The background of the compromise language is important. I received a memo dated November 2, 1990, from Katharine Lyall to Ron Bornstein "Re: Regent Weinstein's Request for Consolidated Tuition and Fee Information." This was shared with the board. It concluded that for 1990-91, UW-Madison's tuition was $390 lower than the midpoint of peers, UW-Milwaukee's was $241 below peers, and tuition at the comprehensive universities was $188 below peers. To reach the midpoint, UW-Madison undergraduate resident tuition would have to be raised by 18.5%, UW-Milwaukee by 15.8%, and the comprehensive universities' by 10.6%. That amount was seen as entirely too great by some of us and caused the "unusual circumstances" language to be added. Despite this history, some of the current proponents of raising tuition exclude proportional state funding as a condition, and ignore previous board resolutions.

Regents ought to consider other factors that Lyall, Hansen, Steil, Davis and other proponents of higher tuition included in their reasoning, and that, in my opinion, militate against raising tuition beyond inflation:

1.   Professor Hansen stated that the *median* family income reported by entering freshmen at UW-Madison was $48,000 for 1990. He compared that with the *national average* of $34,000 and concluded that tuition should be raised for resident undergraduates so that faculty could be paid more. Of course, faculty would be most unhappy and would find it totally unacceptable if in arguing for higher compensation they were compared to the national average, rather than the relevant peer group. Furthermore, median family incomes of entering freshmen, even if accurate, only described the financial circumstances of those who entered the System. It said nothing about the financial circumstances of those who did not enroll, for any number

of reasons, including not being able to afford it. The use of median family incomes ignored other important considerations. For example, Table 1 of the March 5, 1993, UW Board of Regents Meeting Agenda, item 1.1.h.(4), shows the distribution of UW freshman by family income for Fall 1990. Each of the family income categories represents 20% of Wisconsin families. For example, 20% of Wisconsin families had incomes from 0 through $18,575. At UW-Madison, families with incomes under $40,000 were under-represented, whereas families with incomes over $55,220 were substantially over-represented. Regents need to be concerned that tuition not become the gatekeeper to admission.

Table 1

Distribution of UW Freshman by Family Income, Fall 1990

	$0-18,575	$18,576-29,832	$29,833-40,616	$40,617-55,219	$55,220-and over
TOTAL:UW System % reporting:79.4 N=19,125	13.8%	19.8%	24.7%	21.1%	20.5%
UW-Madison % reporting:75.9 N=3,568	8.4%	15.0%	19.7%	22.2%	34.6%
UW-Milwaukee % reporting:76.6 N=1,873	13.9%	20.9%	26.5%	20.9%	17.8%
UW-Comprehensives %reporting:85.9 N=11,504	14.7%	20.6%	25.7%	21.2%	17.8%
UW-Centers % reporting:61.1 N=2,180	17.7%	22.2%	26.4%	19.6%	14.2%

There are at least two reasons why basing a tuition policy on the median family incomes reported by freshmen is not good public policy. Approximately 15-29% of entering freshman did not report. Further, and more importantly, the median family income figure does not accurately describe the profile of family income of entering freshman and their ability to pay. Even for UW-Madison, the median family income hardly describes the economic circumstances of at least 43% of entering freshmen whose family incomes were substantially below the reported median. For other campuses, the percentage of entering freshmen whose reported family incomes fell below $48,000 was substantially greater than that of UW-Madison.

A tuition policy for undergraduate students based on the purported family income of entering freshmen assumed that the parents were supporting not only the freshmen but all undergraduates. The family income of entering freshmen hardly describes the economic status of the great majority of students, who may not rely on family support. As an illustration of who may or may not be receiving family support, here is the age breakdown of undergraduates for the System 1991-92:[50]

Age 19 or less	26.2%
Age 20 to 24	53.3%
Age 24 and over	20.5%

In addition, for the System, the breakdown of full-time and part-time students for the same period was:[51]

Full-time	76.6%
Part-time	23.4%

Many part-time students are older and do not receive support from their parents.

Tying a tuition policy to the median family income of freshmen ignores the fact that for 1991-92, most undergraduates were not freshmen:[52]

Number of Freshmen	37,648
Number of Sophomores	30,304
Number of Juniors	26,606
Number of Seniors	34,550

Resident undergraduate freshmen constituted only 27.6% of all resident undergraduates.[53]

2.   Others proposed that tuition for undergraduate residents in Wisconsin be compared with undergraduate resident tuition charged by peer institutions. While peer group comparisons for some factors were relevant, they were not for all. Peer groups were developed to compare faculty compensation. It was a way of establishing a *relevant competitive market* that had nothing to do with tuition. Resident tuition charged by public universities in other states was not relevant for Wisconsin residents, since they would be charged

non-resident tuition in those states. Of what interest was it to a Wisconsin family that Michigan residents pay more than they do for in-state tuition? For example, for 1990-91, the California public four-year university tuition was $731 less than that in Wisconsin. At the public two-year schools, it was $1,120 less.[54] I did not hear any of the peer group proponents suggest that since California was among Wisconsin's peers, tuition should be reduced. Tuition for undergraduate residents should, in my view, be based on what is reasonable under *all* the circumstances in *our* state. Peer group comparisons are relevant only for out-of-state students.

3.   Of greater importance than the median family income of entering freshmen or peer group comparisons is the fact that Wisconsin is not a rich state. Wisconsin's per capita personal income in 1990 was 6.3% below the national average and ranked 22nd in the nation.[55] For 1991, *The Wisconsin Taxpayers Alliance* reported, "In per capita personal income, Wisconsin continues to be below the U.S. average, just as it has been for at least the last 25 years."[56]

University administrators and regents ought to study the "Distribution of Wisconsin Adjusted Gross Income and Net Tax Liability by Adjusted Gross Income Class" for 1991.[57] 68.5% of the tax returns filed showed adjusted gross income below $30,000. An additional 10.8% of the returns showed adjusted gross income between $30,000 and $40,000. Only 20.9% of the returns showed adjusted gross income exceeding $40,000.

Even those with median family incomes of $48,000 would be hard-pressed to save for the university education of their children, as Regent Davis suggested. The $2,000 that he referred to was the tuition at UW-Madison, which was the smallest portion of the cost of attending. For the period 1990-91, the total annual cost for a resident undergraduate student at UW-Madison was $5,273, including university housing and meals, but excluding books and other living expenses.[58] That was approximately 12% of the after-tax income of a family of four that earned $48,000. In addition, Wisconsin taxpayers pay more per $1,000 of personal income to support public higher education than the national average, and for the period 1989-90, Wisconsin ranked sixth in the nation for the amount of state and local taxes paid per $1,000 of personal income.[59] Those additional amounts must also be taken into consideration in determining tuition policy.

4.   Wisconsin residents have been hit pretty hard already. Whereas the Consumer Price Index increased cumulatively by 85.4%-88.6% from 1979-80 to 1990-91, tuition for Wisconsin residents attending UW institutions increased by 147%. At the same time, Wisconsin per capita personal income increased by only 112.6%.[60] UW-Madison tuition covered 31% of "actual cost of education," whereas the average nationwide was 26%.[61]

In 1973-74, Wisconsin resident undergraduate students paid 26% of instructional costs; by 1991-92, that percentage rose to 35.2%[62], due to the fact that state support per resident undergraduate student in constant dollars was dropping, as was the state's share of cost per student.[63] Students and their families made up the difference through increased tuition and fees. UW System Vice President for Academic Affairs Stephen Portch pointed out that "... had the UW System not embarked on enrollment management, the decline in support per student would have been precipitous."[64] In my view, it already was.

The Chronicle of Higher Education Almanac reported on August 26, 1992 (p. 7), that tuition and fees charged by Wisconsin's four-year public institutions were $63 higher than the national average, and those of Wisconsin's public two-year institutions were $410 higher than the national average for 1990-91. When viewed in terms of personal income of Wisconsin residents, which is below the national average, tuition is no longer a "bargain."

5.   There is no evidence that raising tuition would not result in a further reduction in state funds unless it was specifically conditioned on maintaining the current ratio of tuition to state support. The ratio had not been maintained.

6.   Students whose families cannot afford the tuition resort to loans, grants, or work. From 1980-81 to 1987-88, federal student aid went from 55.8% grants and 40.4% loans to 50.4% loans and 46.9% grants, putting a greater burden on students. The balance was work programs.[65] As far as the System is concerned, the report to the regents dated May 1991 states, "Loans have been the major source of aid dollars available to UW students since 1981-82."[66] For the UW System, student debt at the time of graduation had risen from $5,884 in 1982-83 to $7,977 in 1989-90.[67] The headline of an October 28, 1992, article in *The Chronicle of Higher Education* says it all: "Hope Fades for Cutting Reliance on Loans as Chief Component of U.S. Student Aid."[68] Time was when grants were the major form of college aid for the underprivileged. The author concludes that this shift from grants to loans will lessen access to higher education. In an article titled "Middle-Income Families Need Immediate Help in Paying for College," Alan Guskin, president of Antioch College and former chancellor of UW-Parkside, wrote:

> Federal student aid appropriations trailed inflation in the 1980's. The Pell Grant, a mainstay of federal aid, has not kept pace with costs. The maximum Pell Grant is only $2,400 per year. In addition, few middle-income families are eligible for Pell Grants in any helpful amount. Other federal aid programs fared even worse. From 1981 to 1992, funding for Supplemental Educational Opportunity Grants fell 11.9%. College work-study monies declined by 32.3%. State Student Incentive funding slid 48.1%. Forced to turn to loans to pay for college, some students are saddled with a five-figure debt when they graduate. Perhaps a high salaried physician or corporate lawyer can overcome that

burden. What, however, is a school teacher or social worker going to do? The real solution to the problem of how to pay for college is for the federal government to understand that it is in the nation's interest to provide adequate financial aid for the middle-income students without detracting from the vitally important aid programs for low-income students.[69]

More troubling to me was that financial aid follows color lines. *The Capital Times*, on June 2, 1992, reported that "78 percent of all Native American and 73 [percent] of all African-American resident undergraduates received financial aid. Hispanic students follow the same pattern." In quoting from the System research brief, the article continues, "Loans have been the major source of aid dollars available to UW students for the last 10 years ... " and 40 percent of resident undergraduates receive some form of financial aid.

In discussing student debt, some argue that since college graduates make substantially more than those without a college degree, the issue of debt is overblown. There is no question that those who attend college will earn more than those who did not. According to the U.S. Department of Labor, Bureau of Labor Statistics, for the year 1987 the "Annual earnings of workers by highest level of education attainment," the average for all occupations was:[70]

Total	$21,543
Less than high school	$15,249
High School	$18,902
1 to 3 years of college	$21,975
4 or more years of college	$31,029

Others observed that for some disadvantaged segments of our society, the amount of debt that would be incurred while earning a baccalaureate degree was totally incomprehensible, and therefore, not acceptable. In writing about the increased amount of student loans, *The Capital Times* reported on March 18, 1992, that "sharp increases in borrowing worry students, not to mention students and parents having trouble making payments during a recession. Total student aid has dropped in constant dollars in the last 10 years ... while public university tuition rose 81% ... ' What's happening is really disastrous. Students are being expected to borrow more than I think is feasible in some cases,' according to Barbara Tornow, director of financial aid at Boston University."

Debt is not only an indicator of a students' ability to pay, but has serious academic implications regarding career choices. A national study conducted by Professor Eileen Zito, UW-Stout, concluded that there was a connection between anticipated loan debt and the choice of a student's major: "We need to go back and look at the grant versus loan issue. The emphasis right now is on more loans than grants. Is that a good move, or are we getting students going into specific majors just so they can pay back their educational debt in the future?"[71]

In commenting on President-elect Clinton's proposal to provide financial aid for students in exchange for performing public service after graduation, UW-Madison Chancellor Shalala said, "It will provide more opportunity for poor kids" and would require the state to appropriate more money to the university to handle the increased number of students.[72] If that is true, then it seems clear that current tuition and student aid policies are a deterrent to some.

7.   A realistic assessment of general economic conditions should be taken into account. The reason the legislature contemplated a reduction in the System's 1991-92 budget was because of shrinking state revenues which resulted from the recession. Wisconsin taxpayers are suffering reduced incomes and paying fewer taxes. An increase in tuition means an additional "tax" on those who attend System institutions, precisely at a time when they can least afford it. The System, and particularly the board, should not operate in a vacuum. In 1992, the governor correctly spoke out against the idea of raising tuition.[73]

8.   Before further "taxing" users, serious considerations need to be given to the state's commitment to public higher education. State appropriations per full time equivalent student have been a relevant indicator of state support. It has been substantially lower than the national average. Another indicator of state support has been the percentage of state tax dollars being appropriated to public higher education. Of the seven states that include the public Big Ten universities, Wisconsin ranked seventh in the percentage of total state tax dollars going to higher education for 1990-91, excluding vocational/technical appropriations.[74] Wisconsin appropriated 12.42% of its state tax dollars to higher education versus a midpoint of 16.62% for the seven other states. Based on Wisconsin's tax dollars collected — $6.025 billion — it would take an additional $253 million in appropriations to the System to reach the midpoint of the seven states — more than enough to meet any shortfall.

9.   The more regents raise tuition, the more the System will be scrutinized, even punished, by political leaders. Then the media joins in. It has already happened. Political leaders have a great interest in tuition policy because they must answer to their constituents. The Joint Legislative Audit Committee ordered an audit by the LAB of faculty workloads.[75] Legislators, as we shall see, are critical of decisions that would raise tuition beyond inflation. And they control the budget. The reasons are obvious. Students and their parents will complain publicly. Wisconsin has had a long tradition of low tuition, lower than the peer groups. In the past, comparisons with peer groups were

not a persuasive argument. In 1992, regents "bought into" the peer comparison argument, and raised tuition 6.7% when inflation was running substantially less than that. On the heels of that increase, it was reported that "Members of the Board of Regents and state officials forecast such increases [10% annually] because of tight state budgets and the relatively low cost of a college education in Wisconsin."[76] In response, Representative Stanley Gruszynski, a long-time friend of the System, was quoted as saying, "The Board of Regents and administration look to tuition as if it's the only alternative. We need to make it less convenient for them to do that." The significance of the tradition in Wisconsin for lower tuition and for maintaining a balance between tuition and state funds cannot be underestimated.

I fear the current board and some campus and System administrators are looking to tuition as the only alternative as they speculate publicly about various plans to raise tuition, based on the August 25, 1992, report of *The Governor's Commission on University of Wisconsin System Compensation*. The report seemed to abandon the current tuition-to-state-funding ratio. It turned to peer comparisons for tuition, but left much unsaid. In part, the report concluded, "Given the constraints, at least in the short run, on dramatically increasing GPR funding for the UW System, tuition revenue will need to play a bigger role in supporting the overall needs of the UW System. Dramatic annual increases in tuition rates should be avoided. Tuition rate increases should be accompanied by proportionate increases in student grant assistance. Tuition increases should not be offset by decreases in state tax revenue to the UW System."[77]

What is meant by "dramatic?" How much of a greater share of overall costs should tuition be? What would be the source of the increased student assistance? The commission concluded that the source of the problem was the lack of state funds. It recommended that the legislature retain a role in establishing tuition and "set guidelines regarding the tuition levels Regents can approve. ... One reasonable set of guidelines would be a requirement that resident undergraduate tuition be no higher than the median of resident undergraduate tuition at the other public Big Ten institutions."[78] The tables that accompanied the report showed that tuition would have to be increased by 32.57% for UW-Madison to reach the median. Is that not "dramatic?" Two state representatives, expressing their concern that wage settlements have been in the 2 to 3% range, and that the regents could price the university "beyond the means of most people in the state," have asked that tuition be added to a special session of the legislature.[79] It was reported that the state fiscal bureau concluded that tuition would have to be increased 14.2% each year to reach the median in five years.[80] Is that "dramatic?" In October 1992, the board adopted the System's proposal to recommend a tuition increase of about 8%. The reaction was immediate. State Representative Peter Barca said, "The writing is becoming clear. A University education will become a dim prospect for lower- and middle-income families in the future."[81] The co-chair of the powerful Joint Finance Committee said that if approved, the tuition increase would further restrict access.[82] The United Council president, representing students, said, "The (tuition) increase will naturally turn away many of Wisconsin's citizens who will not be able to afford it. ..."[83]

The commission's findings regarding shortfall in faculty and academic staff compensation seemed clear enough. Commission Chair Neshek was quoted as saying that it would cost an additional $25-$30 million a year to provide the "ultimate" solution.[84] That is roughly the same figure provided to me by UW System Budget Analyst Nate Peters. How much of an increase in tuition is needed to raise $30 million? With 135,000 FTE, the increase would amount to $222 per student. It's a far cry from the difference to reach the median of the Big Ten, but it would still amount to about a 10% increase.

The commission referred to other alternatives. "The Commission stresses that an important objective for the UW System is to reduce administrative costs."[85] I predict there will be increased pressure to reduce administrative costs and find other alternatives as the board considers raising tuition beyond inflation. Charges of inefficiency, insufficient faculty instructional workload, and high administrative costs will come under attack. That is the price they will pay for raising tuition higher than what the public and political leaders perceive as being affordable. Pressure to engage in downsizing in one form or another will increase from inside and outside the board. It will become increasingly difficult for System administration and campuses to defend past practices. For instance, Arnold Hauptman, educational consultant, was quoted as saying that raising tuition is easier "... than making hard choices." He contended that small teaching loads for faculty, caused by "unhealthy competition," were a contributor to the problem of increasing tuition rates.[86]

Conclusion

For all of the reasons stated, I do not believe tuition should be raised beyond the amount of inflation. There may be some modest savings available in administrative costs; there will probably be no increased state funding; private funds may help deal with some infrastructure needs. President Lyall's *Quality Reinvestment Plan*, which ordered that some vacant positions not be filled, and that the savings, amounting to $20-$25 million, be reallocated to meet priority needs, cannot be repeated over and over again. What is to be done to preserve quality? Other strategies are available. That is the subject of the next chapter.

VIII.

Suggestions and Options for Preserving Quality

Conclusion #8: In order to preserve the quality of the UW System, the regents should define the elements of access and quality, establish standards, and design and implement strategies, keeping in mind that all elements of quality are not related to funding.

Problems and the Solutions

It is now time to consider the future and provide suggestions and options for regent and System administration consideration.

No meaningful discussion of quality can take place, no goals can be established, no solutions can be adopted and implemented, without first defining the elements of access and quality. Access and quality have elements of their own. Some are intertwined with funding and some are not. It is important to stay focused on quality. We will do so by examining the elements of quality and discussing how various strategies to preserve quality have an impact on elements of access. That will help determine which choices are more acceptable than others.

In addressing the issue of quality, I will rely on the three-step approach to management. To begin, you need to keep the mission, or *goal*, in mind. Earlier I pointed out that the mission of the UW System consists of instruction (undergraduate and graduate), research, and outreach (public service). Undergraduate education is primary. The challenge before the board is to make certain that all aspects of the mission are being carried out in a quality manner. Quality is the *standard*. When faced with a choice between quality and access, quality had to prevail, since access without quality is not considered to be good public policy. On the other hand, those students who can qualify should have access. It was never the intention of the board to keep such students out.

If existing assumptions are not challenged, no progress can be made, and we are back defending the status quo. Whenever an organization wants to change (or must), all assumptions should be challenged. I will do just that, and suggest the assumptions have outlived their usefulness and ought to be abandoned.

Elements of Access

Geographic Access

No one argues that Wisconsin does not provide superb geographic access by maintaining two systems of post-secondary education, as well as a large number of institutions for each system located throughout the state. In the UW System, students and their families benefit from this geographic access because it offers them the opportunity to more easily control the costs of travel and room and board. The ability of the state to afford geographic access is another matter. Maintaining 27 institutions necessarily duplicates programs and administrative costs. It is an issue the board has not addressed. The conflict between quality and maintaining this access to institutions and programs remains unresolved. I will consider the implications of geographic access along with other "Options" at the end of this chapter.

Financial Access

Access for individual students depends on ability to pay. As previously discussed, Wisconsin has had a tradition of low tuition. It had long been the policy of the state to ignore comparisons with peer groups and to concentrate on the goal that ability to pay should not be the gatekeeper to university admission. Yet as we saw in the previous chapter, whenever funding issues are discussed, raising tuition has always been at the top of the agenda. I believe there is little regard paid to how raising tuition impacts access. Regents should not carry on serious discussions about raising tuition unless they also discuss how this will affect the financial access of our students.

Academic Access and the Relationship to VTAE

When I was a freshman at UW-Madison in 1941, the only academic access criteria was a Wisconsin high school diploma. Access to public universities was considered a matter of right. The unstated policy was, "Let them in and flunk them out." This policy was radically altered by the regents. When the first enrollment management policy was adopted, regents raised minimum admission standards for System campuses. Some campuses followed by raising their institution's admission standards even further. As a result, based on academic performance in high school, access to some or all of the System institutions was denied to some Wisconsin high school graduates.

As of Fall 1992, it was reported that "93% of Wisconsin applicants who complete[d] an on time application and [did] not withdraw before an admission decision [was] made, receive[d] at least one acceptance" to a System institution.[1] Still, as a result, the freshmen class of fall 1991 was the smallest in the System's history. "This reduction in the number of new freshmen enrolling has not been achieved at the expense of access, but echoes the shrinking number of Wisconsin high school graduates. The proportion of Wisconsin residents enrolling in a UW institution immediately after high school graduation was 24.8% in 1976, rose to a high of 31.8% by 1986 and [stood] at 31.4% for Fall 1991."[2] High school students entering the System were better prepared. That was exactly what the regents had hoped to accomplish by raising admission standards.

The second enrollment management initiative required overall enrollment reduction of 4.3% from fall 1991 to Fall 1994. The number of projected high school graduates in Wisconsin was expected to drop by 5%, so access would not be affected unless there was a surge in the percent of high school graduates who applied.[3] However, "The number of high school graduates is projected to increase sharply beginning in 1995. At that time, access to UW [institutions] will drop back unless increased resources again allow enrollments to expand."[4] This assumes that admission standards will not be increased. Based on retention rates, they should be.

What about those 68.2% of high school graduates who don't qualify or choose not to go to college? How about access for them? While it is true that they may not have access to the UW System, they have not been shut out of access to post-secondary higher education. It is estimated that half of American workers who do not attend college will lack the skills to perform the jobs of the 21st century.[5] Their training will clearly be the role of the technical colleges. The relationship between the UW System and the VTAE system is crucial. To the extent that there is competition between the two, it should be replaced by cooperation so that the public can be better served. It is an issue of funding that I will discuss in this chapter.

Access to Class Sections, Facilities, and Faculty

Once enrolled, a student needs access to class sections, so that graduation can take place in a timely manner. Students need access to laboratories and computers as well as to the faculty. These elements of access are related to funding and faculty teaching loads.

Elements of Quality

The overriding issue that will confront the System continues to be quality versus access. The board, I repeat, has stated as a matter of policy that quality must take precedence over all else. "However, when faced with a choice between maintaining educational quality and decreasing access to its programs and resources, the University of Wisconsin System must choose to maintain quality. For if academic programs, research, and public service are not first-rate, access to the institutions will be of little value."[6] It is understood that given a finite amount of funding resources, quality will diminish if enrollment numbers are allowed to increase indefinitely. That was the rationale behind the enrollment reduction initiatives. Knowing when the proper relationship has been thrown out of balance is another matter. It is often assumed by those within the System that the level of quality and access is determined only by the amount of funding. While in a general way that is true, there are elements of quality that are not determined solely by funding. Therefore, quality, like access, must be defined. It cannot be dealt with meaningfully in generalities.

Objective Measurements of Quality

What is quality? Can one rely on so-called objective, outside assessments that will measure the quality of one institution against another? In the search for such criteria, students and parents often turn to published guidelines. It would be helpful if the guidelines could agree on the elements of quality. Unfortunately, no such agreed upon set of criteria exists. As the criteria change, so do the conclusions.

Example: *Money Guide* magazine published the "Best College Buys" in its 1992 edition based on 1990-91 data.[7] In order to make the list, institutions must "possess outstanding students, faculty and facilities." The magazine attempted to equate the relationship between price and quality — what a school charges and what it delivers. Cost consisted of tuition and mandated fees. Quality, which the editors admit is "trickier," was based on 12 factors:

- Student/faculty ratio.
- Faculty strength — i.e., the number of full-time faculty and the number with Ph.D.s who are available to teach undergraduates.
- Library resources.
- Instructional and student service expenditures.
- Entrance exam results.
- High school class rank of entering freshmen.
- Acceptance rate — number of students accepted for Fall 1990 divided by the number of applicants, an indicator of the school's reputation and ability to choose highly qualified students.
- Freshmen retention rates—the percentage of freshmen who return for a second year is an indicator of student satisfaction.
- Graduation rate — the percentage of entering freshmen who received a degree within four or five years.
- Percentage of students who go on to earn a graduate or professional degree.
- Percentage of students who earn a doctorate degree.
- Business success — based on the alma mater of the top 70,000 corporate executives.

Based on these criteria, the University of Wisconsin-Madison ranked 31st out of the top 100, above the University of California-Berkeley, the University of Iowa, the University of California-Los Angeles (UCLA), and Columbia University.

U.S.News & World Report omitted tuition and fees, and used the following criteria to determine "the best education for the money" as of Fall 1990:8

- Academic reputation
- Student selectivity
- Faculty resources
- Financial resources
- Student satisfaction
- Average or midpoint ACT/SAT scores
- SAT/ACT 25-75 percentile
- Freshmen in top 10 of high school class
- Acceptance rate
- Faculty with doctorate
- Student/faculty ratio
- Total spending per student
- Graduation rate
- Freshmen retention rate

As could be expected, the results were quite different from those reached by *Money Guide*, which factored in tuition and fees. Harvard, Yale, and Stanford, which have very high tuition, were ranked 1, 2, and 3 in *U.S. News & World Report*. Yale ranked 16th, and Columbia ranked 74th. Harvard did not rank among the top 100 considered by *Money Guide* to "deliver the best education for the money." UW-Madison did not make the "top 25" list of *U.S. News & World Report*, but was ranked in the first quartile of the other universities studied, in 52d place.

In *U.S. News & World Report*, UW-Madison ranked lower for the following reasons: In measuring the percentage of freshmen who were in the top 10% of their high school class, UW-Madison had 33%, while the top 25 universities had 76% and higher. One could conclude that UW-Madison was too severely judged because the top 25 included private colleges, which are more selective than public universities. However, it is important to point out that some public universities have much higher admission standards than UW-Madison does. The University of California-Berkeley, for example, reported that 95% of its freshmen were in the top 10% of their high school class. For UCLA, it was 90%, the University of Michigan 69%, and University of Virginia 72%. The acceptance rate is also lower at the other public universities mentioned above than at UW-Madison.

There seemed to be no great difference between UW-Madison and the other public universities in faculty/student ratios, the percent of faculty with doctorate degrees, total spending per student, or freshmen retention rates. But there was a difference between graduation rates with UW-Madison at 60%, Cal-Berkeley at 70%, Virginia at 88%, Michigan at 79%, and UCLA at 63% — which is understandable in view of the percentage of freshmen in the upper 10% of their high school class.

One of the most popular rankings is *The Gourman Report, A Rating of Undergraduate Programs in American and International Universities.*[9] It is readily available in bookstores and on the shelves of high school career counseling offices. The report ranked UW-Madison as "Strong," the highest rating given. Other UW System institutions ranked "Adequate" (the fourth lowest ranking), and just above "Marginal."[10] Teacher education programs at UW-La Crosse, UW-Oshkosh, UW-River Falls, and UW-Whitewater were ranked below the "Marginal" range.[11] On August 19, 1988, I wrote the editor of the *Gourman Report* on Regent stationery and asked for the criteria used to rank administrations and governing boards, since the UW System was not included among the "Leading institutions."[12] I did not receive a reply. On September 30, 1988, Regent Grover wrote to Dr. Jack Gourman asking for the basis of the ranking of teacher education programs. He did not receive an answer to his letter.

The 1992 *Standard & Poor's Executive/College Survey,* according to a newspaper account, ranked the "UW System second among university systems that issue undergraduate business degrees to people who later became business leaders."[13] "... When it came to systems or universities that issue master's degrees in business administration, the University of Wisconsin ranked 10th in terms of graduates who became business leaders." When both graduates holding a bachelor's degree and master's degree are considered, the UW System ranked fourth. "The survey is based on individual information provided ... by 70,000 executives." Ellen Hartery, who was in charge of the project, was quoted as saying,[14] "While some would argue that the standard is worthless, others would argue that any national ranking that places the UW System among the top 10 in the nation is splendid news, indeed." A faculty member observed that those business leaders probably graduated 10-20 years ago, and, thus, the report is out of date relative to current measurements of quality.

It can be anticipated that campuses will take exception to reports that do not rank them high and will embrace those that do. When UW-Madison did not rank in the top 25 universities listed by *U.S. News and World Report,* 1991, UW-Madison administrators pointed to the *Fiske Guide to Colleges 1992,* a

New York Times-related handbook that gave eight universities five stars. UW-Madison was included in that five-star category.[15]

Defining Quality in the UW System

Regents will not find much help in these national rankings for determining quality. Even though there are no consistent outside assessments of objective standards of quality, the board must, nevertheless, define quality and establish standards. I am convinced that unless the regents are willing to take this responsibility they cannot deal with the issue in any meaningful way. This became abundantly clear to me at the October 5, 1990, meeting of the regents. System administration presented a paper on undergraduate education. It seemed to me and to others that the paper was so vague that it was essentially useless. I suggested that we needed to define the components of quality of undergraduate education and deal with each — quality of the faculty, students, and facilities. Everyone agreed. James Sulton, special assistant to the president for minority affairs, suggested that we add quality of campus environment. Agreed. It has since occurred to me that quality of administrators is also an important component of overall quality.

In sum, my approach is that if there is going to be a meaningful discussion of quality, regents must examine its major components — administrators, faculty, facilities, students, and campus environment — and then establish standards. Taken together, they determine the quality of our System and any one of its institutions. Unless this is done there is no way of knowing how we are doing, where we ought to be going, and whether or not we are getting there.

Quality of Administrators — The Huli Syndrome

I am not suggesting that current administrators are incompetent. As a matter of fact, I believe that in most cases the opposite is true. Nevertheless, as the board looks to the future, regents must take into account the fact that quality of an institution includes the quality of its administrators. Administrators' ability to manage budgets, downsize some departments and expand others as needs change, plan programs, avoid duplication, employ competent and skilled personnel, deal with personnel issues, encourage innovative ways to deal with old problems, and implement regent policies will all play a role in determining the ultimate quality of the institution.

Who is likely to possess the necessary skills and training that would ensure the ability to carry out administrative responsibilities? *The Chronicle of Higher Education* devotes a section in each issue to advertising available positions in higher education, "Bulletin Board: Positions Available." It is instructive to read the advertisements. They provide insight into how universities define the qualities of leadership. Two examples: Neosho County Community College in Chanute, Kansas, and Rockford College in Rockford, Illinois. At the former, applicant for the position of president was expected to be "... a leader who will work with the Board of Trustees and the College community to provide an open and objective atmosphere for policy making and participatory management. Ability to provide a vision that looks to the future opportunities and changes for the College. Experience in higher education administration. Experience and skills in budgeting, financial management, economic development, strategic planning and organizational development. An earned doctoral degree is desired." Rockford College, in looking for its president, wanted someone with "experience as a successful independent college president, with a Ph.D. or equivalent." It expected the applicants to have "strategic planning experience and entrepreneurial perspective. High energy and goal orientation. Proven marketing and enrollment management experience. A participative management style."[16] While I understand the difficulty of writing a job description, I often wondered as I read these advertisements if the writers were describing more than one job! Those in academic life certainly know what a president or chancellor of a campus does. It would make more sense to me to describe the university in some detail and indicate that the applicant must demonstrate relevant experience and relevant skills.

Campus administrators are selected by search and screen committees that represent a cross section of the institution. These committees are heavily influenced by faculty, since they often make up a majority of membership on the committees. I believe it is important, therefore, to understand the basic assumptions that faculty make about who is best qualified to occupy administrative positions. Those assumptions not only find their way into the advertisements but dictate the outcome. In the summary section of the article, "Integration of administration and faculty," written by former chairs of the UW-Madison University Committee, it is noted that, "Administrators in academic line positions *must* be faculty members, chosen through processes that assure predominance of faculty interests. Administrators often return to their faculty duties after completing terms in administration; consequently they retain their faculty viewpoint and a continuing interest in faculty welfare, and need not be educated on the special needs of the faculty" (emphasis added). The assumptions here are that administrators must come from the faculty, since only faculty can understand the needs and interests of faculty; that faculty alone understand the institution; and that having completed their administrative duties, administrators will return to the faculty. All of these assumptions should be challenged.

Allow me to digress. In 1991, my wife and I visited Papua New Guinea. Hulis, or wig men, live in the Central Highlands of Papua New Guinea. The Hulis are considered to be among the most primitive groups of people. What fascinated me about them was their attitude about territory. I found the similarities among the Hulis, faculty, and some administrators to be striking.

The Hulis live in extended family groups or clans in a compound. Each compound is surrounded by a nine-foot wall made of mud and clay. On the inside of the compound, next to the wall, is a trench. The trench hides the Huli warrior in time of war. Any intruder or stranger entering the compound without permission is considered an enemy and enters at his or her own peril. This includes Hulis from other compounds. Each group has its own folklore, oral tradition, and language. As a result, the "insider" - "outsider" distinction is strong, bringing me to my comparison. For so it is with many faculty and administrators. The borders of the university surround the faculty and administrators. Those on the "outside" are strangers. In this case, the definition of stranger may include regents, legislators, the public, the media, and the governor. "Outsiders" are not to be trusted, because they do not understand the folklore of the "clan" or the "special needs of faculty." Therefore, to hire a key administrator, such as a dean or vice chancellor, who did not come from faculty ranks would be unthinkable. That would be tantamount to allowing a stranger, perhaps an enemy, into the Huli compound.

In practice, however, there is an interesting inconsistency that is usually not talked about. When I served on the board, the System executive vice president and two of the four System vice presidents had faculty rank. One System president of the two who served while I was on the board had faculty rank. While having faculty rank is always considered to be a condition for administrators with the title of chancellor or vice chancellor for academic affairs, or for deans of schools, the search for the System president, the most important administrative position of all, resulted in the hiring of Kenneth Shaw, who did not seek or receive tenured faculty status. The search and screen committee, dominated by faculty, submitted his name among the finalists. They were obviously looking for someone with administrative skills rather than a record of scholarship. Yet for their own campuses, they would not reach such a conclusion. Our consultant, an expert in the field of academic administration, told us that Shaw was the "new type" of academic administrator. While he had earned a Ph.D. in Sociology, he did not have a distinguished research or publication record as required of those seeking tenure. Shaw made it clear to us that he saw his future in administration, not as a tenured faculty member. Eyebrows were raised because his predecessor had held a tenured faculty position. And yet Shaw was the more superior administrator. When Syracuse University was searching for a chancellor, Shaw was selected at twice the salary he was earning as president of the UW System. His lack of tenure at Wisconsin was not a negative as far as Syracuse was concerned.

What is there in the training of faculty that is relevant to skills needed for administration? Faculty members are, supposedly, trained and hired to teach and do research and outreach. Administrators are hired to manage. Each discipline requires substantially different knowledge and skills. Researchers are taught to reach tentative conclusions until further research is done. Administrators often cannot afford the luxury of waiting until all the data are in. Problems must be solved and decisions made. If the solutions are not perfect, they will be modified. The skills one needs to balance conflicting points of view, deal with personnel issues, control budgets, develop long-range plans, reach unpopular decisions, and implement them are not those required of Ph.D.s who choose to be faculty. Some former faculty members make excellent administrators, not because they were faculty members, but because they had the interest and learned administrative skills. Some administrators I encountered who were faculty members did not have the skills although they had the responsibility. In a word, there is no relationship between the two.

I fear that the assumption that those who come from the faculty make good administrators is based on another assumption, namely, that administration is not a very complicated matter and can be learned on the job. Those of us in the private sector know this to be false. The skills needed by the administrator of a large modern institution have little, if anything, to do with academic disciplines. And learning those skills on the job is not the most efficient method. It is often costly to the institution in the long run.

Currently, administrators who have tenure can, after spending years away from their academic department, leave their administrative post and return to the department as tenured faculty. It's not difficult to imagine what that person's colleagues think about his/her ability to contribute to the discipline after having been away from it for a number of years. No area of study remains static. Keeping up is time-consuming. To suggest that one can maintain both an important administrative position and stay current in an academic field is an insult to those who devote full time to the field. It makes light of academic responsibilities. The department's scarce financial resources must incorporate the returning faculty member and find space that is already in high demand. More than one academic has said to me that there ought to be a limit on the number of years a tenured faculty member can occupy an administrative position and return to his or her tenured status in the academic department. They should not be allowed to have it "both ways." In fact, regents joked after learning that an administrator was returning to the academic department after many years, "What will that person do, having been away from the department for so many years? Write yet another book about the history of the university!" I have heard it argued that setting a limit would make the university non-competitive, and good faculty would not be attracted. That assumes qualified faculty will not enter the System unless they are assured they can be candidates for administrative positions. "If we were to say that faculty would lose tenure after X number of years in administration, no one on the faculty would want to go into administration." This argument is based on the assumption that faculty make the best administrators.

Suggestions regarding the quality of administrators that are unrelated to funding:

- Before filling administrative positions, the board should carefully scrutinize the descriptions. These documents ought to accurately reflect skills required of candidates. A person with tenure may, indeed, be desirable, all other position requirements being equal, but that should not be a requirement.

- Regents ought to take another look at the assumption that only tenured faculty are able to adequately carry out the responsibilities of major administrative positions. I suggest this because in the new environment of higher education, institutions will need to make hard fiscal choices. Among those choices will be the necessity to downsize departments, a choice that has a direct impact on faculty. Isn't it expecting too much to ask tenured faculty-administrators to make unbiased decisions about these hard issues? Why should that be a problem? Because there is the understanding that these individuals, when no longer interested in administrative duties, will return to their departments. Are they really in the best position to make such choices? In addition, this assumption that only tenured faculty should occupy major administrative positions severely limits the pool of qualified applicants while raising the price at the same time.

- A systemwide policy is needed that limits the number of years a faculty member may be granted leave from his or her academic department as an administrator. Should the faculty member choose to remain in administration, then he or she should forfeit tenure. This should be incorporated into the "Leave of Absence" policy.

- System President Shaw inaugurated annual reviews of the chancellors, based on yearly goals, and reported his conclusions to the regents. He also asked the board to review his performance on an annual basis. The regents should require that the annual evaluations of the System president and chancellors include an analysis of the performance in carrying out goals *and* regent policies; and merit raises should be tied to performance of both.

Suggestions regarding the quality of administrators that are related to funding:

- Compensation for the president, vice presidents, chancellors, and vice chancellors is currently governed by state law. Studies show that the compensation is not competitive in the relevant national market, that is, what peer institutions pay for comparable positions. On the other hand, state law does not limit compensation for deans and faculty. The result is an absurd situation where deans earn more than vice chancellors and even vice presidents. State law should be changed so that regents are given the authority to set compensation for all administrators. Regents must insist that administrative quality be related to compensation. Compensation paid must be competitive with peers. That is true whether administrators are tenured or not.

A few years ago, I suggested to a high-ranking state official that the governor appoint a task force for the purpose of determining relevant markets for each classification of state employees. I expressed concern that some people in state government were being overpaid, while others, especially university administrators and faculty, were being underpaid. He thought it was a good idea and said he would think about it. In 1991, the governor did appoint a commission to study faculty and academic staff compensation, but not that of administrators. While the appointment of such a committee is long overdue, the simplest way to solve the problem is to change state law.

Suggestion relating both to funding and non-funding regarding the quality of administrators:

- The regents need to be concerned with the short length of service of the System president. A study sponsored by the Association of Governing Boards of Universities and Colleges concluded that "Presidential terms now average approximately seven years; this is too short to serve effectively some of the major interests of an institution."[18] Strategic plans must look into the future for 10 or more years to be beneficial, and persons charged with carrying out the plans should be in the position long enough to see them implemented. The study recommends that "Each board should structure the presidential relationship toward a longer term than now typically exists between the president and the institution. This means giving careful attention particularly to the selection of and to the support for the president, but also to conditions that can enhance longer tenure of positions."[19]

Quality of Faculty

An important determinant of educational quality is the quality of the faculty. They are responsible for carrying out the missions of teaching, research, and outreach. In order to attract quality faculty, UW System institutions must be competitive in terms of "perks" offered to faculty as well as the level of compensation. Tenure is the most important perk. How it is awarded will affect quality.

Tenure: In Chapter V, I spoke of tenure as an obstacle to change. I referred the reader to the appropriate sections of the Wisconsin Administrative Code that describe tenure and the circumstances under which it can be revoked.

While I served on the board, concerns regarding the awarding of tenure and post-tenure review arose in three areas:

1. The weight given to instruction of undergraduates in the granting of tenure, and in post-tenure review, and how that affected the quality of undergraduate education, especially at the doctoral campuses.

2. Alleged discrimination against women and minorities in the granting of tenure.

3. The weight given to outreach in the granting of tenure, and in post-tenure review.

While tenure can surely be an obstacle to change, it is here to stay unless it is abandoned nationally and ceases to be a competitive issue when hiring faculty. Nevertheless, our focus here is on preserving the quality of the three-part mission, and faculty do play an essential role. They must be part of the solution. There does not have to be conflict among tenure, post-tenure review, and quality as long as the basis for awarding tenure and post-tenure review procedures is consistent with the missions and the established standards of quality. The board bears ultimate responsibility for quality. That is why regents must be involved. It is a diversion to have faculty argue that regents should stay out of such discussions. They simply cannot and should not.

There is a national discussion in progress regarding the merits of tenure. I know from past experience that any interest expressed by the board about awarding tenure and post-tenure review results in accusations of attempts to destroy the faculty, interference in faculty governance, and the destruction of the quality of the institutions. One can imagine what the response would be if the regents were to engage in a discussion on whether tenure has outlived its usefulness! Tenure is the Holy Grail!

Back to our mission of teaching, research, and outreach. Wisconsin Statutes established that undergraduate education was of preeminent importance. Regent policy confirms that. Faculty are key to carrying out our mission. It's obvious that how we award tenure and conduct post-tenure review determines whether or not faculty will address the issue of undergraduate education adequately. I have spoken to faculty who believe the entire area of tenure and post-tenure review is out of bounds for the board — they believe tenure is an internal affair best handled by those who understand the process. Faculty believe that regents are not qualified to determine whether faculty should receive tenure. The same arguments apply to post-tenure review. Others are defensive when the issue of undergraduate education is raised, and declare that this is uppermost in the minds of faculty. They dismiss the national discussion taking place about the quality of undergraduate education and citizen complaints as overreacting. Regents should not "rubber stamp" the awarding of tenure, and oversight of post- tenure review must be pursued diligently. Regents have a role to play both from a statutory and a public policy point of view.

Statutory basis for regent involvement in tenure and post-tenure review: Chapter 36.13, Wisconsin Statutes, makes it clear that regents are assigned an active role in both the granting of tenure and post-tenure review. Section 36.13[1][b] states: " 'Tenure appointment' means an appointment for an unlimited period *granted to a ranked faculty member by the board* upon the affirmative recommendation of the appropriate chancellor and academic department or its functional equivalent within an institution" (emphasis added). The institutions can recommend tenure, but cannot grant tenure. Section 36.13[3] provides; "RULES. *The board and its several faculties after consultation with appropriate students* shall promulgate rules for tenure and probationary appointments, for the review of faculty performance and for the non-retention and dismissal of faculty members. Such rules shall be promulgated under ch. 227" (emphasis added). The faculties *and* the board promulgate the rules for tenure and post-tenure review. The board has yet to carry out these responsibilities.

Public policy basis for regent involvement in tenure and post-tenure review: Before and after tenure is granted, the board must be assured that those with this special status are performing in a manner that is consistent with UW System and institutional missions. In Spring 1991, I was asked to meet with representatives of the Association on Undergraduate Education, which represents the 19 most prestigious public research universities in the nation. I put it to them bluntly: "Is it not true that because of growing pressure to change the role of faculty vis a vis undergraduate education, you are simply circling the wagons in order to ward off any drastic changes, and that until the reward system changes, little will happen?" These are the exact words of their answer: "Sad to say, it's true."

Post-Tenure Review: UW System President Lyall proposed guidelines for post-tenure review that were adopted by the board in May 1991 over the objection of the UW Madison faculty. Adopting the guidelines is only the first step in the management process. Have these guidelines been implemented? What was done on every campus? The regents will never know unless they ask the questions and receive timely reports.

Lyall may also have had the federal legislation on age discrimination in mind when she proposed post-tenure review guidelines. As of December 13, 1993, the federal *Age Discrimination in Employment Act* will outlaw mandatory retirement of tenured faculty members because of age.[20] Patricia A. Hollander, general counsel of the American Association of University Administrators, and a trustee of Western New England College, addressed this issue in 1992. She pointed out that as of the effective date of the act, tenured faculty could still be terminated if they failed to meet "appropriate standards, such as competence in teaching, research, and service." In addition to incompetence, tenured faculty could also be terminated for "just cause." Those criteria, as reported in *The Chronicle of Higher Education*:

'Neglect of duty, such as refusing to follow the curriculum, refusing to teach scheduled classes, or refusing to develop assigned courses, ... insubordination ... unprofessional conduct ... sexual misconduct.' Tenure is not a 'contract for life-everlasting job security.' It is a 'conditional continuing contract. That is, it continues without having to be formally renewed year after year but only so long as the individual meets the conditions of the contract, including satisfactory performance of duties.' [And while tenure does not protect tenured faculty from being terminated for "cause," it does protect termination for] 'reasons related to academic freedom, such as teaching or doing research on unpopular topics.'[21]

While I served on the board, this was never discussed, and I believe that it should have been.

Hollander argues that evaluation in view of the act is even more important. Previous evaluations focused on non-tenured faculty. Tenured faculty must now be included in evaluation processes. She urges universities to establish procedures that "lead to evaluations that are honest and careful enough to persuade faculty members whose performance is flagging to retire without the need for a full-blown faculty hearing." In order to establish such an evaluation process, there must be a review of faculty contracts, handbooks, and governing board policies. "Basic questions must be answered: What is the job description for each faculty position? What are the qualifications for that position? What are the criteria for promotions, salary increases, and terminations? What evidence is acceptable to demonstrate that the standards have been met? Who shall participate in setting evaluation standards and procedures? Who shall participate in doing evaluations? What due-process procedures shall apply?" I would add that there needs to be clarification of the role in teaching and outreach in the evaluation process. Based on the advice of Hollander, UW System regents, System administrators, and campuses have much more to do before a true evaluation process exists.

Suggestions regarding the quality of faculty that do not require funding:

- The board should, pursuant to the mandate of Chapter 36.13[3], Wisconsin Statutes, "[P]romulgate rules for tenure and probationary appointments, for the review of faculty performance and for the non-retention and dismissal of faculty members." What are the criteria for granting tenure? Are they written anywhere? Shouldn't they be? How is this followed up? The board should approve such a document to ensure that criteria are consistent with the mission of the university. Obviously, criteria should not be the same for each campus, since missions differ. On the other hand, is there justification for having unstated criteria? The same should apply to post-tenure review. Student evaluation of faculty is a case in point. Is it true that in some departments, the student evaluation forms are never shown to the faculty?

- Regents should never "rubber stamp" tenure lists. They ought to ask more questions before voting, such as:

  a. Who on the list was granted tenure because of outstanding teaching?

  b. Who on the list was granted tenure because of outstanding work in Extension?

  c. Who was denied tenure solely because of "inadequate research?"

  d. What is the percentage of women on the tenure list?

  e. What is the percentage of minorities on the tenure list?

  f. What weight was given to undergraduate education, outreach, and research?

Regents should review the definitions of "good cause." If they do not exist or are too broad, then tenure becomes a lifetime appointment regardless of competence. While I agree that there ought to be a presumption of competence, the outcome of any dismissal or disciplinary hearing will depend on the definition of "good cause" and who enforces it. Why should this be different than the day-to-day application of the rules negotiated in a union contract, in which employees are responsible for carrying out company policy and dismissal for "cause" is spelled out? Tenured faculty should not be permitted to ignore or fail to implement regent policy.

- The failure to carry out regent policy is, in my view, "just cause." Tenure can be revoked for "just cause," according to the Wisconsin Administrative Code. It is an area the board ought to define. Tenure is a perk, not available to the vast majority of citizens. It should not be defended with religious fervor. Faculty, like all members of our society, are hired for a purpose — in this case to carry out the System's missions and board policies. Performance of faculty should be reviewed just as we all have our performance reviewed. Tenure and accountability are not incompatible.

Improving undergraduate education: In Chapter VI, I discussed attitudes of some tenured faculty about their role in undergraduate instruction, and the efforts of regents to deal with the weight given to undergraduate education in awarding tenure and in post-tenure review. Our major accomplishment was that the issue was put on the agenda, and following hearings, regents adopted a series of initiatives that were spelled out in the document *The Undergraduate Imperative*. Much remains to be done.

What did we learn as regents that can help the board see where it needs to go in the future?

1. We learned that despite denials, faculty did not teach in a significant percentage of the entry-level courses on the doctoral campuses. Graduate teaching assistants were often not supervised, and in many cases they did not have adequate verbal skills in English.

2. We learned that there was no consistent response to the mandate of Chapter 36, Wisconsin Statutes and regent policy that undergraduate teaching was "at the core" of the university's mission. Faculty on the doctoral campuses insisted that research remain the primary criteria for awarding tenure. As a matter of fact, to do otherwise, they said, would make the campus uncompetitive with peer institutions. At the meeting with the UW-Madison Faculty Committee (described earlier), I asked what was being done to improve undergraduate education, a subject that had received national attention and a great deal of the board's attention. I told committee members that at the hearings, we had heard that faculty did not spend enough time in the classroom, that they had turned a good deal of teaching over to graduate students who were neither trained nor supervised, and that many freshmen did not have contact with a faculty member at all. The response was that if we wanted them to teach more, we would have to pay more. I couldn't believe what I had heard. I suggested that they not repeat that in public. Undergraduate education was not an insignificant part of the mission and they were already being paid to carry it out. This was another example of faculty not being able to come to grips with the reality of change, and not understanding that if they would not address the need to change, others would.

3. The vast amount of literature that had appeared nationally suggesting that research and scholarship must be redefined so that undergraduate education could play a larger role had essentially been ignored. Dr. James Rhem, executive editor of *The National Teaching Forum*, wrote, "... research was [and is] esteemed far more than teaching. When it comes to tenure, promotion and pay raises, it is generally one's research record that counts most. It's the interdependence of teaching and learning that makes scholarship exciting and higher education worthwhile."[22]

4. There was no disputing the fact that unless the awarding of tenure gave greater emphasis to undergraduate instruction, little would change. Yet there was no evidence that the basis for awarding tenure had changed. When discussing issues with System administrators in the past, I was reminded that in the early phases of confronting issues, denial of the existence of the problem was not unusual. There is always a conflict between maintaining the status quo and change. It was refreshing, therefore, to read that former UW-Madison Chancellor Donna Shalala believed research institutions such as the UW-Madison, were

criticized for concentrating on research at the expense of undergraduate education, and that change was necessary.[23] I applaud her observation and wait for implementation from her successor, David Ward.

5. We learned that, by and large, the weight given to undergraduate education had no institutional or System standard, and had been left to each department or college to decide.

Had the attitudes of faculty changed? Had the attitudes of the regents and System administration changed? The national debate persuaded the board that it needed to examine the UW System. Testimony heard at the hearings and the reports that resulted came as a surprise to us. It was clear that Wisconsin was not immune.

There was an obvious turnabout in the System administration with the addition to the staff of Vice President for Academic Affairs Stephen Portch and President Lyall. Proposals made by the regents in September 1991, through the "working groups" discussed earlier, met an immediate response from System administration in the *The Undergraduate Imperative*, which the board adopted in December 1991. President Lyall took a lot of flak from faculty, and the board was correct in supporting her with a unanimous vote adopting *The Undergraduate Imperative*.

Now that the blueprint for change is in place in *The Undergraduate Imperative*, the challenge will be to implement it. That is not likely to happen unless the regents receive regular updates and refuse to give in to the time-worn arguments of the past. The Teaching Quality, Evaluation and Rewards Committee of UW-Madison reported in November 1992, "The reputation of the university in other academic circles will continue to be based on our research, and we don't want to change that. But the university needs to provide more recognition for teaching."[24] It was recommended that departments allocate at least 20% of the merit award to faculty with excellent teaching records, and that there be annual evaluations in teaching for non-tenured faculty and evaluations every three years for tenured faculty. The Faculty Senate will reconsider the report and vote on it in February 1993. *The Undergraduate Imperative* was adopted by the board more than two years prior. There did not appear to be any suggestion made as to the weight given to teaching in making tenure decisions, nor does there appear to be a sense of urgency to implement the plan.

The additional challenge confronting the regents is described in a 1991 article in *The Chronicle of Higher Education*. The headline read, "Professors Feel Conflict Between roles in Teaching and Research."[25] The article reported on a survey that was based on responses from 35,478 professors at 392 institutions who agreed that there was tension.

In 1990, the Carnegie Foundation for the Advancement of Teaching recommended that scholarship be defined as the discovery, integration, application, and teaching of knowledge. Traditionally, only the discovery of knowledge counted at promotion and merit raise time.[26]

Some may find solace in a 1992 article written by Bryan Barnett, an academic program administrator at Rutgers University. He wrote that the modern university was divided into two "separate realms ... one centered on the sciences, the other on the arts and humanities" with "different cultures ... different administrations, budgets, sources of financial support, academic standards, and sometimes even campuses."[27] He noted a new division emerging — "one part devoted to undergraduate education and another to full-time research." As evidence of this emerging division, he pointed to the "increasing amount of teaching done by non-tenure track instructors, either graduate students or semi-permanent visiting lecturers," as well as the

> recent proposals for 'teaching track' for tenure (at the University of Colorado), or the creation of separate undergraduate teaching colleges within the university (proposed by faculty members at the University of Michigan). While these developments are suggestive ... other reasons exist for thinking that they foretell a larger shift toward two separate institutions of research and teaching. Several generations of official rhetoric notwithstanding, the present requirements for high-quality undergraduate education ultimately are incompatible with the sort of research programs now required to secure tenure, promotion, external support, and scholarly reputation and status. High-quality research and high quality undergraduate education are not compatible for a variety of reasons:

> One cannot produce the quality or quantity of research needed to establish a significant reputation among peers as a part-time pursuit. Therefore it is wrong to suppose that the division now emerging in academe will be avoided if central administrations decide that teaching deserves more attention from faculty members than it has been receiving. ... [T]he skills and abilities essential to prolific publication have little to do with good teaching. Good teachers can retain their intellectual vitality without publishing [or at least without publishing much] ... Research-based reputations most often are built by intensive work in a very narrow specialty. However, the needs of undergraduates are for introductory-level work, broad exposure to several disciplines, and integrated knowledge. ... [T]he overall mission of the university might ultimately be better served by the open and conspicuous separation of the two.

He proposes separate research and teaching sectors, separate administrations, budgets, and faculties, either within each school or department or by a:

literal division of the university as a whole into an undergraduate college loosely associated with a collection of research institutes. The members of those institutes might continue to provide instructional services ... in the form of lecture programs, but ... would have no responsibility for testing or grading students' work ... Each of these activities [research and teaching] would have to justify itself independently of the other. Research that produces nothing of evident value would no longer be able to get a free ride on the public's need to finance undergraduate education. Freed from dependence on the research interests of faculty members, curricula could be developed and arranged principally with the needs of the students in mind.[28]

How would this be viewed in Wisconsin? During a discussion I had with UW System Vice President for Academic Affairs Portch on June 9, 1992, he expressed the view that research and teaching undergraduates was, indeed, compatible. I suspect that the political leaders and public agree. That being the case, the board must insist on movement to improve undergraduate education.

The national discussion continues. "More Time in the Classroom — Colleges Face New Pressure to Increase Faculty Productivity." This headline appeared on a page 1 story in *The Chronicle of Higher Education.*[29] Agencies in a dozen states were seeking information about the number of hours faculty members spent with students. Of course, there are those who would argue that campuses cannot demand more teaching hours than those required by their peers, if they were to attract quality faculty. And more teaching would mean less research. Faculty do not understand the seriousness of the inquiry. "This is a subject that isn't going to go away," says Robert Zemsky, director of the Institute for Research on Higher Education at the University of Pennsylvania.

"Higher education is not going to be exempt from the economic, technological, and demographic pressures that are causing every type of institution we have to reconsider how to organize itself to get the job done," says Patrick M. Cullen, a former vice president of the Education Commission of the States. "... [F]aculty members seem to be in denial," Zemsky continues. "Higher education has been remarkably successful at not keeping records on this subject. It's simply impossible to document what everyone knows — that teaching loads have declined." This does not bode well with the public or the legislature since instruction is seen as the major mission of the university.

The underlying reasons for the problem have been stated by those within academe. James S. Fairweather, senior research associate at the Center for the Study of Higher Education at Pennsylvania State University, and associate professor of higher education, in a first-of-its-kind study concluded from data from a full range of four-year institutions, research universities, and doctoral institutions, that "[T]he more time you spend on teaching, the less the compensation. The more hours in class per week, the lower the pay. The greater the time spent on research, the higher the compensation. Faculty who teach only graduate students get paid the most. The greater the number of refereed publications, the greater the income." His research supported the widely held belief that an "institutional drift" was occurring as professors at various types of colleges increasingly sought to emulate the research focus characteristic of leading doctoral institutions.[30] It is precisely this culture that regents, System administrators, and campus administrators must overcome if real progress is to be made. All of the other initiatives are important, but they pale in significance to the assumptions made by tenured faculty about their role in undergraduate teaching. Recognizing "distinguished teachers" is hardly an appropriate way to deal with so fundamental an issue to the mission of our System or to the education of 137,594 undergraduate students. In 1992, 65 such individuals, out of a total faculty of 7,361 — less than 1% — were recognized as "distinguished teachers."[31] That says a good deal about the commitment to the "core" mission.

Suggestions to improve undergraduate education that do not require additional funding:

- The board should receive regular reports on progress being made in the implementation of *The Undergraduate Imperative*.

- The board, by adopting the policies contained in *The Undergraduate Imperative*, concluded that there is no fundamental incompatibility between faculty engaging in quality research *and* quality undergraduate education. That being the case, there must be an understanding of and a response to the faculty reward system now in place. It is natural for people to do what they are expected to do and for which they are rewarded. The reward system sends a powerful message about expectations. It ought to be obvious that if faculty do not see undergraduate teaching as important in terms of tenure and career advancement, it will be underplayed. Rhetoric is not enough. Regents need to value undergraduate teaching for those being proposed for tenure. At the last regent meeting I attended in June 1991, I asked the System vice president of academic affairs, when we were presented with the list of tenure nominees, what assurances he could give us that undergraduate education had been an important part of the decision to nominate the individuals for tenure. He responded that he had asked the chancellors to certify in writing that undergraduate teaching was included. Is this enough? Hardly. In September 1991, the board adopted the recommendations of the working group on *Rewards, Incentives, and Policies for Undergraduate Teaching* listed in Chapter VI. UW System response in December 1991, also adopted by the regents, charted new ground. The follow-up will make the difference. Without that, it will be business as usual. Why shouldn't there be a minimum standard to the weight given to undergraduate teaching for each institution in considering people for tenure? Undergraduate instruction, tenure, and post-tenure review must be linked together. It is naive to believe that after six or seven years in the tenure process, with research far outweighing all other aspects of evaluation, that in the post-tenure period there will be a sudden turnabout in attitudes learned over a long period of time.

• Distinguished faculty should be encouraged to teach freshmen and sophomores. Who better can "turn them on"?

• Teaching assistants should not be allowed to teach undergraduates unless they are qualified to do so and are closely supervised.

• Lapsed academic positions should go back to the chancellor, so that the campus can respond to changing needs.

• The board should receive regular reports from across the System on teaching loads of faculty broken down by faculty rank. An October 1992 study, "Trends in Faculty Teaching Assignments," concluded that faculty teaching loads from 1981 to 1991 remained about the same.[32] That leaves unanswered the question: What should the teaching loads be? After a full discussion, there should be consideration of establishing *minimum* standards of time in the classroom for each institution. The issue will not go away. It is better for the board to deal with this issue than the legislature. The Legislative Audit Bureau (LAB) has been ordered to do a study in 1993 of faculty teaching loads. State Representative Robert J. Larson has contended that faculty do not teach enough. In 1989, he introduced a bill that would have required *every* faculty member to teach a minimum of 12 hours per week.[33] (At least one faculty member agreed with Larson that a 12-hour teaching load would not interfere with "serious scholarship.")

In response to Larson, I requested an accounting of teaching load. On March 7 of that year, we received the report. It showed that at the UW-Madison, the average teaching load was 5.6 course hours per week "per FTE [full-time equivalent] instructional staff." Peers ranged from 4.8 to 7.5, with an average of 5.8. Comparisons for other System institutions showed that they were in line when compared with the average of their peer groups.[34] ("Instructional staff" included faculty and others who teach.)[35] Because the campuses in the System compared favorably with the average of peer institutions, there was no suggestion that any changes be made. In response to my question regarding the mechanism for assuring teaching quality, System President Shaw responded, "... [T]here are three major ways in which the UW System ensures a quality education for students and fosters quality teaching among faculty. These mechanisms include the UW Board of Regents' policy on student evaluation of instruction, a program of grants and activities designed to help faculty improve their teaching techniques and materials, and faculty development and renewal opportunities." Nothing was said about the reward system based on subsequent regent hearings; the response was too narrowly drawn. I wrote to various legislators voicing my objections to Larson's uniform standard. Representative Larson replied that he had served as a tenured member of the faculty in the System for 10 years, that similar legislation had been introduced in New York, and that it was time the regents dealt with this issue.[36] If they do not, I predict a legislative mandate.

- Regents need to set the standard that quality of undergraduate education and the involvement of the faculty will be considered in the granting of tenure and in post-tenure reviews: There is no more money for this portion of the mission and, yet it is a crucial part of faculty responsibility. Language in the guidelines for granting tenure, adopted by the regents, should include teaching as one of the criteria. The issue for the board is not to improve the language, but to ensure there is proper weight given to teaching. It would be a mistake for the board to ask the state for more money to carry out the "core" mission. That is already being paid for by the state and the students. More attention should be given to innovations. Some already exist, such as using emeritus faculty to teach undergraduate seminars. Distance learning techniques should be employed. Some faculty described how they bring undergraduates into their laboratories and combine research and teaching. Campuses should be encouraged and rewarded for innovations.

Finding ways to combine technology and learning is often neglected. There are opportunities here that could enable universities to become more productive and cost-efficient without increasing the size of the faculty. We are used to thinking about faculty/student ratios as the measure of educational effectiveness. Thus, as the student population grows, as it is predicted to do again in the mid 1990s, there will be a cry for more money to hire more faculty. I indicated in an earlier chapter that the likelihood of the System receiving a greater share of state revenues is not great. Universities, like other organizations, need to be innovative, and must take advantage of modern technology. George Keller, former faculty member and college dean at Columbia University and an assistant to three chancellors and presidents of the State University of New York and the University of Maryland, observed (1986) that "there was one major revolution in teaching in the history of the world" — the printing press. Before that, teaching was oral and people would have to travel "by mule or on foot to sit at the foot of Erasmus or Thomas Aquinas or somebody in Paris or Bologna. With books, you could take the professor's ideas and move the books around, and you could start new universities ... all over the place. To this day we still live in the 15th century mode; we talk and we have readings."[37] He described the second revolution in teaching — films, satellites. According to Keller, Columbia University uses a satellite dish to tap into Soviet TV soap operas, to help students learn colloquial Russian. "Students may find a cassette by a world famous scholar to be preferable to mediocre instruction in person."[38] He was in a large auditorium in a Pennsylvania college where a thousand students were watching TV monitors. A professor from Chicago was lecturing. "This is clearly a very productive way of teaching. It's cost-effective."[39]

The UW-Extension now has the capability of originating a program in one city and having it received statewide. It combines audio and visual interaction between the instructor and the students. "WisView" has been used with seven courses, "primarily continuing education classes for engineers."[40] There are computers in each of the state's 13 UW Centers as well as two locations on the UW-Madison campus. Classrooms can originate anywhere. Computer software and hardware are rented to the user. In addition, students at 10 UW Centers are taking an engineering mechanics course being taught by Frank Gonzalez at UW Marathon Center in central Wisconsin. Students from around the state who have registered for the course use computers that display graphics. The instructor can receive input from the students and they can read his comments on their screens. Professor Jim Davis, UW-Madison, will be teaching courses in Technical Japanese using "WisView," according to *Teleconference Times*.

The Educational Communications Board of Wisconsin commissioned a comprehensive Distance Education Technology Study.[41] The study is being coordinated by UW-Extension, VTAE system, the Wisconsin Department of Administration, and Wisconsin Department of Public Instruction. Every UW campus is represented. The purpose of the study is to determine what technologies will meet distance educational needs of the state.

Extensive new in-service programs were recently announced. These "video-in-service programs ... "are delivered via satellite in a live, interactive format in Wisconsin and throughout the country by the 24-state SERC (Satellite Educational Resources Consortium) partnership of educators and public broadcasters. These courses carry Continuing Education Units, and will include such diverse subjects as environmental education, parent-teacher and school-community relationships, tech-prep programs, teacher transition to middle schools, and multicultural literature.[42]

The Wall Street Journal reported that 21 universities, "including Washington State, the University of California at Berkeley and Pennsylvania State ... offer credit courses they transmit on the [cable] channel. ... [S]tudents can earn full-fledged degrees from the University of Maryland, George Washington University and Colorado State."[43] The cable channel, "Mind Extension University," reaches 18 million homes and aims to reach 50 million homes by 1996.

Discrimination in the granting of tenure: I referred to the March 1992 Wisconsin Law that gave regents authority to grant tenure when it was denied for impermissible reasons, including discrimination. At the May 1992 meeting of the UW Board of Regents, a System report showed that there was a "revolving door" for women because of relatively low pay, harassment and discrimination, and a "non-supportive environment." These conclusions were based on exit interviews of 111 minority and women faculty. If things continue at the current rate, it would take 25 years for female faculty members to approximate their proportion of doctorates earned.[44]

Suggestions regarding discrimination in granting tenure that do not require funding:

- The law as previously described is in place and must be taken seriously. Regents must schedule regular compliance reports. They can be sure that the Legislative Audit Bureau will be back to follow up on the effect the legislation has had. It is in the public interest that discrimination stop and that the citizens of the state not be required to pay out huge awards resulting from non-compliance. The sponsor of the legislation, Representative Barbara Notenstein, D-Milwaukee, was reported to have warned that she would push legislation to force tougher investigation and monitoring of discrimination if the university failed to do so on its own.[45]

- Those who have discriminated must be disciplined by the regents. Currently, when a department or group of faculty has been found to have discriminated against a person in the granting of tenure because of race or sex, there has been no disciplinary action taken. Yet the citizens of the state pay the jury awards or pre-trial settlements. Tenured folks ought to be held responsible for their actions. The rules of tenure should not preclude such action.

- Regents receive reports on a regular basis, showing the composition of the faculty at various campuses. More detailed reports that reflect the information by department are necessary. System administration should investigate department chairs who make no progress, and give a report on them to the board.

- At its December 1991 meeting, the UW-Madison Faculty Senate adopted a requirement that departments provide probationary faculty with written criteria for tenure and an annual written evaluation of their performance. In addition, each department executive committee is required to establish written criteria and standards that can be used in recommending tenure.[46] The board should require this of all campuses and ask for regular follow-up reports.

- All merit pay considerations should take into account department progress toward compliance with regent policy in this area.

Extension services: Not only were regents concerned about the weight given undergraduate education in the awarding of tenure and in post-tenure review and about the alleged discrimination against women and minorities in the granting of tenure. Regents were also concerned about the weight given to outreach in the awarding of tenure and in post-tenure review.

In viewing Extension in the future, there will always be those who will argue that there would be cost savings if Extension were abolished and all budgetary and programmatic functions were carried out at the campus and departmental levels. It will be argued that that is a more efficient way to deliver Extension services. In Chapter VI, I described how the board dealt with this argument and concluded that if outreach services were to remain viable, the central extension office should not be abolished but strengthened.

What weight should outreach services receive in the awarding of tenure? Should the regents establish a standard? In January 1992, the National Association of State Universities and Land Grant Colleges acknowledged that "although the disciplines and institutions expect such activities (service) they often fail to encourage and recognize them." Institutions that expect their faculty to carry out the three missions might weight them as follows: teaching and scholarship each 40%, service 20%. "In fact, junior professors at research universities are routinely told to forget about service activities if they want to achieve tenure. ..."[47]

Jeffrey Boutwell, associate executive officer of the American Academy of Arts and Sciences called upon the million faculty members and administrators employed in the nation's 3,500 colleges and universities to share their expertise on key national issues.[48] He pointed out that when faculty are evaluated for tenure and promotion, research and teaching continue to be valued much more highly than "community service." "Further disengagement by colleges and universities from active contacts with their local communities exacerbates the sense of 'we' and 'they.'" He proposed that administrators institutionalize speakers' programs. "If our democracy and society are to remain vital and responsive to the challenges facing us, colleges must not ignore their responsibility to help continue the education of all our citizens." In the future, as regents review the activities of Extension, the observations of Derek Bok, president emeritus of Harvard University, are relevant. He stated that universities could begin to regain public confidence by taking part in the national agenda. "We must associate ourselves more prominently with solving the problems that concern Americans the most."[49]

We should not take the future of Extension for granted. As far back as 1986, Michael Quinn Patton, futures editor, Minnesota Extension Service-St. Paul, warned, "Extension's future isn't guaranteed. The land grant values undergirding Extension are in peril in many universities. Resources are diminishing. The response of most Extension Services seems to be retrenchment, circling our wagons, and learning to cope with downsizing. ... Great opportunities for Extension lie in a marriage of informal educational methods with a universitywide content. The future of Extension will be determined in part by our ability to broaden the Extension process to include all knowledge in the university — not just our traditional program areas."[50]

Suggestions regarding the quality of Extension services that do not require funding:

- As with undergraduate education, the board needs to establish and monitor the implementation of standards for the weight to be given to outreach services in the awarding of tenure and in post-tenure review, including merit pay.

- UW System Regent Lyon was correct in asking at the December 8, 1989, regent meeting whether there was a monitoring of tenure being granted to faculty who hold collaborative appointments as compared to faculty who hold other appointments.[51] Because tenure is the ultimate reward, the answer should be sought on a regular basis.

- The functions assigned to a strong central Extension administration, articulated in previous regent resolutions, have validity for the future, and should be reaffirmed by the board. In order to insure the greatest benefit to the citizens of the state through Extension, many of the essential functions that must be performed cannot be carried out at the campus level. For example:

  1. There are Extension offices in every Wisconsin county. There are county agents in those offices. These must be coordinated centrally in order to avoid utter chaos.

  2. There are two doctoral campuses, 11 comprehensive campuses, and 13 centers in the UW System. To the extent that they are involved in outreach services, there needs to be a central planning and coordinating body that allocates budgets as they are needed and can reallocate when desirable.

  3. The Extension services being offered by the various campuses need to be coordinated. Campuses tend to compete with each other rather than work together cooperatively. Coordination and planning function for a statewide system must be done centrally in order to ensure effectiveness and avoid unnecessary duplication.

4. The Extension budget, which exceeds $100 million should be spent in a manner ensuring that campuses and departments are fulfilling the outreach mission requirement. The power of the purse strings is crucial.

5. A regent resolution of April 1982, which was reaffirmed in 1988, provides one other function that realistically can only be carried out by a central office.[52] "The recently developed program evaluation process, wherein every program is evaluated within an eight-year cycle, should continue to have as one of its objectives a determination whether the program being evaluated is consistent with the mission of UW-Extension, does not inappropriately duplicate programs being offered by other state agencies, including specifically VTAE and DPI, or more appropriately should be offered by others. Continued interaction and cooperation between UW-Extension and other state agencies are encouraged." This is consistent with Chapter 36.31, Wisconsin Statutes, which speaks directly to the subject of the relationship between the board of regents and VTAE.

6. A regent resolution of May 6, 1988, for the first time made it clear that UW-Extension should play a role "in personnel decisions for integrated faculty and staff holding Cooperative and General Extension appointments in the UW institutions."[53] That language is meant to underscore the importance of outreach programs that are provided by institutional departments. It gives the chancellor of Extension a voice in departmental tenure decisions. His control of the budget makes this a meaningful role.

7. In order to deal with the issue of duplication, Joint Administrative Committee on Continuing Education (VTAE/UWS) should be strengthened by appointing lay members.

Has tenure become too great a burden? James O'Toole, while professor of management at the University of Southern California in 1978, wrote a scathing article attacking tenure.[54] He felt so strongly about his position that he gave up tenure. I agreed with his observation that, "Tenure has for too long been the dirty little secret of academia." He is not alone in his opinion. The results of a 1991 survey of 35,478 professors at 392 institutions concluded that 37% of all professors and 29% of those with tenure felt tenure was an 'outmoded' concept."[55]

James A. Winn, professor of English and director of the Institute for Humanities at the University of Michigan, suggested consideration of a system of six-year renewable appointments, with a guaranteed sabbatical at the end of each contract period, as an alternative to tenure.[56] In listing the advantages of such a system he pointed out that departments that are fully or nearly "tenured frequently experience intellectual arteriosclerosis: They cannot hire new people, and they therefore miss the opportunity to hear new ideas. The same courses, the same methods, and the same feuds continue until someone dies or retires. What price such deadly 'stability?'" He pointed to other advantages of ridding ourselves of tenure. Faculty would have an opportunity to negotiate pay at contract renewal time, and there would be administrative flexibility by having some departments grow and others shrink based on changing needs. He pointed to one of the unfortunate results of the current tenure system, which leads to "wholesale hiring of part-time or non-tenure track faculty, ... whose plight should concern every conscientious academic."

In addition, a culture that holds that the positions are "owned" by the departments reduces flexibility of chancellors to guide program offerings of the institutions. Add to that a system of lifetime appointments, and it is clear why changes in attitudes and programs come about so slowly.

What about Wisconsin? Wasn't tenure designed to assure faculty members academic freedom? Haven't the Wisconsin Statutes and the Wisconsin Administrative Code adequately protected the rights of the faculty by law? Chapter 36.13[5], Wisconsin Statutes provides that people having tenure "may be dismissed only for just cause and only after due notice and hearing." The Wisconsin Administrative Code states:

> Any faculty member having tenure may be dismissed only by the board and only for just cause and only after due notice and hearing.[57]

Section UWS 4.01[2] of the code provides:

> A faculty member is entitled to enjoy and exercise all the rights and privileges of a United States citizen, and the rights and privileges of academic freedom as they are generally understood in the academic community. This policy shall be observed in determining whether or not just cause for dismissal exists. The burden of proof of the existence of just cause for a dismissal is on the administration.[58]

In order for a dismissal to occur, there must be a timely investigation. The faculty member shall have an opportunity to discuss the charges with the chancellor, and must receive a written statement of specific charges from the chancellor along with a statement of the appeal procedures available. The process for dismissal involves a faculty hearing committee, due process provisions, procedural guarantees, and review and recommendation by the chancellor to the president of the System, and then to the regents. During the process, the faculty member normally would not be dismissed, and in all cases salary would continue until the board makes a final decision to dismiss.[60]

Haven't the Wisconsin Statutes and the Wisconsin Administrative Code adequately protected the rights of the faculty by law?

Tenure was originally meant to confer on the faculty political and academic freedom. It is argued that since the courts, the personnel codes, and accepted practice now protect these freedoms, tenure has lost its reasons to exist. What is left is an archaic, preferential status system unavailable to others in our society. Tenure has become a goal in and of itself. Some people say tenure results in distorting the pattern of career growth, makes the bureaucratic tendencies of universities worse, leads to retention of the least creative faculty, and discourages flexibility.[61]

On the other hand, others will argue that recent history tells us that all is not well and faculty need the protection tenure provides. One need only recall the days of Senator Joseph McCarthy to understand that from time to time there are those who believe that faculty members who teach unacceptable views, usually referred to as "left-wing," "Marxist," or "PC" need to be purged or monitored, or exposed publicly, in order to stop their "deviant" behavior.

These censorship movements reappear from time to time. There was growing concern about an organization that called itself Accuracy in Academia (AIA). The July 11, 1985, issue of *The Daily Cardinal*, a student newspaper at UW-Madison, reported that Reed Irvine, president and founder of Accuracy in Media (AIM) Inc., said his new group, AIA, would send people into the classrooms to monitor lectures and challenge professors on "questionable" facts. Wisconsin Student Association co-President Brian Fielkow was reported to have said, "That assumes that students are balls of silly-putty that don't understand what professors are saying." Irvine was quoted as saying that the notoriously "liberal" departments were political science, history, economics, and social studies. "That's where they get fed a lot of baloney, and don't know it."

According to a letter written to UW-Madison Chancellor Irving Shain by the national office of the American Civil Liberties Union (August 17, 1985), Accuracy in Academia was being organized in order to combat the indoctrination of students through the "dissemination of misinformation."

The letter reported that the plan of AIA was to enlist students who could identify problem courses and make tape recordings or notes of statements made by teachers who were believed to be in error, and to ask that corrections be made in the classroom in order to expose such inaccuracies. AIA was also to enlist the support of "mature adults" to enroll in courses and serve as auditors for AIA, challenge questionable statements in the classroom and provide alternate reading material to the students. The ACLU letter related that professional educational organizations feared that AIA threatened "... to impose an orthodoxy and conformity on the academic community. ..." From my point of view, the ACLU was on target in pointing out the anomaly of this concern expressed by AIA about a "left-wing" bias at the same time conservative student political groups and publications were on the rise. Indeed, it was a time in our history when Ronald Reagan, the darling of the conservatives, was in the White House.

In the October 5, 1985, issue of the *UW-M Post*, the student newspaper at the UW-Milwaukee, a page 1 story reported that the local chapter of AIA had targeted UW-Milwaukee Associate Professor of Sociology James Otis Smith as presenting lectures and course material with a "liberal bias."

In a front-page article of the same newspaper, dated October 31, 1985, it was reported that a temporary charter had been granted to the local chapter. "A group claiming many college professors exhibit 'leftist' and 'Marxist' bias in the classroom will soon begin monitoring UW-M classes for content and 'historical inaccuracies.'" The article pointed out that this was one of more than 100 chapters nationwide.

On December 9, 1985, Madison's *The Capital Times* asked, editorially, "Are we witnessing a return to the red-baiting days of the infamous Senator Joseph McCarthy?"

At the December 1985 UW Board of Regents meeting I publicly commended the UW-Green Bay student newspaper for making its readers aware of this organization and its purposes. In a letter to the editor of *The Capital Times*, dated December 20, 1985, I suggested that a more appropriate name for the group would be "Censorship in Academia."

In a *Wisconsin State Journal* article, dated December 10, 1985, Katharine Lyall, then UW System acting president, was reported to have compared AIA activities to McCarthyist tactics of the 1950s. "I would have thought that our experience of the 1950s would have been proof against this kind of effort in the 1980s. Disagreement and debate are the stuff of which learning is made."

In a *Wall Street Journal* guest article, dated December 12, 1985, David Brock, a history major at the University of California, Berkeley, and a *Wall Street Journal* summer intern, wrote that, "The evidence of Marxist influence is extensive. ... To transmit knowledge and democratic values, a university must allow opposing views to be expressed, even those inimical to itself. It is one of the contradictions of freedom."

In a letter to the editor of the *Washington Post*, dated November 18, 1985, a student at George Washington University wrote, "I know that unless I completely understand my ideological opponent's mind, I will never be able to defeat him."

What is the proper balance? Doesn't the Wisconsin Administrative Code and court cases provide enough First Amendment protection? What has been the experience of faculty? In addressing the board of regents on September 6, 1991, Acting President Lyall said that while "tenure lies at the heart of academic freedom and provides faculty the security to pursue long-term projects with delayed payoff, to espouse untraditional and unpopular ideas, and to write and revise courses and curriculum in response to evolving scholarship," it is not intended to protect the faculty from regular review of its work or to allow them to escape from their responsibility to carry out the mission of the university — quality teaching, research, and public service.[62]

Because of competitive circumstances, tenure, at least at the present time, is here to stay. Tenure is certainly one of the most important "perks" available to faculty. The UW System cannot attract quality faculty unless it maintains tenure. Tenure is being offered by 85% of all American colleges and universities, and 59% of all full-time faculty have tenure.[63]

Since tenure often stands in the way of change, its continuance is an issue that needs to be debated openly. Whether it will remain part of the faculty's "perks" is not predictable. But in the meantime, the System must be governed and its quality maintained. There must be a proper balance between the rights and obligations of the tenured faculty, the obligation to carry out the missions, and the board of regents' responsibility to govern.

Postscript to tenure — telling tales out of school: I have had an opportunity to discuss tenure with many faculty. Some regard tenure as a right and compare their lifetime appointment to that of a federal judge. They are not interested in the protection offered by the Wisconsin Administrative Code. Others argue that it is a matter of being competitive with other universities — everyone offers it. Others have complained that it is difficult to get rid of "dead wood." Merit review is not meaningful when there is no merit pay money available. Some have said, "Don't ask me to defend it. Those that are good don't need it; those that aren't want it."

Faculty Compensation: In addition to the System being competitive in terms of the "perks" that it grants faculty, the System must also compensate faculty in a manner that is competitive with peer groups if it is to attract quality faculty. But that alone will not ensure quality. Faculty, not unlike others, must be subject to periodic review to determine whether their performance meets the quality standards set by the System, regents, and campus. That review should not be the sole province of other faculty. Having said that, faculty compensation has not been treated seriously enough by the media or the lawmakers.

Some members of the media delight in printing front-page stories that read, "57 UW staffers have salaries of $100,000+."[64] The full story on page 3 explained that administrators dominated the list. Also listed are the names of some faculty members, including the only Nobel laureate in the System. What is the point of the story? Nowhere is there any comparison of what other comparable institutions pay their administrators or faculty. There is no statement that would explain what most faculty members in the System earn. Nor is it explained that UW-Madison alone (there are 12 other institutions in the System) has a faculty of 2,448. Is the number earning over $100,000 out of line? Those reports do not tell the full story; that full professors (the highest rank for faculty) at UW-Madison average $61,330 per year, excluding the medical school; at UW-Milwaukee they average $57,151 per year; and at the other four-year campuses $47,368 a year.[65] Systemwide, the average pay for full professors in 1991 was $47,368, for associate professors $38,821, and for assistant professors $33,813.[66]

In order to deal rationally with the issue, there must be an agreement on the basis for determination of compensation. Tying faculty compensation increases to those of other state employees made no sense since higher education institutions are in competition nationwide. In the early 1980s, Governor Earl appointed a task force of legislators and System representatives. Their goal was to establish "peer groups" for each of the campuses. These "peer groups" were universities of like mission and quality, with whom UW System institutions supposedly competed for faculty. It has been said in labor negotiation circles that if both sides come away unhappy, the negotiations have been successful. So, too, with the conclusions of this task force. It was argued by many, me included, that the task force had made too many compromises. The premier private research universities with which UW-Madison competed for faculty and federal funds were not included in UW-Madison's peer group. Furthermore, the stated goal was to bring faculty salaries of the System to the mid-range of the "peer group." If, for example, UW-Madison was to maintain its national and international reputation as a world-class research institution, why the mid-range and not the upper range as the goal? (The "peer groups" were listed in the February 10, 1992, report of the "University of Wisconsin Compensation Commission.")

The significance of establishment of "peer groups" was not to be underestimated. While it was not perfect, it did, for the first time, separate the calculation of compensation for faculty from other state employees. Based on the "peer group" study for faculty, the board urged adoption of a "catch-up" plan that would bring System faculty compensation to the mid-range of the "peer groups." It was adopted by the governor and passed by the legislature, and funded over a period of years. It was never contemplated that every faculty member would receive the amount listed. Rather, it provided the System with a fund it could use to compensate faculty as needed. Some faculty would require more than others. Unfortunately, the amount provided for "catch-up" to get to the mid-range of the "peer groups," was funded over a period of years, and the annual increases did not keep up with the "peer groups." As a result, System faculty fell behind again. A second round of "catch-up" was adopted. By 1991, the faculty fell behind once again.

Not only did the state not appropriate sufficient funds, but the original study was ignored. New arguments surfaced — since the cost of living in Wisconsin was less than that of some of the peers, the original peer comparisons were flawed. It must be remembered that Wisconsin institutions were targeted at the mid range of the peers, not at the top, so that cost of living comparisons were irrelevant. In the meantime, UW System failed to produce hard evidence that being behind peers in compensation actually meant that faculty left UW institutions or that recruiting new faculty was more difficult. During a meeting with the UW-Madison [Faculty] Committee, I said it was crucially important that we have such hard evidence. Such information was never presented. To make matters even more difficult, during the gubernatorial campaign of 1990, the Democratic challenger, Tom Loftus, stated publicly that the legislature would not go for another catch-up. The argument was wearing thin.

The Governor appointed a University of Wisconsin Compensation Commission on December 4, 1991.[67] Its task was to examine compensation of System faculty and academic staff and make recommendations. In a memo to the Commission, dated February 10, 1992, "Questions and Answers," the methodology for determining the compensation needs of the faculty and academic staff, was detailed, as was the calculated shortfall. The "Salary Peer Analysis" for 1991/92, prepared by the System's Office of Policy Analysis and Research shows the amount needed to bring faculty in the UW institutions to the mid-range of the "peer groups":

UW-Madison

Full Professor	$5,231 (+8.50%)
Associate Professor	$1,372 (+3.05%)
Assistant Professor	$69 (+0.17%)

UW-Milwaukee

Full Professor	$3,993 (+7.05%)
Associate Professor	$2,142 (+5.01%)
Assistant Professor	$-1,062

University Cluster

Full Professor	$4,122 (+8.73%)
Associate Professor	$3,555 (+9.18%)
Assistant Professor	$812 (+2.39%)

Based on these figures, UW-Madison ranked last among the 12 universities included in its "peers" for full and associate professors, and seventh for assistant professors. Perceptions are important. UW-Madison Provost David Ward was reported to have said that the psychological effect of being at the bottom was "pretty devastating."[68] The report showed that since 1983, compensation for faculty was at or above peer median only in one year: 1986, the second year of catch-up. For assistant professors, the entry-level rank, compensation had been at or near the peer median for the previous 10 years. That was not the case for associate and full professors. The conclusion to be drawn was that in order to recruit, peer medians had to be met. This was paid for by depressing the compensation of the more senior categories of faculty.

An additional $31.5 million was needed for the period 1993-95 in order to bring the average System faculty and academic staff compensation to the mid-point of the peer institutions. Using the current ratio of GPR to tuition, the former would be $21.9 million and the latter $9.6 million (69.5% and 30.5%). According to Nathan Peters, budget analyst, in a conversation we had on June 26, 1992, this was in addition to the Quality Reinvestment Plan, which only partially funded the gap. The rest of the Quality Reinvestment Plan was needed for supplies, labs, computers, etc.

State Budget Director Richard G. Chandler was reported to have said that when faculty compensation, *including fringes*, was compared with peers, they were at the midpoint. The original "peer group" exercise was based on compensation only.[69] He also was reported to have said that a recent Legislative Audit Bureau report showed turnover rates of 1.8% for full professors and 2.7% for assistant professors, and that this turnover is, "in many ways, healthy for an organization."[70] I recall the board's attempt to deal with comparisons of fringe benefits as well as cost of living differentials. It was concluded that they were a "wash."

In response to the request of the University of Wisconsin Compensation Commission for hard data regarding the impact of compensation on faculty retention, Professor Diane Kravetz, representing the UW-Madison Faculty Senate, warned the commission, "You can wait until the data are in. You can wait to see if our dire predictions come true. But if you wait, it will be too late. At the point at which we have hard data that we cannot recruit and retain outstanding faculty at the UW-Madison, you will no longer have the opportunity you now have — to take bold steps to help ensure the continuing excellence of this university."[71]

Faculty Compensation Linkage with Academic Staff

In my view, there is yet another reason why competitive faculty pay is difficult to achieve. Early on, faculty and academic staff compensation were linked together by System administration. That was a mistake. The result of the linkage was that the percentage raise requested for one was requested for the other. The distinction between faculty and academic staff is that faculty are on a tenure track or tenured, whereas academic staff are not. Faculty who do not achieve tenure after the probationary period leave. In addition, Chapter 36, Wisconsin Statutes, as originally adopted, provided for a role for faculty in governance. The faculty had the responsibility to set the standards for admission and matriculation and decide what courses are required to qualify for a degree. There is no such role for the teaching academic staff. I'm making the distinction here for "teaching" academic staff and faculty.

In determining compensation relationships, it is important to understand the relevant market for faculty. They will be recruited by universities of comparable quality to those within the System. The situation here is complicated by the variety of roles played by academic staff in addition to teaching. Academic staff may be directors of admissions, financial aid officers, associate vice chancellors, librarians, research assistants, or lecturers. Their relevant peer groups are different than those of the faculty.

When faculty and academic staff compensation requests were lumped together, the amounts requested were substantially larger than those in which faculty had been separated out. My concern is that when confronted with such large amounts, the governor and legislature will continue to reduce line items for salary, leaving less for the faculty. The problem of linkage can be demonstrated by referring to the 1991-93 budget requests. System proposed that both faculty and academic staff receive a 2.4% increase for catch-up (the amount needed to bring the groups up to their peers), plus 6% for "keep-up" (the amount needed for them to remain competitive). For faculty, the biennial total was $26,503,500 for catch-up and $65,838,600 for keep-up, a total of $92,340,100. For academic staff, the amount was $11,206,500 for catch-up and $33,446,900 for keep-up, a total of $44,653,400.

During the budget debate that took place at the regent meeting in November 1990, I was troubled by the amount of the request for academic staff catch-up and asked what evidence System administration had of academic staff turnover. I was told that the study had not been completed. I left the room briefly and was handed a study by someone who claimed to be a member of the academic staff. To my amazement, it showed that for the previous year, out of a total of 7,000 academic staff, only 150 had received outside offers, of which 130 were accepted. This would indicate a turnover rate of about 2%. I gave the study to the System president. He consulted with some of his staff and announced that the study was flawed. I asked whether there was a better study. None existed. On November 20, 1990, I wrote the System president, restated the figures, and stated that the low turnover rate could indicate that we were overpaying academic staff. I asked for evidence proving there should be linkage between faculty and academic staff peer groups. "Unless we can prove our case that they ought to be linked to faculty peer groups, we endanger faculty pay." I never received an answer to the letter.

I expressed this and my other concern that while some academic staff might have the same peer groups as faculty, I doubted that was true of all. Some should be compared with local market conditions, I argued. This was conveyed in a letter to UW-Platteville Assistant to the Vice Chancellor Christopher T. Lind, UW System President Shaw, and the board of regents on November 26, 1990. I do not recall receiving a response.

When I first came onto the board, I heard complaints from members of the academic staff that they were unhappy with their compensation and had no job security. Some belonged to a union and others did not. The board held hearings. The complaints were always the same. I concluded that the complaints and the System would be better off if the complaints became unionized and negotiated directly with the state for wages and working conditions, since they were not going to be awarded tenure or included in the same governance decisions as the faculty. Linking their pay adjustments to the faculty worked to the disadvantage of the faculty.

I was convinced that academic staff had an identity crisis. They knew they were not going to be equated with the faculty, yet they wanted to be given employment terms that looked like tenure. They also wanted to be part of management. As a matter of fact, in 1985, the legislature granted some governance rights to academic staff. System supported this initiative. On January 15, 1992, the System once again appeared before the legislature to oppose a bill that would give academic staff the right to bargain collectively. This would include the right to bargain over wages, which are now established by the System and board of regents, as is the case with faculty. It is a well-established principle in the private sector that those with management rights do not belong to unions. That is because, as Acting Vice President for University Relations Judith Ward pointed out to the legislative committee, "By its very nature, collective bargaining assumes an adversarial, not participatory, model." Union membership is inconsistent with being a part of management. They should not have it both ways.

In response to the pressure from academic staff that they were not being compensated fairly, the legislature ordered that a study be done. Very little time was allowed for its completion. A professional organization was called in to do a "quickie" study. It prepared a classification of academic staff and established comparable peer groups. That study would haunt the regents and academic staff, because even though it concluded that academic staff were being underpaid, academic staff criticized it for not classifying positions correctly, runs together and thus depressing the pay scale for certain positions. It was, basically, a mess on top of a mess!

In addressing the governor's Commission on University of Wisconsin System Compensation on May 13, 1992, Anthony Milanowski, compensation planner, State Department of Employment Relations, said that a large number of academic staff in "Category A" are not "associated closely with the academic mission of the university," are not tied to "a close peer relationship with university faculty," and should be reclassified into the state's civil service.[73]

On August 25, 1992, the commission issued its final report.[74] It verified what was widely known within the System, namely, that the compensation system of faculty and academic staff was not adequate, accountability for annual pay raises was diffused, year-to-year fluctuations existed, morale had deteriorated, and compensation relative to peer groups was low and the gap had widened.

More interesting were the recommendations that addressed the issues of compensation:[75]

1. A decoupling from other state employees of annual pay increases for faculty and academic staff, and reclassifying Category A academic staff to classified service.

2. The board of regents should be given greater authority and account-ability for "management of the operations, including setting faculty and academic staff compensation levels and procedures."

3. "Market analyses should be the principal determinants in setting the target compensation levels for faculty and academic staff. ..."

4. Salary increases should be "awarded primarily, if not exclusively, on the basis of merit," and the regents "should establish a more systematic evaluation procedure for all UW System faculty and academic staff. ..."

Warning that it would take a 14% increase in tuition to meet the commission's goals, Representative Marlin Schneider characterized the report as "blowing smoke." In response, the commission chair stated that the commission had set no time limit on its goals.[76] The debate over flexibility will continue — some will argue that because of limited state resources, the legislature must keep tighter controls, while others will take the opposite view.

The proposals to solve the shortfall in faculty and academic staff compensation through large tuition increases are not likely. Inevitably, the solutions lie elsewhere.

Faculty Workload and Number of Class Sections

I include these subjects under the compensation issue because I believe they are related. What is the "right" teaching load? Can it be increased, thus reducing the number of instructional positions so that those who remain can be paid more? The issue of faculty workload was discussed often while I served on the board. It is an issue that will not go away. Allan M. Winkler, chair of the history department at Miami University of Ohio, summarized the issue recently: "How should faculty members spend their time? How many courses should they teach? And who should make teaching assignments? These questions all revolve around the larger issue of faculty workload, perhaps the most pressing concern in higher education today."[77] He pointed out that "at least a dozen states are examining the academic work week, with an eye toward mandating that faculty members teach more." He urges faculty and others to address the issue "non-defensively," and to be willing to acknowledge that on every campus there are faculty who "should be teaching more." In Ohio, a statewide system of criteria for faculty teaching loads is tied to missions. He concludes that unless such steps are taken, there will be legislative intrusion.

System President Shaw's March 7, 1989, report, "Comparative Data on Faculty Teaching Loads Educational Quality Mechanisms," compared System institutions with the peer group *averages* for the number of course credit hours taught per week. It concluded that based on midpoint comparisons, the UW campuses compared favorably. However, among the eight peer institutions with which UW-Madison (at 5.6 hours) was compared, one had an average of 7.6 hours and another had an average of 7.2. What would be the savings if UW-Madison went from 5.6 to 7.2? For total instructional staff, excluding teaching assistants, UW-Madison is the lowest in the System with 5.6. (UW-Milwaukee is 7.6, UW-Superior 12.7, UW-Stout 11.7, the UW-Centers 13.2, UW-Platteville 10.3, and UW-Stevens Point 10.0. Other campuses vary between 9.3 and 9.9.

Averages are deceiving. In a *Capital Times* article, November 14, 1986, it was reported that, "At UW Madison, more than 70% of tenured faculty teach an average of three hours per week." Ed Emerson, academic affairs director for United Council, opposed the System's request for more instructional positions and an accompanying tuition increase. "We have an adequate number of faculty to students; the real problem is the number of hours they teach."

Take UW-Milwaukee with an average of 7.6. Its peers were institutions with 12.9, 9.0, 8.6, 8.2, and 7.9. What would the cost savings be if faculty increased the hours in class to the upper limits of the school's peer group? If we keep comparing ourselves with the peer group averages, we will never change.

On August 7, 1991, the System provided an information table on student-to-instructional-staff ratios by institution. In seeking clarification, I discussed the table with regent staff. A faculty member who works half-time on research and half-time on teaching is counted for half. No comparisons were provided for peer institutions because of the lack of uniformity in the manner in which instructional positions were counted. For 1990-91, UW-Madison had a ratio of 1:16.7 instructional staff (including teaching assistants) to undergraduate students. For the other System institutions, the ratio varied from a low of 1:17.9 (UW-Milwaukee) to a high of 1:23 (UW-Green Bay). The System average was 1:19. Is there any "right" ratio? Without suggesting any change, I was interested in the effect that moving the systemwide faculty to student ratio from 1:19 to 1:20 would have on the total number of positions in the System and on possible cost savings. There were 116,480 undergraduate full-time equivalent students in the System for 1991-92.[78] A 1 to 19 ratio would require 6,130 full-time equivalent instructional positions, whereas a 1 to 20 ratio would require 5,824 full-time equivalent positions, a reduction of 306. What would be the cost savings? What impact would this have on overall quality? I believe these are questions worth asking.

Traditional concepts of faculty to student ratios need to be re-examined. What is the proper ratio? In his response to the LAB Audit on the System's use of additional instructional positions, President Shaw wrote that one of the goals was to "improve student contact with instructional staff to 1978-79 levels. ... The student to instructional staff ratio of 17:1, which had existed in 1978-79, was selected as a primary goal to be reached over a number of years (the corresponding student to faculty ratio was 23:1). In 1986, the System student to instructional staff ratio was 18.6:1. ... It was 17.2:1 by Fall 1989, and is expected to reach 17:1 by the end of Enrollment Management I."[79]

Why is 17:1 the proper ratio? Why is 18:1 systemwide unacceptable? Assuming an FTE student enrollment of 135,000, a 17:1 student to instructional staff ratio would result in 7,941 instructional staff positions. On the other hand, an 18:1 ratio would result in 7,500 instructional staff positions, a reduction of 441 positions. Depending on the compensation and fringe benefits, the savings could be enormous. It is an area worth exploring. The effect it might have on quality, however, has not been quantified.

On some campuses, a lecture course of several hundred students is considered quality education. On other campuses, small class sizes are in order. The Milwaukee Area Technical College announced that students enrolling in 1992 could earn a 64-credit Associate of Arts Degree in Liberal Arts and Science by taking a combination of video and some campus-based courses. All courses for the existing two-year associate of arts degree are already accepted by the UW System.

Acting UW System President Katharine Lyall proposed a way to balance the need to pay the faculty more even though additional funds were not available. The "Quality Reinvestment" initiative recognized that downsizing could help maintain quality. It should be supported by the board, campus administrators, faculty, and political leaders. The plan contemplated downsizing by not filling positions, and using the savings to support increased faculty compensation and other needs.

Enrollments are of future concern. The System is not alone in anticipating an upswing in enrollment during the latter part of the 1990s. The senior vice chancellor for administration and finance for the California State University System urges the use of technology to provide more off-campus courses. "We may not be able to afford traditional educational institutions for much of this decade or beyond. The infrastructure and the technology associated with distance learning may offer the very best hope ..." Institutions must be "much more productive, efficient, and cost-effective in the delivery of services."[80]

Faculty members at research universities have been quick to point out, according to an article in *The Chronicle of Higher Education* (May 6, 1992) that those who "believe that scholars do research mainly for their own benefit, to enhance their careers, and to avoid the real 'work of teaching' engage in a 'dangerous misconception,' "[81] This is true according to three faculty members from the University of Georgia. "If, under pressure from the public, research universities decreased the time allotted faculty for 'reading professional magazines,' 'consulting with colleagues,' and 'thinking,' and increased the time assigned faculty for undergraduate classroom instruction, they would be making the transmission of received opinion a higher priority than the attempt to understand the world. Furthermore, they would be neglecting the training of graduate students." An associate professor of Spanish at the University of Maine wrote in the same issue of that, "Many of us are expected to deal with students who are not prepared to do real intellectual work, and who frequently have no interest in it. We are teaching at levels that previously would have been considered appropriate for, at best, the secondary level. Legislators, boards of trustees, and administrators have handed this problem to us, and they have a vested interest in not identifying it as such. They, therefore, should not be surprised if we burn out and prefer to retreat to the library."

Suggestions regarding the quality of the faculty that do not require funding:

- Unlink faculty compensation from that of academic staff. There is an ongoing concern that eventually it will become more difficult to recruit and retain quality faculty, because of the inability to compete in the area of compensation. Any extra burdens that come into play, including linkage of academic staff compensation to faculty compensation, ought to be removed.

- Academic staff should be allowed to organize and bargain collectively, and Chapter 36.09[4m], Wisconsin Statutes should be repealed.

- Downsize the number of instructional positions, including faculty positions, and redistribute the savings. Follow up on the "Quality Reinvestment Plan."

- Reduce the number of class sections by increasing the faculty-to-student ratio.

- Re-examine the faculty workload, and analyze why the faculty-to-student ratio and time in class cannot be increased.

Quality of Facilities

Every budget I can recall demonstrated the need to upgrade laboratories, libraries, and computers for students. The final state budgets were less than requested. While the State of Wisconsin approved new buildings for the System, the approval was not accompanied by the funds needed to maintain them. After a period of years, maintenance and the ability to repair suffered.

The Crumbling Academia illustrated the problem nationally.[82] The author noted that a fourth of the buildings now in use were built before 1950. Another fourth were added between 1950 and 1965. It was estimated that in order to refurbish and modernize these buildings, it would take almost $80 billion. The condition existed because state appropriations did not keep pace with needs.

The Capital Times featured a series of articles dealing with these needs on the UW-Madison campus. This was also true for the other campuses in the System. There was general agreement that the research facilities on the Madison campus were in need of repair, refurbishing and construction. A prime example of campus leadership is illustrated by the manner in which UW-Madison Chancellor Shalala moved the issue beyond the talking stage, where it might have stayed for years to come. She proved that chancellors can, by force of their own leadership and imagination, move issues off of dead center.

Shalala appointed a "Council of the University of Wisconsin-Madison," consisting of former regents, state business leaders, and the chair of the economics department on campus. Its assignment was to study the facilities and make recommendations, which it did in December 1990. Its document, "Facilities Advancement for State Technology," concluded that in order to maintain the university as a world-class research institution, a five-year program involving 30 facilities on campus at a total cost of $225 million — $150 million for new construction and $75 million, for renovation of existing facilities — would have to be implemented. UW-Madison would raise 1/3 of the cost of the new facilities, or $75 million from the private sector. The balance would be funded through the state's bonding authority. The board of regents endorsed the report, as did the governor. As of March 1992, $28 million had been raised from private sources.[83] The initiative had been named "WISTAR-Wisconsin Initiative for State Technology and Applied Research."

Earlier, I described the legislature taking auxiliary funds saved for residence hall maintenance. The seriousness of taking care of facilities across the System cannot be overestimated.

Suggestion regarding the quality of facilities that requires funding:

- Regents should not request new buildings unless there is a corresponding funded maintenance budget.

Quality of Students, Retention, and the UW System's Relationship with VTAE

Even if there are quality administrators, quality faculty, and quality facilities, a university will not be a quality institution unless it attracts quality students.

During my term on the board, quality students were not defined. I believe that was a mistake. If having quality students is a necessary condition for a quality university, then there ought to be an understanding of what that means.

In my view, a quality university student is one whose high school academic achievements are equal to the ability to graduate from the admitting UW institution. The consequence of not abiding by that definition is that there is the danger that a university will admit large numbers of students who cannot meet the graduation requirements of the institution they have chosen. Thus, they will spread the school's resources too thin, and affect overall educational quality.

It has been said that universities are not for everyone. As a matter of fact, that has been precisely the case. Based on Fall 1988 data, 48.3% of high school graduates in the United States enrolled in some form of higher education. In Wisconsin, that figure was 52.6%, out of which only 31.7% enrolled in the UW System — the balance being distributed throughout private colleges, the VTAE, and state universities in Minnesota, which has a reciprocity agreement with Wisconsin.[84]

When I attended the UW-Madison in the early 1940s, the success of the individual enrolled was second to what was perceived to be the public policy of open access. "Let them in and flunk them out" was the unstated policy. One wonders if there may have been some other factors at work. Bureaucracies have a propensity to grow. The more students, the more faculty, staff, buildings, offices, budgets, etc.

In any event, that has changed, because funding did not keep pace with enrollment, and growth was unbridled.[85] In 1975-76, the total student enrollment was 143,700, whereas in 1985-86 it was 164,546. That number included part-time and full-time students. The demographers were wrong. They constantly underestimated potential enrollment. It was not until the change of System presidents and more active participation by the board of regents that these issues were seriously addressed.

As previously discussed, the first attempt to reduce enrollment fell far short of the target of 7,000, or about a 5% reduction from the 1986-87 base of 138,710 full-time equivalent (FTE) students, by fall 1990-91.[86] While the actual reduction of 5,500 students was hardly a heroic effort, it was a reversal of previous trends. The second enrollment reduction ordered by the board was for an additional 4% by 1994-95, or about 5,000 FTE students. Both initiatives were an attempt to bring the number of students in the System in better balance with available resources and, thus, maintain quality. To bring about enrollment reductions, as described in Chapter VI, the regents took the initiative to raise admission standards because faculty hadn't. These admission standards set a minimum below which no campus could go, though campuses were free to raise their own standards above the minimum. Some did.

As we discussed this issue, some board members said that we must not become too elite — those who wanted to benefit from a university education should be permitted to do so. But was it elite, some of us argued, to recognize that college is not for everyone? I argued that we should contribute to students' success, not failure. If they could not "make it," why let them in and flunk them out. That was certainly cruel to the individual and disadvantaged those who could benefit the most. The citizens of the state support an excellent, alternate system of post-secondary education — the VTAE system. The UW System should not "oversell" the university to students. For too long, we used the argument that a university education was good and everything else was bad. There was no evidence that the taxpayers were willing to support the policy of unlimited enrollment, regardless of the ability of the students to "make it." If we admitted students at risk, we owed them educational support, or else we contributed to their failure.

The response to higher standards was interesting. The UW Centers had a large increase in enrollment when the four-year campuses closed admission. There are, for example, two-year centers in Manitowoc, Marinette, and Menasha. Their tuition is lower than the four-year campuses, and students can live at home and hold a job rather than paying room and board. When UW-Green Bay closed its enrollment, the center at Manitowoc experienced a 30% increase in enrollment and the Center at Marinette had an 80% increase. "[We] have educationally a great deal to offer: smaller campus; our classes aren't run by teaching assistants, but by faculty who have been trained as professionals; you can keep your job, live at home and go to school."[87] And as already discussed, the credits were transferable to other System institutions.

Regent policy provided a minimum admission standard for Fall 1991. Freshmen would be required to have 16 high school credits from prescribed academic areas. In addition, the American College Test (ACT) would be required of all resident freshmen in Fall 1989. It was hoped that this would "... send a message to all parents and potential university students that [UW System] expects entering freshmen to be fully prepared to begin university study." When the regents were developing these enrollment reduction plans, their horizons were too limited, as I view this in retrospect. It was not until later that the regents were told that high school class rank was the most reliable predictor of graduation from a university institution.

On January 16, 1987, Assembly Speaker Thomas Loftus requested from the Legislative Audit Bureau the results of a study it had done on admissions of freshmen in the System. There was particular concern about exceptions being made at the time of admission. I was sent a copy as president of the board. The report concluded that "between 1980 and 1985, 13,401 (or 9.8%) of the 137,431 freshmen students admitted in the 13 four-year campuses did not meet university minimum rank-in-high school class admission standards." There was a wide variance among campuses — UW-Madison admitted 1.9% below its minimum rank-in-class standard, while 33.1% of UW-Superior's students did not meet the minimum standard. The report also pointed out that of those admitted below the minimum rank-in-class rank standard, 7.8% were minority students. I mention this fact because there is an assumption that this group of students has a negative impact on quality.

The following table, taken from report, shows the percentage of students admitted below the campus' minimum high-school-class-rank admission standards:

Fall 1985

Campus	Required Minimum High School Class Rank	Percentage Admitted Below the Minimum
Madison	top 50%	1.5%
Milwaukee	top 50%	21.6%
Eau Claire	top 50%	20.6%
Green Bay	top 50%	24.6%
La Crosse	top 75%	24.6%
Oshkosh	top 75%	5.4%
Parkside	top 50%	12.4%
Platteville	top 75%	9.4%
River Falls	top 75%	5.5%

Campus	Required Minimum High School Class Rank	Percentage Admitted Below the Minimum
Stevens Point	top 30%	9.8%
Stout	top 75%	13.9%
Superior	top 50%	34.4%
Whitewater	top 75%	4.9%

The report asks: Why is it that minimum standards have been set and yet there seems no rationale for granting exceptions? *"... University staff note that the high school graduation ranking of prospective freshmen students is one of the best predictors, albeit not always perfect, of whether a student is likely to benefit from his or her university experience by graduating from college"* (emphasis added). The System's report on retention rates submitted to the board in 1991 agreed with this conclusion.

In the *Green Bay Press Gazette* of January 28, 1987, campus Vice Chancellor David Jowett was reported to have agreed with the figures in the Legislative Audit Bureau's report, but added that exceptions were granted to inmates of the Green Bay Correctional Institution, those with ACT scores above the national average but without all of the required high school credits, some who were 20-45+ years old, those who were tested and interviewed individually, and some from high schools that did not rank graduates. All in all, however, Jowett accounted for only 268 of the 800 exceptions at Green Bay. He is reported to have asked, "Which of these groups do you want to eliminate? The American way is to give people a second bite at the apple." Of course, that begs the policy question of balancing the costs per student versus the available funds. Indeed, the Legislative Audit Bureau's report alludes to the growing concern that university enrollments are too high given state resources, an issue that is still with the board.

In its response to the Legislative Audit Bureau's report, System Administration attempted to diffuse the thrust of the report by concluding that 93% of new freshmen, based on systemwide averages, met the high school percentile rank (87.5) and an additional 5.5% met "measurable criteria," such as standardized scores, or graduated from high schools that did not provide rankings. This report did not deal with the relationship between high school class rank and retention rates, which both LAB and System agreed was a reliable predictor of success. The systemwide average was artificially raised by UW-Madison, and did not reflect the actual percentage of   campus admissions below the campus minimums.

In December 1987, I asked for a chart showing minimum high school class rank requirements for each campus for freshman for Fall 1986, 1987, and 1988. No changes occurred from 1986 to 1987. Interestingly enough, some changes occurred from 1987 to 1988, the year following the Legislative Audit Bureau's report:

Campus	Fall 1987	Fall 1988
La Crosse	top 75%	top 60%
Madison	top 50%	top 40%
Oshkosh	top 75%	top 60%
Platteville	top 75%	top 50%
River Falls	top 75%	top 50%
Stevens Point	top 70%	top 50%
Superior	top 50%	top 40%
Whitewater	top 75%	top 40%
Centers	Open	top 75%

Eau Claire, Green Bay, Milwaukee, and Parkside remained unchanged at top 50%.

What about the relationship between high school class rank and System graduation rates? It should not be ignored. In planning future policies regarding admission standards, regents should consider retention rates for each campus. If the goal is to admit as many as possible, whether they can "make it" or not, there will be a slide back to the previous policies, and overall quality will be threatened. If the success of the individual is important, then admission standards and the graduation requirements ought to be related to each other.

A System study, "Outcomes of New Freshman Students: Retention, Graduation and Time to Degree" dated March 1991, shows the graduation rate of students based on high school rank. The executive summary states, "The strongest predictor of college graduation is high-school rank in class." Statistics bear this out.

Table 3 of the study (see following page) shows the percentage of freshmen entering in Fall 1980 who graduated from a UW institution by Spring 1990, by high school class rank.[88]

High School Class Rank vs. Percent Who Graduated from UW Institutions

1st quartile	69.0%
2nd quartile	49.3&%
3rd quartile	33.5%
4th quartile	17.6%
No rank	28.3%

Those students who were not in the first or second quartile of their high school class had a less than 50% chance of graduating. For each of those 7,516 students, the state invested approximately $6,000, or $45 million a year. The policy considerations are obvious. While no one argues that we should be an elitist institution, the board needs to think through how to best use limited resources.

Table 6 in the same study shows "Graduation from UW Institutions of Fall 1980 New Freshmen as of Spring 1990" by institution:

Beginning Institution	Total Graduation Rate (Percent)
System Average	51.1
Madison	69.1
Milwaukee	40.5
Eau Claire	58.8
Green Bay	43.1
La Crosse	52.7
Oshkosh	48.9
Parkside	31.1
Platteville	58.5
Beginning Institution	**Total Graduation Rate (Percent)**
River Falls	44.8
Stevens Point	52.1
Stout	55.4
Superior	31.2
Whitewater	55.5
Centers	31.7

Center transfers — 69.8 (students who began at a UW Center and later transferred to a four-year UW institution).

The study concluded that, "The average final graduation rate of freshman in the UW System is 52%. This compares favorably with a national average rate of 50%." Stating the conclusion this way tended to cover up individual campus graduation rates. A System average is deceiving. UW-Madison's high graduation rate raised the overall System average. System administration had no comment to make about those campuses with graduation rates below 50% (six) let alone those with graduation rates below 40% (two), Centers excluded.

Since enrollment reduction initiatives and higher admission standards had been put in place, campuses were reporting an improvement in retention rates; students were better prepared to meet the standards set by the institutions.

The retention study concluded that 48% (System average) of the students admitted in Fall 1980 did not graduate. This raised a serious policy issue which the regents did not address during my term on the board. Is the graduation rate acceptable on an overall average and on a campus-by-campus basis? If only one in two students admitted graduated, then the cost to the state per graduate is double the cost per student. What about the cost per student on a campus where only one in three freshmen admitted graduated?

What do the follow-up studies show? In 1986, 43,372 freshmen were admitted to all System campuses. How many graduated by Spring 1991? If the earlier statistics hold true, then some 20,000 students did not graduate. That is a greater number than the total student enrollment at every System campus, except Madison and Milwaukee, for Fall 1985. That is almost equal to the total enrollment of the next two campuses combined. It is an issue worth considering.

In 1992, Stephen Portch, System vice president for academic affairs, reported on the lowest number of freshmen admitted since 1971, "What we're saying is that we will not take more than we can handle. We're trying to keep enrollment in line with resources. This is positive."[89] I wish he had addressed the issue of retention.

The regents must deal more forthrightly with the issues of retention. Based on past experience, most campuses admit too many students who are not qualified. It is irresponsible in terms of the expenditure of public funds and the ability to provide students with a successful experience. The System and the VTAE need to develop an approach for cooperative recruitment so that all high school graduates are given a realistic opportunity for continuing education. About 70% of Wisconsin high school graduates do not attend a university, yet they all need to receive post-secondary training. The System has an obligation to destroy the notion that if a high school graduate goes to college, that is good; if they do not, it is bad. We must not be afraid to say, no to students who are not prepared. If we have their success in mind, we will be honest with them. When exceptions are made, and they should be, then the campuses owe those students a special obligation to ensure their success.

The continuing obligation of the regents is to consider whether students whose likelihood of success, i.e., the ability to graduate, is less than 50-50 ought to be admitted, given funding constraints. There is no question that if the System is bloated with students, the faculty:student ratio suffers, and availability of class sections and labs also suffers.

Some university administrators, while not arguing with the conclusion that high school class rank is a reliable predictor of one's ability to graduate, will contend there is also a relationship between family income and parents' education. The issue before the board is how it should best arrange priorities given a limited amount of funds. Perhaps in the best of all worlds, everyone would be admitted, given a chance, and charged no tuition. But having to face reality, that is not possible. I am concerned for the individual student who is admitted even though the likelihood of success is slim. Why should we contribute to that individual's failure?

The board needs to know a great deal more about why some students graduate and some do not. What about the other factors, such as the increasing debt incurred by students as well as the necessity to work while attending the university? And should we provide remedial academic support? If so, how?

Remedial education: Remedial education offered by campuses has been an issue before the board. Some questioned why it was offered at all, and that students should take remedial courses elsewhere. Faculty members complained to me that they should not be expected to teach "high school" courses.

In a report to the regents dated October 2, 1985, UW System Associate Vice President of Academic Affairs Vernon Lattin reported:

"The Basic Skills Task Force" estimated that 25% [of freshmen] need additional preparation. It must be remembered that this figure is an estimate of need and that actual numbers of students involved in remedial programs are likely to be less than this percentage."[90]

The importance of high school class rank was further emphasized. "Data from a sample of campuses in 1979 suggest that the likelihood of a student needing remedial work is inversely related to his or her high school rank-in-class. Eighteen percent of the students who ranked in the bottom half of their high school classes were enrolled in remedial course work in English and/or mathematics; only 6% of the students who ranked in the top half of their high school classes were enrolled in similar remedial courses. In addition, the data indicated that students needing remedial work in *both* English and mathematics were more likely to have graduated in the bottom half of their high school classes than were students who needed remedial work in only one of these areas."

Shedding additional light on the need for remedial education, the report stated, "It appears, then, that while need for remedial assistance is clearly related to high school academic *performance* [rank in class], it is somewhat less clearly related to the *numbers of units of preparation* a student has had in high school."[91]

The regents approved a recommendation on remedial education in November 1988 (Resolution 5088). It was implemented in Fall 1990. Its basic provisions:

- "Students who are admitted ... whose scores on English or mathematics placement or proficiency tests indicate a low probability for success in college-level courses ... *should* be placed in appropriate remedial courses" (emphasis added).

- These courses were to be taught on the university campus.

- Students enrolled in remedial courses would not be permitted to take more than 12 credits during the time they were taking such courses.

- No later than Fall 1991, "all remedial courses ... shall be offered on a fee recovery basis."

- In cooperation with the Department of Public Instruction, a plan would be developed for assessing English and mathematics skills of high school students. Students would be encouraged to take appropriate courses in high school to avoid the necessity of taking remedial courses in college.

- A detailed statement of the minimum college-level skills and competencies students were expected to have in English and mathematics upon entrance to the university would be developed by October 1989.

The policy was not implemented. System administration urged a change in policy because only about 60% of students needing English and /or mathematics remediation actually were enrolled in remedial courses. At the November 8, 1991, board meeting, the proposed changes were adopted.[92] The new policy would require "new freshmen ... whose scores on English or mathematics placement or proficiency tests indicate a low probability for success in college-level courses in either or both of those subjects ... to complete successfully the necessary remedial courses prior to completion of 30 credits."

For an interesting departure from the usual approach, the proposals of S. Frederick Starr, president of Oberlin College in Ohio, should be explored. He proposed that universities offer a three-year baccalaureate degree, focus new energy on undergraduate education, "a shift of emphasis long overdue," and stop offering remedial high school education.[93] He contends this would provide tuition relief for students. Remedial education can be provided more inexpensively at community colleges or preparatory schools. "Colleges could even pay this bill for students they want most to recruit, and they still would save money."

If remedial courses were to be taught, then they should, in my opinion, be taught by qualified high school teachers, not UW faculty. Such courses should be taught without credit.

UW System and VTAE Relationships. I include this subject with the discussion of the quality of students in the System because the ability of System institutions to bring admission standards closer to the probability of students to graduate depends on that relationship. The public, the legislature, and common sense dictate it. Let me explain.

Not every Wisconsin high school graduate will qualify for entrance into the UW System institution of his or her choice. Taking a broader view of public higher educational opportunities, the enrollment management approach based on the qualifications of applicants is "positive." First, it is a responsible use of resources. Those who are most likely to graduate are admitted. Second, those who are not admitted are not shut out, because the VTAE system is a viable alternative. College is not for everyone, as we have seen from the retention studies. Yet post-high school education must be made available to everyone. It is understandable that regents and System administrators are so involved in campus issues that they lose sight of the broader picture. "Roughly 75 to 80% of all jobs still may not require a worker to have a baccalaureate degree in the year 2005."[94]

The role of the VTAE is clear, and needs to be seen as part of Wisconsin's overall commitment to post-high school education, along with the UW System. For its part, the UW System needs to forge meaningful, non-competitive relationships with VTAE, so that all citizens benefit. The UW System, the Department of Public Instruction, and the VTAE system must work much more closely, so that potential students understand the criteria for admission to the various institutions, All high school students should be encouraged to continue their education consistent with their previous achievements. To the extent that there has been competition between the UW System and VTAE, and there has been, it needs to stop. The needs of students should be at the forefront. Unless the three public agencies can work together more closely, I predict the state will establish an overall coordinating board of public education. Citizens can understand why every institution of public higher education cannot be open to everyone, as long as there are well-known and understood admission standards and alternatives. They will not understand if there is no institution available for everyone seeking post-secondary education. The System dares not contribute to the perception that it is superior in any way to the VTAE system, or that one institution in the System is more desirable than another. What is important is that the individual student be counseled to pursue a course of action that will lead to success. During my term on the board, I was not able to convince the professionals of either system of the significance of this, nor was there any meaningful formal relationship created. The "Statement of Principles" adopted by both boards is the only true moment of cooperation.

Senate Majority Leader Joe Strohl wrote to me on July 27, 1990, and made the following observation: "Finding skilled, well-trained workers has become one of the greatest challenges facing employers. High schools have traditionally had close ties with colleges but not with employers, even though 60-65% of high school graduates go directly into the work force. Of the 35-40% who go on to higher education, one-half will drop out, and they too will enter the workplace unprepared. The tragic result is that almost 80% of our young people enter adulthood unprepared for the world of work and without the skills needed to land good paying high-tech jobs."

While he was addressing the need for a better relationship between the high schools and the technical colleges, it is good for the board of regents to understand that System graduates a small percentage of the population. The VTAE system is of equal or greater importance in preparing high school graduates for the job market. The two need to develop much closer working relationships in order to optimize the opportunities for the success of the greatest number. The System must help legitimatize the VTAE institutions as a choice of equal significance. On August 29, 1990, Dwight A. York, state director of the VTAE said, "I see a time when the technical colleges are viewed as the first option, the first place people turn to, for training. This will be especially true of women, displaced homemakers, minorities, those in need of retraining, displaced workers and persons new to the job market."[95] It is in the self-best interest of the UW System, recognizing its budgetary constraints, that it work closely with the VTAE.

In a letter to State Superintendent of Public Instruction Grover, I wrote on September 18, 1990:

> Before we define our relationships [between UW System, VTAE, and DPI] we need to understand the "gestalt" of the citizens we are talking about. We need to come to grips with the idea that the majority of high school graduates will not go on to college. We need to embrace the idea that those who do not, still need post secondary education and some of them will use this route to go to college. UWS trains the teachers and counselors for DPI and for VTAE. Do they understand the climate? How do we deal with perceptions that cause some students to believe that the UW System choice is good but the VTAE choice is bad? How do we

educate the public to accept the equality of the two systems? How do we get government to support the two systems? UWS needs to embrace VTAE and DPI — they need to embrace each other. We need enlightened leadership of the three systems to work together, not as competitors. The goal is the success of the student, not of the bureaucrats. We live in a competitive world. So we must compete or lose our place in the world, which we are doing. It is everyone's responsibility to address these issues together.

This issue was only partially addressed by the Regent Working Group on Undergraduate Education and the Relationship of the UW System and VTAE. The working group dealt primarily with agreements having to do with credit transfers.

The March 1991 joint report of the Wisconsin VTAE and the DPI said: "Several labor market studies indicate that by the end of the decade, 80 percent of all jobs will require formal education beyond high school, but less than a baccalaureate degree." It behooves the two Wisconsin institutions of post-secondary education — the UW System and the VTAE—to work together much more closely so that every Wisconsin resident is fully informed and is made available *realistic* options that will lead to the individual's success. The old turf battles and preconceptions about the quality of each system make no sense if we are to be responsible future planners prepared to carry out the public trust.[96]

Secretary of Administration James R. Klauser observed that, nationally, approximately 50% of high school graduates enrolled in college, but only about half ever graduated. "We're not really giving our young people a lot of choices. Technology is changing, and we think we have to give young people more options and alternatives. From the viewpoint of the economy ... it's critical. To maintain our standard of living, we have to develop technical education, technical skills." Superintendent of Public Instruction Grover noted that the school systems "have increasingly neglected the majority of our students that are not college-bound," and announced a high school apprenticeship program, "Tech Prep," modeled after those in West Germany. General student competencies and curriculum topics will be identified around the following major clusters:

- Health Services/Medical Services
- Business/Marketing
- Agribusiness/Agriscience
- Family and Consumer Education
- Technical/Industrial[97]

In reporting on the 1992 "Milwaukee Sentinel's 29th Forum for Progress," the *Sentinel* staff writer noted that "While 70% to 80% of the jobs of the future will require some education beyond high school, most will not require a four-year college degree, according to national statistics."[98]

In 1990, a panel of educators — the chancellor of UW-Madison, the president of Edgewood College (a private Catholic college in Madison), and the district director of Madison Area Technical College — convened to discuss these issues. "[To] educate the best and the brightest — that is no longer acceptable as our only charge. One of our challenges is to educate the under prepared or the average" (president of Edgewood College).[99] The UW-Madison chancellor stated that paying more attention to undergraduate education was the challenge for major research universities. The district director of Madison Area Technical College pointed out that the publicly funded institutions do not have unlimited resources and asked, "Can we continue to do everything for everybody?"

Suggestions regarding the quality of students and UW System VTAE relationships that do not require funding:

- Students admitted at risk should be carefully monitored. If an institution is not willing to put in the extra effort needed to help those students become successful, then they should not admit them. This practice should be monitored by the regents.

- The results of the proficiency test pilot project should be examined to determine whether it ought to be applied systemwide.

- The board should adopt minimum high school graduation standards for *each campus.*

- The board should establish a minimum retention rate for *each campus* at 50% or more. Systemwide averages are meaningless. When a campus has a retention rate in the low 30s, that means that for every student who graduates, two do not. At an average annual cost of $6,000 of state money per student, the cost to the state of graduating one student is substantially increased.

- The board should determine the number of exceptions to minimum admission standards. There should be a redefinition of "exceptions," since current definition of exceptions is confusing.

- Campus centers of excellence should be redone. The centers should not be dependent on additional funding, but should reflect the focus of the campus. What does it offer as its excellence in programs, so that prospective students can make enlightened choices? That would help the board implement a policy demonstrating that every campus cannot be everything to everyone.

- Regents should insist that there be a formalized agreement with VTAE regarding the recruitment of students. There are two systems of post-secondary education in Wisconsin. The VTAE system is an excellent and superior choice for many, including those who could be successful in college. The university is not a superior choice for everyone, and that choice should not be "oversold." One example will illustrate the point. A faculty friend told me that his son did poorly in high school. He would not qualify to enter UW-Madison. He entered the VTAE system where he did very well. He eventually entered UW-Madison and will earn a Ph.D. in 1992. The VTAE can serve as a good transition for some students.[100]

• JACCE and the other UW System and VTAE joint committees should be strengthened by having regents and VTAE board members added.

• It is too early to tell whether enrollment management has improved retention. The regents should follow these figures on an annual basis, so that the graduation rate for each campus can be tracked.

• The board should examine the remedial education policy. How many students who still require remedial work should be permitted to enter the UW System? Tenured faculty should not teach remedial courses.

Quality of Campus Environment

Some regents understand the sensitivities and concerns of minority students and are in the forefront of doing what they can to ensure the quality of the campus environment for all students. Others leave the impression that they don't care, or they allow their personal prejudices to sway their decisions. Chapter 36, Wisconsin Statutes makes it clear that the regents represent all of the students. If the regents do not discharge their responsibility, then the legislature should act.

Students are rightfully concerned about the quality of the campus environment in which they are expected to study and learn. A sampling of some newspaper accounts will demonstrate the point:

February 18, 1992 — "La Crosse is 'institutionally racist,' say members of UW-L group."[101]

February 29, 1992 — "Students charge racism in handling of dorm fight."[102]

March 3, 1992 — "Handling of bias complaints earns poor grades for UW-M."[103]

March 5, 1992 — "UW's [Madison] anti-bias record attacked."[104]

October 8, 1992 — "Administration ponders gay bashings."[105]

There are those who believe that minorities are doing well in this country and that the universities can relax their efforts. That is not the case. *The New York Times National Addition* (January 8, 1992, p. A10) reported the results of the "General Social Survey" at the University of Chicago's National Opinion

Research Center, sponsored by the American Jewish Committee. In polls taken in 1984 and 1989 "adults nationwide were asked to rate the 'social standing' of various groups in the United States" (1 was the lowest and 9 was the highest). The "Wisians" were a fictitious group.

The partial results for 1989 were:

Native White Americans	7.03
Jews	5.55
Latin Americans	4.42
American Indians	4.27
Blacks	4.17
"Wisians"	4.12
Mexicans	3.52
Puerto Ricans	3.32

Anti-semitic attacks — including vandalism, assaults, threats and harassment — in the United States reached record numbers in 1991 — up 11% over 1990 — the highest level in the 13-year history of the nationwide survey.[106] Jewish students on campus are aware of these and of the Ku Klux Klan campaign in Wisconsin during the recent elections.

Gay bashing is not unheard of. The *Eau Claire Leader-Telegram*, March 25, 1992, reported in an article titled "Gay Bashing reported at university," "Authorities today were investigating what appears to be the second assault of a University of Wisconsin-Eau Claire woman that was prompted by her sexual orientation." In a follow-up article on March 29, 1992, the same newspaper reported that members of the Gay-Lesbian Or Bisexual Equality organization received harassing telephone calls. The ROTC discriminates against homosexuals as a matter of official policy.

The Chronicle of Higher Education reported on March 25, 1992, that a recent survey "found that American youths are generally pessimistic about race relations in the United States." Arthur J. Kropp, president of People for the American Way, the organization conducting the survey, said, "The plain message of our research is that racial division is taking root among the next generation of Americans. Our young people have placed themselves in opposing camps, divided by race, and they tend to believe only the worst about youths of other races."[107] And ROTC's policy of discrimination against gay students continues.

While I served on the board, the regents took seriously the issue of the quality of the campus environment for every student on every campus and their responsibility to do what it could to improve it. In addressing the issue, the regents adopted Design for Diversity, revised the student conduct code, and adopted resolutions regarding ROTC.

Were these efforts worthwhile?

When Design for Diversity was adopted, goals were established. 1987 was the base year. Chapter 36.25[14m][b], Wisconsin Statutes provides, "By November 15, 1988, and annually thereafter, the board shall adopt a recruitment and retention plan for minority and disadvantaged students enrolled in the System. ... By November 15, 1988, and annually thereafter, the board shall submit a report on the recruitment and retention plan under this paragraph to the governor and to the chief clerk of each house of the legislature for distribution to the appropriate standing committees under s. 13.172 [3]." At the April 10, 1992, meeting of the board of regents, the *1990-91 Design for Diversity Progress Report* was accepted for submission to the appropriate state authorities.[108] How has the System done?[109]

Fall 1988 marked the first year of Design for Diversity.

According to the Report, the percentage of yardsticks achieved system-wide as of Fall 1991 were:

New minority undergraduate students enrolled	81%
Minority faculty hiring goal	92%

One could argue that without the stated goals, the results would have been the same. My experience on the board lead me to conclude quite the opposite. The goals were necessary for success.

In 1987, before Design for Diversity, 1,397 new minority students enrolled. In 1991 1,447 enrolled.[110] Steve Schultze, reporter for the *Milwaukee Journal*, wrote on April 7, 1992, "That raises the question of whether the program has done much to improve on the ordinary turnover of new minority students." In the same article, System President Lyall was reported to have said that in view of Ku Klux Klan rallies at UW-Whitewater and UW-Madison and the national atmosphere of racial polarization, she was "surprised we came as close as we did." James Sulton, special assistant to the president for minority affairs, was reported to have said that more progress could be made if there were better coordination among campus admissions, financial aid, and minority affairs specialists. Sulton was also reported to have pointed to the campus environment as a deterrent to recruiting minority students. Blacks in Milwaukee and American Indians from the Menominee reservation "tell us 'That university is never going to change' or 'They don't want us there.' We have a tremendous credibility problem."[111] I wonder how helpful are statements from regents, who are reported to have stated that the goals were unrealistic, or that in order to reach those goals the universities are recruiting minority students who are unprepared? "Instead of recruiting qualified students, are we recruiting students who are unprepared?" Regent Phyllis Krutsch was quoted to have said.[112] In a private conversation with Sulton on April 28, 1992, he expressed the opinion that there are "more than enough" students of color who are qualified, if they were actively recruited. But it will make no difference in the lives of those who are responsible for recruiting if they do not perform. There is no reward and no punishment. He was still hearing the argument that "we need a bigger pool."

In examining the results, regents must look behind the averages, as stated above. The Design for Diversity Progress Report, April 9, 1992, provided information by minority groups and by campus. It was important, in my view, to keep everyone focused on the goals. That cannot be done by looking at averages because they distort. For example, from 1987 to 1991, the total number of African American new undergraduates actually declined, whereas the number of Hispanics and American Indians increased. In terms of new minority undergraduate enrollment, there were wide variances in campus achievements versus campus goals. The UW systemwide achieved 81% of the goal; individual campuses varied from 63% to 158%.[113] The same was true for minority faculty hires. The systemwide achievement of 90.4% should be viewed in terms of the variance among campuses of 40% to 127.3%.[114] Of significance were the improved retention rates and the increase of degrees confirmed. Whereas the number of bachelor's degrees confirmed to white students in 1990-91 versus 1985-86 increased by 3.6%, the increase for designated minorities, African-Americans, Hispanics, and American Indians was 42%.[115]

An important indicator of progress is to view total enrollments by race and ethnicity. This would show the results of retention efforts as well as recruitment of new undergraduates. On a head count basis, there has been a steady increase in the number of African American, Hispanic, Asian American, and American Indian students in the System from 1987 to 1991, as follows:[116]

African American	up 13.5%
Hispanic	up 20.5%
Asian American	up 50.5%
American Indian	up 29.6%

Nationally, there seems to be some good news. The American Council on Education (ACE) reported that 33% of black high school graduates 18 to 24 years old were attending college in 1990, up from 26.1% in 1985. The increase was mainly among black women. This compares with 39.4% of white high school graduates, and 29% for Hispanic high school graduates.[117] It is all due to the efforts made campus by campus.

Some regents now proclaim that Design for Diversity was a mistake — that it was social engineering, which is beyond the duty of the board. Some faculty members told me that the only solution to these broader social issues is education, but that the universities do not have this as a priority. Harold E. Scheub, professor of African languages and literature at UW-Madison, wrote, "For the faculty of this university, to understand to remedy hate is the major and first task of the new millennium. ... The faculty must become teachers. ... Teaching is what will eliminate hate. It is our only hope. ... Nothing less than a revolution on the campus is called for: The faculty must take back its prerogatives and it must confront these issues with its students — teaching ideas, discussing ideas, arguing ideas. The moral authority of the faculty must return to the campus. The essential relationship is between teacher and student — the idea, after all, of a university."[118] Not all faculty members agree.

I agree with Professor Scheub. But in addition, regents have an obligation to all students to improve the campus environment. They must be actively involved in the educational process. I am not alone in my views.

Elie Weisel, Andrew W. Mellon Professor in the Humanities at Boston University, and recipient of the Nobel Peace Prize and the United States Congressional Gold Medal of Achievement, said in an interview that, "People should know the real meaning of racism. People should know the consequences of anti-Semitism. People should know that it is dangerous and too destructive."[119] Weisel lectured at the Madison campus on April 9, 1992. I attended. He said that people are more ignorant than before. Like Scheub, he believes that only through educating young people will we move beyond ignorance and hate. "One cannot say that one is born with hate, one learns it. So just as you teach hate, you can teach not to hate. The universities have the greatest role. They prepare people for adulthood. They must prepare the next teachers. Professors, scholars, and students share the most important role in moving beyond hatred."

Commenting on the UWS student conduct code (UWS 17), Weisel said, "I think it is a good decision. Absolutely. What is education—it is an opportunity for people to become more civil. I would like to think that this law that you have is simply to encourage civility. And respect." In commenting on the role of the university in dealing with intolerance on the campus, he said, "Teaching is to sensitize. Sensitive people are tolerant and become messengers of tolerance."

I explained in Chapter V how some faculty members disengage themselves from regent policy by "stonewalling." I used Design for Diversity as an example. It is alleged by some that political correctness drives these initiatives, and that they threaten the quality of the institutions. Judy Goldsmith, special consultant to the chancellor for equity and affirmative action at UW-Stevens Point, cited a recent survey done by the American Council of Education at 359 colleges and universities. Only 10% found "significant controversy over the political or cultural content" of addresses by guest speakers and about 5% reported professors being pressured to change course content or texts. She pointed out that 30 years ago most colleges were 94% white and two-thirds male. Now the student body is 53% female, nationwide, and nearly 20% are students of color. "Energetic debate, discussion and dialogue are alive and well on our campuses. What is not is somebody's pipe dream called 'political correctness.' We are all wrestling with the best ways to live and work and learn together."[120]

The Future of Design for Diversity: Specific aspects of regent conduct in the future related to the campus environment will be discussed later in this chapter under the headings "Student Conduct Code" and "ROTC." No progress will be made, however, unless the regents maintain a resolve to deal with the issue of quality of campus environment. I predict an ongoing struggle on the board. There will be those who will attempt to scuttle all of the previous efforts. It will depend, in the end, on the board's collective mental baggage. In discussing multiculturalism and the role of the campus, Mary Kalantzis and William Cope, senior research fellows in the Centre for Multicultural Studies at Australia's University of Wollongong, wrote:

> In higher education, such changes are necessary not just for the moral well-being of our students, but also for our collective economic well-being ... students must be prepared to face the challenge of multiculturalism as an intrinsic element of their future productive lives. Who, after all, will be their clients and co-workers? Multiculturalism, the reality of living with diversity, is not a matter of momentary controversy. Indeed, it may well prove to be the issue of our epoch.

In an article titled, "Opening the Minority Pipeline,"[121] Joni Finney, director of policy studies at the Education Commission of the States, concluded that, "Without forceful and effective leadership from college and university trustees, it is unlikely that American higher education will be able to improve the education of minority students." The mistake, she points out, is to focus primarily on access by providing economic assistance instead of understanding that many of the minority students come from some of the nation's worst high schools and are not prepared academically. (p. 16)

Finney suggests the following, based on campuses with successful programs for graduating minorities:

- Promulgate board policies that "emphasize grants over loans, ... mandate simplified applications for financial aid, and provide for coordinated financial aid and admissions processes." (p. 17)

- Increase the chances for academic success by"[w]ork[ing] collaboratively with public schools to ensure that students are aware of and prepared for the academic challenges of college." (p.17)

- "Help elementary and secondary teachers incorporate performance expectations and required courses into school curricula." (p. 15)

- "Create a campus climate that welcomes and values the participation of all students, and provide more role models by recruiting, developing, and supporting a diverse faculty and administration." (p.18)

- "... focus on improving undergraduate teaching and learning ... use assessment (at entry and after the general-education portion of the college program) to understand what and how students learn and to improve undergraduate teaching ... provide learning assistance to students with identified weaknesses ... evaluate incentive and reward policies to encourage faculty research and innovation that support improved teaching ... reward faculty who place a high priority on student learning ... [while] integrating multicultural perspectives into the general-education program." (p.18)

- "How do campus and Board leaders support and provide incentives for change? Simply put: Leaders make it a high priority and then shift resources, rewards, and incentives. Boards can set institutional goals for minority enrollment and graduation rates and can systematically monitor progress. The purpose of such goals is to provide a bench mark — not quotas — against which to assess the institution's success and the effectiveness of its strategies and programs. The goals should be supported by plans that set forth specific steps to remove barriers to achievement, that help under-prepared students succeed, and that improve teaching and learning." (p.19)

Holding senior administrators responsible for progress should be incorporated into performance reviews.

Student Conduct Code: Design for Diversity grew out of the concern regents and administrators had for the quality of the campus environment. They recognized that the quality of the environment is an important indicator of institutional quality. Campuses across the nation have been paying more attention to this aspect of quality.

An extension of Design for Diversity was the revision of student conduct codes. If students felt alienated, harassed, or threatened, their ability to take full advantage of educational opportunities was diminished.

The issues surrounding student conduct code and ROTC present interesting case histories of how regents dealt — or failed to deal — with controversial and explosive issues.

The amendment to the Student Conduct Code, UWS 17, discussed in Chapter IV, has been seen as an important step in attempting to improve the campus environment. It sent a strong message to all students that the regents were willing to do what they could within constitutional constraints. The U.S. District Court ruled our efforts unconstitutional. Acting President Lyall put it very well in discussing the court's ruling at the November 8, 1991, UW Board of Regents meeting. She pointed out that while the System will protect free speech on its campuses, it is equally determined to ensure freedom to learn in an atmosphere of civility. It believes that every student has a right to engage in these activities free of harassment. "I want all currently enrolled students, prospective students, and parents of students to know that conduct intended to demean a person or prevent them from pursuing an education has no place in the UW System." That was clearly the challenge the board faced. A redraft to satisfy the objections of the court was undertaken by UW-Madison Law School constitutional scholars.

The redraft differed from the original language in two ways:

1. It was more limited in scope so as to comply with the "fighting words" doctrine.

2. It allowed System administration to oversee how the rule would be applied at the campus level. While the court did not say so in so many words, it was believed that the enforcement at the campus level was badly handled.

The redraft was scheduled for a hearing before the regent Education Committee on March 5, 1992. It was widely speculated that the regents would not approve the revision because of the more conservative nature of the board that was reflected in the new appointments. There were the expected newspaper editorials assailing the redraft. One editorial argued that the System should approach the subject of racism and bigotry by teaching students "... to respect people from different backgrounds. ..." They branded the rule as "thought control."[122] Similar editorials were written at the time the regents debated the original revision of the code.

The Education Committee met on March 5, 1992. All regents were invited to attend. Anyone who wished to appear and be heard was invited. Since I had been one of the major proponents of the original resolution and had testified on behalf of the board to the joint legislative committees that approved it, I was asked to appear before the Education Committee.

I debated with myself as to what was appropriate. I was tempted to again debate the First Amendment issue. I was tempted to argue once again not to accept that there were arbitrary legalisms. If a black student and a white student worked in the student cafeteria, the white student was prohibited by law from verbally abusing the black student because of that student's race. Yet the white student was guiltless if the abuse took place in the cafeteria after working hours.

During the debates that surrounded the initial language, I listened to the arguments used against any speech code. I was invited to discuss this on radio and TV. After listening to individuals with no constitutional expertise expound upon their theories of free speech, I became convinced that they had created a myth about the First Amendment. Of course, the First Amendment is an important and fundamental right that needs to be protected. But it is not an absolute right. I recall a debate in which I asked whether it was true that there was no such thing as an unlimited right to free speech. Courts and legislators have ruled that when it is in the public interest, speech can be limited. I provided examples such as laws against sexual and racial harassment in the workplace, laws that prevented employers from threatening employees who join a union, and court decisions that dealt with language that would incite to riot, such as yelling "Fire" in a crowded theater. The only response I ever received was, "Well, that's different." I do not believe it is different. One should be free to express odious opinions, but in my view the line is crossed when the expressions harass and intimidate others, or create a hostile environment that interferes with their equal rights to an education.

I was further strengthened in my position by constitutional scholars from UW-Madison Law School, who believed that it did not violate the First Amendment to limit certain kinds of speech, specifically those covered by the revision. Had I been on the board at the time of the court's adverse decision, I would have argued that the decision be appealed. All this went through my mind as I thought about testifying before the Education Committee.

I decided that launching into a First Amendment discussion made no sense, since the Law School faculty members were experts and would testify. And besides, I had three minutes to make my point. So I shifted the emphasis. I argued to the Education Committee that this was not a constitutional issue for the board, but was best left to the experts; I urged them to accept the advice of the constitutional experts; that they not hide behind the First Amendment as an excuse not to deal with the issues being raised by students; that the board had an obligation to the students — an obligation to do what it could to provide every student a "level playing field," an opportunity to study and learn without being harassed, de-meaned, and tormented. Finally, since the board had previously determined that the student conduct code should relay to students how the board felt about abusive language, it had no choice but to adopt the redraft. If it did not, it would surely send the message to the students that the board did not care. They should set aside their predetermined views, their mental baggage, and listen to the testimony of those whom they represented — the students.

It was known that five members of the board would vote no. Some had already expressed their views publicly. There was concern that others who had voted for the original were changing their minds. The media predicted that this "new conservative" board would vote against the redraft. Later that afternoon, I received an excited call from a member of the System staff. The vote by the committee was seven yes, five no, and one abstention. The full board carried on the debate the next day. The vote at the full board was nine yes and six no. Two board members were absent. One board member who could not attend, called the regent president to say that had he been there, he would have voted yes.

One board member expressed the opinion that all of this was an exercise in futility because the redraft would be challenged in the courts. That argument missed the point. The board needed to be concerned about the needs of the students — all students. To the extent that the board can help create a better environment, it is obligated to do so. A law school faculty member put it very well when he said there is a difference between understanding hurt intellectually and emotionally. Unless one had been at the receiving end of demeaning, hostile, intimidating behavior by others because of one's race, ethnicity, gender, sexual orientation, etc., one can only understand it intellectually. The board of regents has to stretch beyond its members' life experiences and attempt to understand it emotionally, as though it was happening to board members. I would refer those board members to *A Season for Justice*, by Morris Dees. It deals in detail with prejudice towards minorities in the United States.[123] Dees helps those who have not been subjected to prejudice, intolerance, and intimidation because of race better understand what effect such actions can have.

The board debate expressed a wide cross-section of views. A sample follows:[124]

Regent Erroll Davis: "Is the message, 'Come to Wisconsin, where regents believe calling people names is a valuable part of the educational experience?' "

Regent Lee Sherman Dreyfus: "Students now will have less freedom of speech than non-students."

Regent Ness Flores said he was "flabbergasted at the notion that all noise that comes out of human beings is considered speech. That has never been the law."

Regent George Steil called it "an exercise in futility. And rest assured it will be challenged on constitutional grounds."

Regent Davis: "Our responsibility is not to play lawyers and exchange legal opinions. Our responsibility is to create an environment where our children can get an education."

Regent Sheldon Lubar: "I've given it great thought. The rule is ethically and morally correct."

Having passed that hurdle, formal hearings were scheduled for May, and the board reaffirmed its previous vote and submitted the redraft to the president of the Wisconsin Senate. The president assigned it to the Senate Higher Education Committee. Joint hearings were held on June 10, 1992, by the Senate Higher Education Committee and the Assembly Committee on Colleges and Universities. I was asked to testify in favor of the revision, and I did, along with the System president, the immediate past president of the board of regents, the special assistant to the president, the dean of students at UW-Madison, Professor Ted Finman of the UW-Madison Law School, and some students. The opposition came from the same sources it had come from before. No new arguments were heard on either side. As expected, the same legislator that opposed the first revision, declared publicly that he would oppose the redraft, and he did.[125] The ACLU appeared against the proposed amendment to the code. It was always my feeling that both the senator and the ACLU would oppose any limitation, no matter how carefully drawn. The opposing arguments presented were, from my point of view, disappointing because they did not deal with the rights of the victim, but fell prey to the legalisms or argued that human behavior can only be modified by education, not dictates of law, forgetting all of those laws that deal precisely with human behavior that society finds unacceptable. Those who argued for education did not explain what they had in mind. They were not privy to a conversation I had with a prominent member of the faculty who declared that teaching tolerance was not a priority at the university.[126] I argued that legislators have no difficulty passing laws that modify overt behavior, whether those who are so constrained are educated or not. That is the case with work place rules prohibiting sexual harassment. One hopes that while protecting the victims, those who formerly engaged in such practices will become educated.

Some newspapers could not wait to attack the regent decision to support the redraft. One newspaper commented editorially, "Free speech loses again."[127]

Normally it would be expected that after the debate is finished and the vote has been taken, regents would support the majority position. Unfortunately, the board reversed itself at a later date. System President Lyall explained that the board's action to repeal the rule was motivated by a recent Supreme Court decision which caused some to doubt the rule's constitutionality and others to point to the reluctance of the board to spend money to defend the rule in court. "I'm disappointed," Lyall said. "If we're not prepared to spend our money in defense of important human principles, we've come to a sad day."[128]

At the October 9, 1992, meeting of the board, Regent President Steil announced that he and President Lyall would appoint a statewide committee of student affairs officers to follow up on the repeal resolution of the board. On December 11, 1992, the board voted 9 to 7 to repeal the rule. It does make a difference who serves on the board!

ROTC: Because ROTC discriminates against gay and lesbian students, the ROTC debate is, in my view, a component of the campus environment. As described earlier, land grant universities were required by law to offer military training. The Morrill Act significantly pre-dates ROTC, however. ROTC has become the way the mandate of the law has been fulfilled. UW-Madison is the only land grant institution in Wisconsin. Yet ROTC is an educational option being offered on other System campuses without the force of the Morrill Act.

Students who sign up for ROTC are asked to declare their sexual preference. If they identify themselves as gay or lesbian, they may take courses but will not receive the scholarships or be commissioned in the armed forces upon graduation.

The chronology of the controversy is as follows. (Unless otherwise noted, the references were enumerated in *Wisconsin Week*, UW-Madison, September 11, 1992, p.5.) The issue was reopened while I served on the board and resulted in considerable debate:

May 1979 — Faculty Senate, UW-Madison, added sexual preference to discriminatory prohibitions.

April 19, 1985 — In response to the vote of the UW-Milwaukee Faculty Senate opposing ROTC, state Senator Donald K. Stitt wrote to the chancellor, "Your faculty members have asked for 'catch-up' and regular raises. ... Is this vote the way to show their gratitude? The faculty vote made a mockery of academic fairness and the University's responsibility toward its students. ... I am asking that you veto this decision."[129]

October 29, 1985 — *The UW-M Report*, the faculty/staff newsletter of UW-Milwaukee, reported that the Faculty Senate had voted 157-111 to reverse the earlier action of the Faculty Senate.[130]

April 1987 — The UW Board of Regents in referring to the change in state law enacted in 1982, acknowledged that discrimination based on sexual preference "... is not to be tolerated in Wisconsin." That same year, the regents resolved that ROTC programs do discriminate against "... applicants based on sexual preference."

February 1988 — The UW-Madison Faculty Senate adopted a resolution urging the university to renegotiate its contract with ROTC, so as not to permit discrimination based on sexual orientation. It also asked that the Department of Defense be lobbied to change it policies against gays and lesbians.

1989 — Chapter 36.12, Wisconsin Statutes, "Student discrimination prohibited," was adopted by the legislature. Chapter 36.12[1], Wisconsin Statutes provided: "No student may be denied admission to, participation in *or the benefits of*, or be discriminated against in any service, program, course or facility of the system or its institutions or centers because of the student's race, color, creed, religion, sex, national origin, disability, ancestry, age, sexual orientation, pregnancy, marital status or parental status." Chapter 36.12[2], Wisconsin Statutes mandated that the regents direct the institutions to "establish policies and procedures to protect students from discrimination, ... provide criteria for determining whether ... there has been a violation, and "provide remedies and sanctions for violations. ..." Chapter 36.12[2][b][3], Wisconsin Statutes required the board to report by September 1, 1991, 1992, 1993, and 1994 to the chief clerk of each house of the Wisconsin legislature the number of complaints and requests for review and the disposition of them.

December 4, 1989 — After more than 100 UW-Madison faculty members had signed a petition calling for a full meeting of the faculty to consider the ROTC issue, the faculty voted 386 to 248 for the regents to terminate ROTC contracts if discrimination based on sexual orientation did not end by 1993. The resolution called on the university to identify ways it could meet its land grant obligation for military training without such discrimination, and called on the president of the System to work with the state's congressional delegation. It also said the chancellor and the University Committee should lobby in Washington for a change in policy.

Winter 1989-90 — In a concurrent preference poll of the 2,396 UW-Madison faculty members, 40% of the 1,007 respondents favored terminating ROTC by 1993 unless the discriminatory practices stopped.

December 1989 — The UW-Madison's Wisconsin Student Association voted to have the regents terminate ROTC contracts by 1993, unless the discriminatory practices ended.

December 1989 and January 1990 — The Academic Staff Assembly, UW-Madison, asked for non-ROTC alternatives for military training and approved lobbying the congressional delegation, but opposed terminating ROTC.

January 1990 — The Madison chancellor and System president recommended to the board of regents that ROTC be retained, but endorsed an intensification of the lobbying efforts.

February 1990 — The regents endorsed the System president's recommendation and rejected the faculty's recommendation of December 4, 1989, to terminate ROTC by 1993.

March 1990 — UW-Madison University Committee appointed a task force to lobby for ending the military's discrimination against homosexuals.

April 1990 — About 100 students conducted a five-day sit-in outside the Madison chancellor's office. They wanted the university to print a disclaimer in all university publications stating that ROTC discriminates contrary to state law and university policies. The chancellor rejected the demand and stated that the focus should be for change in the Defense Department, consistent with the regent action. Students organized a sit-in at UW System administration offices demanding that the regents reconsider the ROTC issue. They were forcibly removed by the police.

May 1990 — The presidents of four national higher education associations wrote to the secretary of defense arguing in favor of changing the current policy. The official response was that homosexuality was incompatible with military service. The request for a meeting was denied.

May 1990 — System President Shaw responded to UW-Madison Wisconsin Student Association, which sought an appeal from the chancellor's refusal to include in all relevant publications a disclaimer that would say that ROTC, in accordance with federal regulations, excludes students based on sexual orientation and that the policy violated the UW-Madison Faculty Senate resolution of May 7, 1989, and the regent resolution of April 10, 1987. Shaw pointed out that the chancellor had agreed to include a two-page letter on the ROTC issue in student orientation materials and include portions of the letter in the student handbook.

May 1990 — Students at UW-Madison and UW-Milwaukee threatened a lawsuit against the board of regents, unless the board "moves to get the ROTC to abandon policies that exclude homosexual graduates." The suit would be based on the newly enacted state law, Chapter 36.12, Wisconsin Statutes, referred to above, which "prohibits discrimination against students" attending System or VTAE institutions based on sexual orientation. It was reported that the senate of the University of Kansas, in Lawrence, proposed that ROTC courses no longer be counted for credit toward graduation unless the Department of Defense changed its policy.[131]

January 1991 — The UW-Madison and 17 other universities met to discuss a national strategy and the merits of taking legal action.

April 1991 — The UW System president reported to the board, "It seems unlikely that Congress will consider ... a revision in the DOD's (Department of Defense) existing policy of exclusion in the near future."

August 1991 — At the request of the regents, the UW-Madison chancellor reported to the board that developing an alternative military tactics program did not appear to be viable. She was concerned that the inability of an alternative program to grant commissions could affect the land grant status of the institution.

September 1991 — The UW-Madison chancellor reported that a senior Department of Defense official was going to meet with a group of Big Ten presidents and chancellors.

June 10, 1992 — *The Chronicle of Higher Education* reported that the American Civil Liberties Union "asked 250 college presidents to join its campaign to end the military's policy of denying homosexuals admission into Reserve Officers' Training Corps leadership courses." The article reported that the ACLU had already won the support of the American Council on Education, the American Association of College and University Housing Officers, the American Association of Collegiate Registrars and Admissions Officers, and the American Association of University Professors. Robert M. O'Neil, general counsel of the American Association of University Professors and former president of the UW System, was quoted as saying, "If colleges and universities seem increasingly uncomfortable in signing on with ROTC and in enforcing these abhorrent policies, it is not only because students may protest or faculty may express indignation," but also because ROTC policy is an intrusion on "jealously guarded" academic freedoms.[132]

June 19, 1992 — *The Capital Times* reported that, "A new congressional study strongly challenges the U.S. military policy of excluding homosexuals and lesbians, estimating the cost of replacing uniformed men and women kicked out of the services for homosexuality at 27 million [dollars] in 1990 alone." The article reported that several European countries, according to the study, allow homosexuals to serve and that "some police departments in the United States have reported a 'positive impact' since they began hiring gays and lesbians. The investigators found virtually no scientific or sociological evidence to support the Pentagon's arguments that the gay ban is necessary to ensure 'good order, morale and discipline.' " It was reported that some experts believe that the policy "appears to be based on the same type of prejudicial suppositions that were used to discriminate against black people and white women before these policies were changed." The GAO study reported that the "Defense Department's own internal studies largely have erased the notion that gays in uniform constitute a security risk," an attitude also endorsed by Defense Secretary Dick Cheney.[133] It will take either an act of Congress or the will of the president of the United States to change this prejudicial policy.

No one has satisfactorily reconciled regent policy and state law with the ongoing discrimination of ROTC. As for UW-Madison, which because of its land grant status is required to offer military training, the regents have relied on the theory that federal law preempts state law on this subject. As to the other System campuses that offer ROTC, no such requirement exists. Professor Joseph Elder, UW-Madison, in an article he wrote for *Wisconsin Week*, September 11, 1992 (p. 4), reported that the Massachusetts Institute of Technology (MIT) had set a deadline and Harvard and Yale had refused to reinstate their ROTC programs as long as discrimination continued. He suggested that the board of regents seek an opinion from the state attorney general. I would add that if the board wanted to show good faith, it would cancel ROTC on those campuses where military training is not required by the Morrill Act.

Of interest to regents and campus administrators should be a 1992 decision by the Federal Court of Canada. A lesbian had been discharged from the Air Force. The court ruled that it was against the "Charter of Rights and Freedoms" for the military to place restrictions on gays. General John de Chastelain was quoted as saying, "The Canadian Forces will comply fully. Canadians, regardless of sexual orientation, will now be able to serve their country in the Canadian forces without restriction."[134]

Other initiatives: Other initiatives were taken to deal with campus environment, including mandating the teaching of ethnic studies courses to every student, mentoring admitted at-risk students, and improving counseling services to minority students. Individual campuses adopted programs specific to their institutional missions. UW-Madison, for example, established a Multicultural Center, and reorganized the governance of fraternities and sororities in order to prevent discriminatory acts.

Some students claimed the university broke its promise and was not delivering as advertised. In the August 13, 1991, issue of Madison's *Capital Times*, page 3A, under a headline that read, "Minority students chastise UW," students were reported to have claimed that racism on the campus and in the community "... detracts from minority students obtaining the education they're seeking ..." A graduate student claimed, "We're basically counseling ourselves and encouraging each other." In early 1992, an alleged fight took place between a white student and a black student at a women's dormitory at UW-Madison.[135] Heather Nelson, co-president of the Wisconsin Black Student Union, was quoted as saying, "The response [from the campus administration] has been far too slow. I think it is incidents of this nature that explain why we are not coming [to the UW] and why those of us who are here would like to leave." James Sulton, special assistant to the president for minority affairs, said, "We would like to think that higher education is exempt from [racism], but it is a part of it."

The other element of campus environment has been how faculty and students perceive attitudes toward women and minorities on the faculty. If the perception is that discrimination is not stopped, that perception will continue to contribute to a negative environment. As regents address the campus environment, I hope they will realize that unless they represent the needs of *all* students, no one will. They will have to guard against those who believe that universities have gone too far or that the initiatives are not relevant to the times. Arguments that appeal to many — and that could be the unraveling of the various multicultural programs in place, which are an important factor in determining the quality of the campus environment for all students — are expressed by a growing voice in the nation. How much should we do for those who claim to be disadvantaged? What is enough? We have an open society and those who want to participate can do so. If you want to make it, you simply have to work hard. If you don't make it, you haven't tried.

The board does not recognize that by the year 2000, one-third of our population will be "minorities." If they are not all part of the mainstream of American life, there is a limited future for us. While it is true that the university cannot take the place of the greater society in dealing with the quality of the K-12 system, the ravages of broken homes, ghettos, drugs, etc., it can do a great deal by setting an example for others to follow if it has the will. We must set an example by behaving better than society at large. We should do what we can to increase the number of minority and disadvantaged students in our universities by active recruitment and by engaging in pre-college programs. We must train teachers who will work in the inner cities. And once students are brought onto our campuses, we must make sure they find a supportive and accepting environment. That includes mentoring when needed, offering remedial education courses, and taking action allowed by law to deal with discriminatory behavior. We should pursue exchange programs with black universities so that there are more African American faculty on our campuses. We should actively recruit such faculty. We can do this for African Americans, Native Americans, and Hispanics. Then we would be "mainstream" America.

Will it make a difference? There is evidence that it will. UW-Milwaukee's experience shows that retention can be improved. UW-Madison has proven that minority faculty can be recruited where there is a will emanating from the chancellor's office to do so. Black students and Jewish students are more willing now than before to carry on a meaningful dialogue, a sign of improving the campus environment for both. The ugly "Fiji" nights and "Slave auctions" are gone from UW campuses.

Hard-headed American corporations such as Phillip Morris, Lilly Endowment, and the Ford Foundation understand the need to address these issues, and provide universities with substantial funds for program development purposes.[136] One does not have to be a "raving liberal" to endorse these initiatives, nor does one's proclaimed conservatism prevent one from understanding the need for regent action.

When regents speak publicly, they need to be mindful of the impact of their statements, so that they do not, unwittingly, add to the hostility and intimidation that already exists toward minority students. Read the words of some regents and judge for yourself whether they send a message of caring to all students:

- "I believe in fairness for everyone, including minorities. I believe in rewarding those who deserve to be rewarded and I believe in competition. All of those things are a part of me as a businessman, and I think it applies to the university system. Using some of those principles might help more than all the things we've tried to do to make Design for Diversity work."[137]

- "My feeling is we have gone too far in providing social services and things that could be tightened up, to the detriment of our basic task of providing our children with an education."[138]

- "It bothers some of the conservatives on the Board of Regents that we spend a lot of time, money and commotion on special interest groups."[139]

- In speaking of the proposed conduct code revision, one regent was quoted as saying, "The composition of the board has changed. ... Some of my friends on the board who feel like I do have said, 'Let's drop it.'"[140]

Compare this, if you will, with then Acting President Lyall's public statement made at the board meeting on November 8, 1991, after reporting that the court had overturned the code revision: "I want all currently enrolled students, prospective students, and the parents of students to know that conduct intended to demean a person or prevent them from pursuing an education has no place in the UW System. And I call upon students, faculty and staff at all of our institutions to make it your personal responsibility to convey this to all at your institution. We, and I mean all of us, are accountable for the society we create on our campuses; tolerance and civility are principles we will not and must not abandon."[141]

So that we don't become too pleased with our progress to date, let me remind you of the results of a survey conducted by People for the American Way. It found that 50% of American young people said that the state of race relations in the United States was generally bad.[142]

It became clear to me early on that a System staff position assigned the responsibility of ensuring that regent policy be implemented was the way to ensure that campuses viewed minority inclusion as a priority for the board and the System. When the regents held hearings before adopting Design for Diversity, those at the campus level who were assigned the responsibility for minority recruitment and retention often complained that they had received little or no instruction on how to perform their duties. They said they lacked

supervision, and that there was little, if any, coordination between departments. Some met each other for the first time at the hearings. That indicated
to me and others that some campuses were only paying lip service to the
regent policies. The presence of a special assistant to the president would
make a crucial difference in how diversity policies were carried out in the
future. To abandon the position or to reassign it to the vice president for
academic affairs would send a strong, negative message regarding the
resolve of the System administration and the regents.

**Suggestions regarding quality of campus environment
that do not require funding:**

- Joint recruiting by the UW System and VTAE in the high schools would
  go a long way toward helping students make proper choices.

- Regents and System administrators need to implement more cooperative efforts with the VTAE system as an integral part of overall goals to
  help minority students. Sulton reported that by the year 2000, one-third
  of the U.S. work force will be people of color, and by the year 2050 that
  will be true of about one-half of the work force. It is essential that all
  avenues be used to educate this work force. "There is no reason to be
  selfish in minority education." In order to achieve these goals, he said
  that the System must work with VTAE and independent colleges. He
  went on to say that minorities enrolled in any form of post-secondary
  education would be considered a victory.[143] On June 15, 1989, I wrote
  Regent President Schilling urging such cooperation, including getting
  the message out early that post-secondary education is important and
  that each of our systems has virtue. On July 5, 1989, the VTAE state
  board adopted a policy reaffirming its priority of recruiting and retain-
  ing minority students and encouraged support of "joint VTAE/UW ...
  and VTAE/DPI initiatives.[144] I hope the board formalizes these relationships.

- Design for Diversity continues to need a special assistant to the president if it is to be implemented. Regents should not tolerate inaction at
  the campus level.

- Annual reports on the progress of diversity initiatives mandated by the
  legislature must be monitored by the regents.

- ROTC should be discontinued at all campuses except UW-Madison, until such time as it stops its discriminatory behavior. As for UW-Madison,
  the attorney general should be asked whether ROTC is the only lawful
  program for meeting the mandate of the Morrill Act.

Options for Downsizing/Retaining Quality — An Overview

Most of the suggestions I have made do not require additional funding,
but, nonetheless, deal directly with quality issues. Even if all of the

suggestions I have made are adopted and implemented, there will still remain a shortfall in funding needs. Given a realistic assessment of funding sources, I believe that downsizing in one form or another is inevitable in order to avoid horrendous tuition increases, which are, at the very least, politically unacceptable and unfair to students. Board members should not be afraid to ask questions and demand answers, because if they do not, the legislature will. General answers, such as, "That won't save much," are not enough. How much is "much"?

Ideally, it would be wonderful if the status quo could be preserved, and the legislature would provide more money, and/or the students and Wisconsin taxpayers would willingly pay substantially higher tuition. None of these scenarios is likely to happen. Old solutions won't work. Internally, there will always be resistance to change. The resistance to downsizing will be even greater because employees will feel threatened. The board will be charged with micro-managing and attempting to destroy the quality of public higher education. That is the expected response from those who do not want change. There will also be political falling outs. Legislators will hear from their constituents if there are any major changes that affect students, such as a reduction in the number of class sections, consolidation of programs, or adoption of higher admission standards. This is to be expected when public institutions change.

The business community will also be heard from when the board announces plans to downsize. It happened in the past and it will happen in the future. The board has to make it clear that its statutory obligation is to preserve and enhance the quality of the System's mission — instruction, research, and outreach. Bringing business to the community is not part of the System's mission.

The board must examine *all* options in order to show they are serious about preserving the quality of our education system and are not taking the easy way out by focusing only on tuition and the state to answer funding needs. I will provide some options. It would be appropriate to have the regents speak with the political leaders as various options are being discussed so that there are no surprises. This is the approach that worked with enrollment management.

There is no one option that will solve all of the problems. Since it will take a combination of options, all should be seriously considered. These options were not adequately addressed during the time I served on the board. I sense a new resolve on the part of the System administration and, hopefully, the regents, to consider them now. To begin, I believe emphatically that no matter how downsizing is approached, the savings realized must stay in the System. If not, the desired result will not be achieved and the effort will be for naught.

The options I will discuss are:

- Closing campuses.

- Consoliding or regionalizing programs.

- Consolidating some administrative costs among campuses close to each other geographically.

- Converting some baccalaureate campuses to two-year campuses.

- Eliminating substandard programs.

Some options may impact access in one form or another. That has to be weighed against preserving quality.

Option: Close campuses

Because closing campuses is a political hot potato, the issue is ignored. Until the figures are developed, the debate cannot take place in any meaningful way. I believe it should — and soon.

Some would argue that since 80+% of the costs for maintaining a campus are personnel-driven, little would be gained by closing a campus. While the issue was discussed informally during my term on the board, it was never dealt with seriously because of fear of political implications. What legislator would favor closing a campus in his or her district? In the hope of depoliticizing such a decision, the statutes were amended to give the regents authority to close campuses. Will they? A financial analysis should be provided the board that includes a detail of fixed and variable costs for each campus. While it may be true that personnel costs account for the largest portion of costs, they are by no means fixed. For example, those employees who perform administrative functions may not all need to be replaced if a campus were closed and students attended other System institutions. It follows that to the extent resources are spent on fewer institutions, the quality of those remaining will be enhanced.

The *Isthmus*, a Madison newspaper, reported on December 6, 1991, that political commentator William Krause recalled that UW-Parkside and UW-Green Bay were built as a result of "... pure politics. The numbers were all hoked up. ... The campuses, obviously, should never have been built." State Senator Fred Risser is quoted as saying, "... [H]ad the enrollment projections been what actually transpired, I don't think the [old UW] system would have expanded."

Legislator David Clarenbach is quoted as saying, "There is no question that the quality of the UW System and UW-Madison are both diluted by the large number of campuses and the inefficiencies that are created by conflicting and overlapping programs. As tuition skyrocketed to pay for this diffused system, and as enrollment caps continue to deny access, I think there will be growing recognition that something else has to give. But right now, campus closures are not even on the radar screen yet."

The *Wisconsin State Journal* reported on April 16, 1992 (p.1A), that Regent President Steil said the System might consider closing or merging several campuses in western Wisconsin, where there are three in close proximity to each other. *The Capital Times* quoted Steil as saying, "There may be a need to consolidate River Falls, Stout and Eau Claire. I wonder if we can afford all three." The article says Steil noted that UW-Superior is near the University of Minnesota campus in Duluth, which Wisconsin students could attend without paying out-of-state tuition because of the reciprocity agreement with Minnesota.

This quoted comment met with an immediate negative reaction. The UW-Superior Student Senate, understandably, circulated a petition stating, "We ask that all officials in the UW System eliminate all discussions related to any possible closing of UWS [UW-Superior] or the reduction of any present academic program."[145] Governor Tommy Thompson said, "I do not support any consolidation or closing any campus."[146] A state senator from the area stated, "It's obviously a terrible idea." System President Lyall was quoted as saying, "Our campuses are full and we have no plans to close or merge any of our institutions" (*Milwaukee Sentinel*, April 16, 1992). She said in a television interview a few days later that closing a campus would not save "much," but didn't define "much." The *Oshkosh Northwestern* commented editorially on April 19, 1992, that UW-Oshkosh was not being "targeted by Steil or by the system for any substantial changes." Steil stated later that he did not advocate closing any campus, but rather the merging of some academic programs.[147] On May 1, 1992, *The Capital Times* (p. 1B) quoted Steil, "It was out of context, that's all I can say. ... A campus brings some degree of economic help, wherever it is. At the same time, we have an obligation to the citizens of Wisconsin to provide education for them, if we can do it." On May 3, 1992, Steil said he did not expect any campus closings in the near future, but favored consolidating some programs.[148]

The *Green Bay Press Gazette* commented editorially on April 19, 1992, that closing campuses was a bad idea, because, among other considerations, "A university makes a substantial contribution to economic development in a community and region." In looking for savings, closing campuses should take a "back seat" to other efforts, such as having UW campuses "explore additional ways to cooperate with each other and with the state Vocational, Technical and Adult Education System." The introduction of the economic argument is not new. When the regents announced the first enrollment management program, bankers from Whitewater attended the hearings to complain that a reduction in enrollment at UW-Whitewater would hurt the economy of that community. That argument ignores the mission of the System, as explained previously.

Option: Consolidate programs

The Superior Evening Telegram, on April 15, 1992, quoted System President Lyall as saying that while merging campuses was not being talked about, the System "has and will continue actively to explore and look for ways to eliminate a duplication of programs. ..." *The Daily Cardinal*, a UW-Madison student newspaper, reported on April 16, 1992, that Lyall pointed out the difference between closing a campus and consolidating programs, which she apparently favors. "We could take teacher education from one program and combine it with a teacher education program at another campus, creating a regional teacher education program. That's not the same as closing campuses." Those programs ought to be identified and action taken.

The consolidation program exercise could take two forms. When programs can be consolidated regionally, they should be. Programs that are graduating more students than they can place should be consolidated. It is a reasonable way to deal with limited resources. One example is worth noting. "For 1990-91, 4,686 students completed teacher certification programs in UW System institutions," whereas in "1991-92, Wisconsin public schools hired 2,583 inexperienced teachers who were prepared in the UW System institutions."[149] Is it not time to consolidate teacher education programs? By doing so would we improve the quality of the education received by teachers of tomorrow? Would we not free up needed funds for other programs? I believe we would.

Option: Consolidate administrative costs among campuses

Refer to the previous discussion in Chapter VII's "Reduce System and Campus Administrative Costs." It is an option worth looking at.

Option: Convert some four-year campuses to two-year centers

The board of regents should study the impact of converting some four-year campuses to two-year centers. They should specifically consider UW-Parkside, which is very close to Milwaukee, and UW-Superior which is close to Duluth. Because of Wisconsin's reciprocity agreements with Minnesota, the University of Minnesota-Duluth is an acceptable alternative.

Option: Eliminate substandard programs

While I served on the board, we attempted to deal with this issue. An example of our effort was the determination that MBA programs not qualifying for accreditation would be eliminated. Once a substandard program is eliminated, that program should not be reinstated until there is overwhelming proof that it is needed on that campus. The regents need to establish standards and methods to identify such programs.

Summary

I have offered 44 suggestions that, in my view, would enhance quality. Most of them would not require additional funding. I have also proposed four options that would help the System deal with a realistic assessment of state funding and avoid tuition increases beyond inflation. Now it is up to the board to take action.

IX.

Moving the "Battleship" in the Future by Changing Attitudes

Conclusion #7: In the last analysis, those within and outside the UW System need to change their attitudes and assumptions. Our way is not the only way. The lack of System flexibility is counter-productive to the public interest. There is a need for a new strategic plan that will take the System into the 21st century. All of this is necessary if we are to maintain the quality of the System, the state's most important asset.

Regents

We all have "mental baggage." That is difficult to overcome. If we recognize our "mental baggage" for what it is, we can put it aside in the best interest of those we agree to serve. I urge regents to step back from their preconceived ideas about the role of public higher education in our society and leave their political loyalties outside the board room. They have distinct roles to play if the quality of public higher education is to be preserved. No one else can play the roles of governance and advocacy. Regents are not regulators responsible for the state's commitments outside of public higher education. That is the role of the executive and legislative branches of government. Regents must be advocates for university administrators, faculty, staff, and students.

As citizens, members of the board, and advocates for students, regents have an obligation to first examine all options before looking to the state or students for more funding. That is particularly true in these times. Tuition must be kept from rising faster than inflation; otherwise, ability to pay will be the gatekeeper of admission.

Based on the most recent budget discussions, it seems obvious to me that the board must deal with change in a radically different manner. At the November 1992 meeting, the board approved the budget for 1993-1995. It contained an 8% tuition increase and 5% faculty compensation increase. Both the regent president and vice president doubted that either proposal would be supported by the governor and said so publicly. Other regents, even though they supported the budget proposals, expressed their concern that higher tuition would keep prospective students out, that program consolidation should move forward more quickly, that the LAB audit of faculty workloads, scheduled for 1993, would reveal "real problems that we have in this university," and that business as usual was out.[1] I asked a board member why, in view of these publicly expressed concerns and doubts, the board would approve the budget? He replied it was done in self-defense, since other state agencies were requesting large increases.

The board must display a sense of urgency. It is not credible to state publicly that the quality of the System is in jeopardy and then "study" options endlessly. Timetables for completion of studies should be shortened.

System regents have a rare opportunity to make a difference. System President Lyall has set out the challenges. She now needs the full support of the board if the obstacles are to be overcome. The regents need to exercise their authority, as stated in Chapter 36, Wisconsin Statutes. Issues such as faculty workload and tenure are properly within the jurisdiction of the regents because they affect the quality of the mission.

In my view, it *is* time for a new strategic plan. The board must deal with the issues confronting the System in a substantially more productive way. It is time to back off and look at the total picture rather than work on small pieces. The board should direct System administrators to present a strategic plan based on the following assumptions:

- The System will receive approximately the same percentage of state tax revenue as it has in the past, plus or minus adjustments for general economic conditions.

- The current tuition schedule will remain in effect with adjustments for inflation.;

- Faculty and staff will be paid competitively.

- All missions, including undergraduate education, will be carried out in a manner consistent with quality.

Given those assumptions, the budget, based on current funding levels, will be well in excess of $2 billion per year. What kind of a model can be structured? How many students can be educated while maintaining quality? What should be the minimum retention rate for each campus? What about faculty teaching loads, faculty student ratios, etc.?

System and Campus Administrators

Managing our great public universities is an awesome responsibility. I respect those who serve in those positions. I do believe that to be responsible leaders they must help the board confront the obstacles to change and challenge the status quo. While campus administrators may come from the faculty, their loyalty must be to the institution and must not be limited to the faculty. Above all, they must remember that the students are the "customers." In the private sector, we say that when employee satisfaction takes precedence over customer satisfaction, we go broke.

System and campus administrators, faculty, and staff need to shed their paranoia about "outsiders," meaning political leaders, the media, and regents. The System is a public institution, and the public has a right to know what is going on. When a mistake is made (and they will be made), admit it and correct it. As my father would say, "If it's raining outside, don't tell me the sun is shining!" Those within the System who cannot shed their views that anyone not on the "inside" is an "outsider" and cannot be trusted ought to get out. They do a great deal of harm to credibility with the public. In addition, System Administration must become much more comfortable relying on regents to carry the message to governing bodies, the media, and the public at large. They will be seen as "honest brokers," whereas university employees are often seen as self-serving.

In presenting the budget to the board, governor, and legislature, System Administrators should not ask for more money to carry out the core mission — undergraduate education — but rather explain what *other* services it may have to reduce in order to fund the core mission.

System and campus administrators must be careful how information is presented. Public institutions are subject to public scrutiny, and how positions are presented does make a difference to our supporters and detractors.

There must be accountability at every level. That means that those who do not carry out regent policy must be held accountable, tenure not withstanding.

Faculty

Robert Birnbaum, associate director of the National Center for Post-secondary Governance and Finance and professor of higher education at Teachers College, Columbia University, wrote:

> The days of amateur administration when faculty temporarily assumed administrative positions and then returned to the classroom are long since over at most institutions. As institutions become large and more complex, knowledge of legal precedents, federal regulations, management information systems, student financial aid procedures, grant and contract administration, and many other areas of specialized expertise is needed to accomplish many administrative tasks. Faculty and administrators fill different roles, encounter and are influenced by different aspects of the environment and have different backgrounds. ... Administration and management can become so complex that even those faculty who are interested in governance may not have the time or the expertise to fully understand the processes of decision making or resource acquisition and allocation that are at the heart of many governance issues.[2]

Faculty in Wisconsin are eager to point out that shared governance was invented here. If shared governance means faculty veto over regent or administrative decisions, then, with all due respect, it is an idea whose time has passed. On the other hand, if it means faculty will devote themselves to carrying out the missions of the university — instruction, research, and outreach — and the reward system of tenure and post-tenure review actually reflects that devotion, then shared governance is, indeed, a concept that will keep the university great and responsive to the needs of citizens and students. Faculty have had difficulty understanding and coming to terms with the duties and obligations of the board of regents as defined in Chapter 36, Wisconsin Statutes. I hope this book is helpful in adding to their understanding.

Political Leaders

Our way is not the only way. I suppose every political body believes its way of doing things is the best. It is good to keep in mind that other states manage their public universities quite differently than Wisconsin does. We can learn by examining those differences.

Michigan, for example, is one of 11 states where one or more of the universities were created by the constitution rather than the legislature, as is the case in Wisconsin.[3] There is a major difference in perception. "Constitutional provision for a public university is based on the theory that education should be a fourth branch of government, and, inasmuch as it underlies the well-being of the whole society, should be separated from the other, essentially, political activities of government. Opponents of this theory contend that the nature and scope of all of education is a matter of public policy and, therefore, should be the responsibility of the governor and the legislature."[4]

In Michigan, the university submits a total budget to the legislature, which it can adopt or change. The determination of each line is made by the governing board, not the legislature. "The board must, of course, appeal to the legislature for funds, so that practically, a way is available for an aggressive or hostile legislature to influence the institution by threatening to cut its appropriations. The courts have repeatedly ruled, however, that once funds have been appropriated to the institution, it becomes the prerogative of the board to administer them."[5]

In Wisconsin, by contrast, the legislature often gets into such details as faculty and administrative compensation, supplies and expense budgets, and tuition, and the governor can "line item" veto the budget. As a result, the System cannot possibly achieve the same degree of flexibility that a constitutionally created university system can, which would permit it to move amounts from one line to another in order to respond to changing compensation pressures, etc. We need to move in the direction of greater flexibility. Because the System was created by the legislature, we need its agreement and support to make this happen. We can improve our way and still protect the public. Even though it is not likely that the Wisconsin constitution will be changed to alter the status of the System, there is much that could be done to bring about needed change in the manner in which the System is managed.

A 1992 article in *The Chronicle of Higher Education* carried the headline, "In Tough Times, Some Colleges Find Conservative Management Pays Off."[6] While the experiences related won't change the past, they may help show the way for the future. In observing that some campuses did not experience layoff and enrollment reductions, the author explains that those institutions avoided the "excesses of the 1980s" by "choosing to grow cautiously and selectively." That may be well and good for private institutions, but public institutions are subject to the pressures of government officials and the public, who want unlimited access, top quality, low taxes, and low tuition.

In view of changing circumstances, everyone will have to be realistic about what is possible. That was my purpose in making suggestions and proposing options. None of that will work if everyone denies that there is a problem or that every proposal is politically unacceptable. All of the slick slogans and statistical manipulations will not solve the problem. At risk is the quality of public higher education in Wisconsin and in the nation. That is why attitudes have to change. If political leaders insist that the size of the System, in terms of campuses, programs, and students, must remain unaltered, and at the same time, they will not provide more funding, then quality will be jeopardized. Wisconsin Statutes were amended to allow the board to close campuses. That was done in order to remove that issue from the political arena. It should not be brought back into that arena.

I find little disagreement with the notion that public bureaucracies are not efficient and flexibility is needed — there are too many layers of oversight that slow the process down. For example, buildings cost substantially more because of the elaborate bureaucratic hurdles that drag out the process. Bureaucracies tend to get larger and larger and, finally, become difficult to manage. They need to be broken down into manageable units. If that is done, then how do we achieve accountability and control in order to protect the public's interest? On the other hand, it is argued that it is in the public's interest to slow the process down, get more people working on the decisions. It produces a better end product and achieves accountability. The public has a sense of ownership and does not want to give it up.

What does it mean to protect the public's interest when we speak of public higher education? Carried to its absurd conclusion, every taxpayer ought to attend every board of regents meeting and participate in all the decisions. Instead, the legislative and executive branches of government represent the public's interest and assure accountability, so the theory goes.

Public officials need to redefine their roles vis a vis public higher education. They cannot govern it, as much as they try. That is why it is important that the Senate confirm regents who have a commitment to and knowledge of the System, and who are willing to work to maintain quality. After that, regents must be given the authority to maintain quality. Public officials do have an obligation to hold the board accountable for the quality of our System institutions. But accountability cannot be demanded without authority. Attempting to establish and oversee every line item of the budget very substantially erodes regent authority. Once the budget has been approved, regents and System administrators should be allowed to govern. That may involve some unpopular decisions, such as downsizing by reducing enrollment or closing a campus. It is better to allow the board to make those decisions, if for no other reason than they are politically unpopular. In addition, the board must have the authority to set compensation levels for faculty, academic staff, and administrators. The current method does not work, and leaves the universities non-competitive with peer institutions. The need to engage in periodic "catch-up" is demoralizing at best.

We must be bold enough to deal with the issues of accountability and flexibility in a way that will ensure the quality of public higher education and still protect the public. I have no fears that governing boards will "give away the store" or that university administrators are basically incompetent. On the contrary, I believe that both governing boards and administrators are capable of doing a better job if there were a restructuring of the budget process. Specifically, the language of Chapter 36, Wisconsin Statutes should be changed to permit the board of regents to set the compensation of all System employees and permit reallocation of base budgets when deemed necessary by the board. If the System is to maintain its quality, establishing competitive compensation for faculty, staff, and administrators is a must. The current process has resulted in unwarranted delays in responding to needs, and it results in a non-competitive and lopsided compensation system.

Line item budgeting is counter-productive. On July 9, 1992, I wrote System Regent President George Steil and offered my help in bringing about these changes:

> There is no question in my mind that the present method of budgeting is counter productive. Once the System and the board knows how much money it has to work with *in total*, it can plan accordingly, keeping in mind the proper level of compensation for faculty, staff, and administrators, as well as supplies and expenses, maintenance, etc. No group is better able to deal with these issues than the board, which is supposed to be the representative of both the public's and the university's interests. In

order to balance both, tough decisions have to be made, some of which will not be popular politically, but necessary, none the less, to maintain the quality of the System. What body is better prepared to make those decisions and take the 'heat' than the board? It would be a great day if the political leaders would take the position that they hold the board accountable for the quality of the System, and, at the same time, give it the full authority to make it happen.

Wisconsin political leaders should consider having the State Building Commission, working with the System, develop statutory changes that would shorten the timeframe for completing building projects. The oversight of those buildings should be turned over to the System. In the alternative, the supervisory function of the System and campuses should be increased.

The System does not have flexibility in personnel matters, and has little incentive to be efficient. For example, System administrators can move non-personnel items in the budget to the personnel line, but not the other way around. And if personnel is increased above the pay plan set by the state, the System must justify the increase for each person based on merit. Both are unnecessary.

Public officials do not help when they accuse the UW System of being inefficient or unresponsive but then refuse to allow reallocation from the base budget as proposed by the "Quality Reinvestment" plan. Of course, there are inefficiencies and unresponsive behavior in the university, just as there are in any other public or private bureaucracy. When I was president of the board, I worried a great deal about the inefficiencies, because I felt an obligation to the taxpayers to spend their money wisely. I compared our System with those of other states and concluded that we were generally more efficient than others. That did not mean we could not improve. Indeed, the regents appointed a special committee from among their members to deal with this issue on an ongoing basis. But no matter how many committees are formed, how many Legislative Audit Bureau reports are published, there will always be some inefficiencies. It is naive to think otherwise. But to "beat up" on the System for being inefficient is unproductive, to say the least.

"Strengthening Leadership in Colleges and Universities," a report sponsored by the Association of Governing Boards of Universities and Colleges, concluded that based on 848 interviews of current and former presidents and spouses, trustees, faculty members, executives of search or consulting agencies, and state and federal officials, that, "Undue public intrusion still exists in many — perhaps most — states."[7] The report recommends that public authorities can be "particularly helpful" by:

* Eliminating line-item budgeting. "Post-audit is better than pre-audit."

- Appointing people to the board who have the long-term welfare of the institution in mind.
- Keeping partisan politics out of the institutions.
- Periodically reviewing what is best subject to public control and what is best subject to institutional control.

The Wisconsin Governor's Commission on Compensation in the UW System recommended more flexibility for the regents to set tuition, "management of the operations, including setting faculty and academic staff compensation levels and procedures," while having greater accountability measures in place for "effectiveness, efficiency, quality, access, diversity, stewardship of assets and contribution to compelling state needs."[8] While in my view, the report was flawed with its emphasis on raising tuition, nonetheless, it did propose a fundamental change in the approach to governance and accountability, which some of us have urged all along.

Now it is up to the governor and legislature. It will be interesting to listen to the debate over more flexibility balanced by accountability, as the Commission suggested. Some will argue that because there are limited state resources the legislature must keep tight controls on the System. Others will argue the exact opposite, contending that precisely because of limited state resources, the regents need more flexibility. Some will argue that based on past experience, the System cannot be trusted. In the end, the issue will be resolved based on trust. Past relationships between the System and political leaders will play an important role. Milton Neshek, former regent and commission head, said, "The whole thrust of the recommendations are to give the university the ability to manage without being micro-managed by external agencies."[9]

The regents have been given the statutory authority to make decisions to preserve the quality of the System. They cannot make those decisions if they are "vetoed" by public officials even before they are considered.

The Media

The media ought to be a bit more thoughtful in how it presents information about the System, which in my view is the state's most important asset. It is easier to destroy the System than to maintain its quality. The media could play a significant role in maintaining quality by helping educate the public and legislature about the difficult choices.

Conclusion

In his book, *Choosing Quality, Reducing Conflict Between the State and the University*,[10] Frank Newman observed:

- "Despite the assumption of different goals, the greatest prestige and most rewards accrue to the research university. The result is an inexorable drive within the faculty to try to turn each institution into some form of a research university ... to move from teacher's college to state college to state university to research university [and to Division I athletics]."[11]

- The governance structure can be a positive force in maintaining the quality of the university if leadership "establishes a clear vision of the role, mission, and standards of the whole system as well as [a clear vision] for each university campus and recognizes the difference between them. Political leadership is required from the heads of the governance structure," which includes the board president. The system or board must set clear rules and priorities, including priorities for each campus. The system or governing board must enforce the rules set for the campuses.[12]

- In order to be great, a university must not only excel at research. It must also "excel at undergraduate education." It must define its particular niche and focus its resources accordingly, since it cannot be everything to everybody. Where it does not aspire to greatness, it should not spend its resources. Campus leaders must "set standards, evaluate results, eliminate outmoded or ineffective programs and search relentlessly for ways to improve." Universities must take action in order to avoid frustration of the state, which may take inappropriate action. "Academics need to remember that left without a solution to a pressing problem, the political system will create one."[13]

- Governing boards can encourage greatness by making sure that their agendas focus on policy issues. They must ask the hard and fundamental questions about the improvement of quality, improvement of faculty, "who is admitted and why," how much students are learning, the retention of majority and minority students, and the university's contribution to the state's economy. Boards should see actual programs in order to understand the needs of students.[14]

- States can encourage greatness by avoiding mandates and creating incentives, reducing unnecessary regulation, defining more clearly university responsibility, and insisting that the missions of each university be consistent with current and future needs of the state. The governor and legislators "must support boards, chancellors, and presidents who take the risks inherent in building a great and responsive university and analyze state actions to prevent unthinking disincentives to risk taking," and must "insist on a university of quality."[15] Newman quotes T. Edward Hollander as saying, "States should lead, not regulate; challenge, not dictate; set initiatives and climate, but leave the institutions free to respond."[16]

Vision for the Future — Confronting the Status Quo

Is the System planning for the future so that those who can benefit from a quality education and receive a college degree will not be turned away? Is there a vision for the future?

I have outlined a number of suggestions and options to indicate that there are ways of dealing with the quality issues that do not involve more funding. In addition, it is time for a new and different strategic plan. While some will continue to pressure for more faculty, more students, and more funds, it is clear to me that there must be a departure from the status quo.

I wrote about the need for "outsiders" and "insiders" to change their attitudes in order for the status quo to be confronted. It is easier not to make major changes. But that is precisely what is needed.

In a feature article in *Time* magazine, "Campus of the Future," some interesting observations and predictions based on budget deficits and the need to plan accordingly were made:[17]

- Critics of universities are asking whether students are receiving good value as tuition rises faster than inflation.

- Some of the small liberal arts schools with meager endowments and largely local reputation will have closed their doors or merged with larger, more stable schools.

- Some new schools will open (two-year community colleges), emphasizing service-oriented courses.

- Neighboring schools will share facilities and courses.

- There will be growing pressure to have the curriculum be more practical and less theoretical.

- Students will be under growing pressure to take two foreign languages, with growing emphasis on Chinese, Japanese, and Russian.

- All universities, including world-class research institutions, will place greater emphasis on the quality of classroom teaching. There will be growing pressure on the faculty to spend more time with first- and second-year undergraduates.

- Universities will have to adapt to a more diverse student body — not only women and minorities, but older and part-time students.

- A growing number of students will earn degrees — without ever setting foot on campus — through the use of computers, fiber optics, satellite dishes, etc. Distance learning is already taking place at the University of Minnesota and Penn State. Ball State University has wired 200 classrooms and laboratories with a fiber-optics video information system. This has not only increased student interest in the courses, but allow the courses to be transmitted to off-campus locations. Out-of-town speakers can be beamed directly into the classrooms.

- As there is a growing interest in new kinds of alliances with business, so there will have to be a re-examination of conflict of interest and ethics rules.

- Many colleges will have to offer a narrower range of courses.

- The code word for the future is "accountability."

- Some schools have chosen to dismantle their bureaucracies to devote more resources to labs, libraries, and classrooms.

- Critics of academia say universities have for too long emulated government, which means they have been run badly and have bureaucratic bloat. Boston University's John Silber said, "Harvard doesn't have a financial problem, it has a management problem."

Is public higher education up to the challenge? Is the UW System up to the challenge? During August 1991, Kenneth S. Shaw resigned his position as president to become chancellor of Syracuse University. After a nationwide search, the UW Board of Regents, in April 1992, appointed Katharine C. Lyall to the position of president. She had served as acting president between the time Robert O'Neil left and Shaw was appointed, and again when Shaw left. She had served as System executive vice president and vice president for academic affairs. My term on the board expired May 1, 1991, so I could not vote for Lyall although she was my favorite candidate. I made no secret of it and expressed it to anyone who cared to listen. The reasons were simple. I knew her quite well from my experience on the board. She was responsible for seeing to it that the *Future* strategic plan was begun; she and I had many discussions about management issues and the needs of the System. She was always frank, knew what had to be done, and stated her positions clearly. She has been unafraid to spell out her positions on many issues:

- Balance enrollment against funding levels.[18]

- Fight for competitive faculty salaries.[19]

- Reduce tension between lawmakers and UW officials.[20]

- Put quality ahead of access.[21]

- "If we don't change, change will roll over us, anyway."[22]

- Increase efforts to attract more minorities.[23]

- Consolidate programs and "stop trying to be everything to everybody."[24]

- Regionalize fields of study to specific campuses.[25]

- Establish a five-year tenure review of every tenured faculty member. This is critical to the credibility of the university.[26]

- Combine research programs directly with classroom teaching activities, rather than maintain the current system of independent research.[27]

Lyall knows what has to be done, can articulate it, and can make it happen. She is resourceful. Her "Quality Reinvestment Plan" directs campuses to reduce the size of the faculty and reinvest in priority items. An economist by training, she understands budgets; being a member of the academic community, she understands the culture of the campus. And from dealing with her in the past, I know her to be tough-minded. She understands the obstacles to change and is willing to confront them. Will the board support her? The going will not be smooth. It is essential that those who lead the System in the years ahead have an understanding of its problems, the skills to explain them, and the resolve to address them. I envy those board members who will have the opportunity to work with President Lyall.

The UW System — The State's Most Important Asset

I knew long before my term on the board expired that the UW System is the state's most important asset. The level of funding and the criticism it receives from the policymakers should not lead us to believe they do not agree. They have the impossible task of balancing priorities.

Those problems that are visible at the moment cry out for immediate attention. Those problems which may develop in the future are put on the back burner. For example, eliminating crime in the schools (K-12) and maintaining the quality of our universities are both competing for state resources; the needs to build prisons and support public universities are in conflict over funds. Will the public believe that by our policies today we can destroy the quality of our universities tomorrow? As we say on the street, "It's a hard sell!"

Mark G. Yudof, dean of the School of Law, University of Texas-Austin, commented on the relationship between the public university and the state. "Anguished cries from universities for higher budgets ... by themselves, will be of no avail. I suggest a higher-education compact. State universities should agree to establish realistic institutional priorities, to eliminate weak programs, and to act aggressively to reduce waste and duplication of effort. An institution's priorities should include providing high-quality under-graduate education. In return, state governments should agree to rededicate themselves to support the core public functions of the academy, functions that will never receive adequate support from other sources."[28] Given the limited resources of the University of Wisconsin System, I am constantly amazed that it continues to include within its institutions truly world class programs and scholars in research, instruction, and outreach. In addition, I know from my personal experience and that of my family that the UW System contributes immeasurably to the quality of life of the citizens of this state. What kind of a state would Wisconsin be without the UW System? What would the cultural life of our citizens be without the presence of System institutions in our communities? Where would small businesses turn for expertise? Where would farmers go for the latest in technology? And where would the critically ill turn for the most advanced medical care?

I am aware of a recent survey done in our state of 1,013 adults selected at random to answer questions about the UW System. It reported that "Overall, 93 percent said they had a very favorable or somewhat favorable impression of the UW System."[29] To the extent that I am critical, like my father asking us if there was a grade better than an "A" and knowing that there was, I am motivated by the belief that we can do better — we must do better. The old solutions will not work. The old assumptions need to be carefully scrutinized. Above all, we must remain focused on the goal of maintaining and improving the quality of public higher education.

Robert M. Rosenzweig, president of the Association of American Universities, said, "It's very hard to take an institution that has been around for 100 or 200 years, grab it by the scruff of the neck, shake it, and make it try to do something different. Change does happen, but slowly and incrementally."[30] Those of us who served on the board of regents know that only too well. Our efforts were directed toward speeding up the process so that currently enrolled students would benefit from the changes.

I am optimistic because the administrative leadership of the System understands the needs of our institutions and has the courage to deal with the options. The chancellors of the campuses are, by and large, talented and dedicated. If the regents assume the responsibilities assigned to them in Chapter 36, Wisconsin Statutes, the needed changes will take place — the battleship will be moved.

X.

Postscript — Donna Shalala: The Consummate Campus Administrator

In a previous chapter, I urged the UW System Board of Regents to deal with quality by dealing with quality's components: administrators, students, faculty, facilities, and campus environment.

On Friday December 11, 1992, President-elect Bill Clinton nominated UW-Madison Chancellor Donna Shalala to serve in his cabinet as secretary of the Department of Health and Human Services, the largest of the federal agencies. Because it is unprecedented for a chancellor of the UW System to be nominated for such high federal office, I believe it is appropriate to end this book with comments about Shalala, who was, in my view, the consummate campus administrator.

If bringing about change in a large university system is comparable to moving a battleship with one's bare hands, then bringing about change at a major research campus such as the UW-Madison is comparable to moving an air craft carrier with one's bare hands! While governing boards can make a substantial difference, campus administrators can contribute a great deal to overcoming the powerful forces that seek to maintain the status quo. Shalala was that kind of administrator.

My relationship with Shalala goes back to her selection as chancellor of UW-Madison. At that time, I was serving as president of the UW System Board of Regents. The former chancellor of UW-Madison, Irving Shain, retired. In accordance with Chapter 36, Wisconsin Statutes, the board of regents select the chancellors, the chief administrators of campuses in the System. We began the search process for UW-Madison's new chancellor.

UW System President Kenneth Shaw appointed a search and screen committee. Next, a "short list" of prospective candidates was sent to the board of regents. It was my responsibility as president of the board to appoint a special regent committee to interview those on the "short list" and recommend a decision to the full board after consulting with the System president. As president of the board, I also served on the special regent committee that conducted interviews with the finalists and unanimously recommended Donna Shalala to the full board.

We knew that Shalala had boundless energy, was highly intelligent, and had extensive experience in academic and governmental leadership roles.

253

We knew of her commitment to social change. During the interview we learned, to our delight, that she already understood the challenges that would face her as chancellor of the System's largest and most prestigious campus. What we had yet to learn was how forceful an administrator she would be.

President-elect Clinton was on target, in my opinion, when he said that Shalala had an unusual natural talent for leadership. She does possess an uncanny insight into good administrative practices. Her tenure as chancellor at UW-Madison proved that beyond a doubt. She understands that leaders must first establish goals, set standards, and implement them through specific programs that must be monitored. Shalala's tenure at UW-Madison provides a case study in effective campus leadership.

During the five short years she served as chancellor, Shalala transformed the role of her office and changed the culture of the campus. That was accomplished through the three-step process of management I outlined earlier: establish goals, implement them, and control the results through follow-up. Shalala made it clear early on that she had goals: every program would be of the highest quality or it would be discontinued; the campus was a *community of scholars and students* that would be inclusive in terms of students and faculty; the university must be a role model for the general society; in order to maintain its world-class status, UW-Madison must substantially increase private sector fund-raising; the infrastructure needs of the campus must be addressed; the university was a community within the greater community.

Shalala understood that establishing goals and setting standards was only half the battle. They have to be implemented. That meant dealing with problems that had been allowed to fester unaddressed. It meant changing the attitudes of campus administrators and faculty as well as putting together a team of her own that would buy into her goals. She had the courage of her convictions and proceeded accordingly. For those unfamiliar with UW-Madison, her goals may not sound particularly ambitious. But as we examine the goals in greater detail, we will see how bold they really were.

Goal: Program quality. Shalala demanded that every program be of the highest quality. Athletics were not exempt. The athletic department had been losing money when Shalala arrived on the scene. The board had been told repeatedly that the program was being turned around. Yet, income projections were overstated and expenses were understated. Matters became worse. Shalala fired the athletic director and the football coach, hired top people, backed them publicly, and the turnaround began.

She did not accept the often heard argument that the issue of quality of undergraduate education was being exaggerated. She said publicly that it *must* be a priority. She championed improvement of undergraduate education. To set an example for faculty, she taught a freshman course. She encouraged emeritus faculty to teach undergraduate seminars, and they did.

Another example — the Department of Dance had been a world-class department in earlier years. Its reputation had diminished dramatically. Shalala closed the department until she could find proper leadership.

The University of Wisconsin Hospital and Clinics for years had been attempting to deal with state bureaucracy. State government had prevented the institution, one of the top 25 in the nation, from responding to changing research and health-related issues in a timely manner. Shalala ordered a study, in which I participated. It concluded that the hospital needed more flexibility in matters affecting personnel, facilities, and equipment. Shalala embraced its conclusions and became a strong advocate for restructuring the governance of the hospital. She came under heavy criticism from some union leadership and media editorial writers alike. The plan to restructure the governance of the Hospital and Clinics was consistent with her goal of excellence for all programs. She was unafraid. And if time-honored procedures had to be challenged, so be it.

Goal: A university is a community of scholars and students. It must be inclusive in terms of students and faculty. It must be user-friendly, and serve as a model to the larger community. Shalala understood that a large campus, with an enrollment of over 40,000, could be threatening to some students. She determined that the campus must be "user-friendly." Long-studied plans for computer registration were finally implemented. Freshman orientation week took on a new flavor, with the added feature of Shalala teaching new students the words to "Varsity," the university's alma mater.

She described the campus as a community where *all* were welcome. But words were not enough. Immediately after coming to the campus, she learned of UW-Madison's plan to encourage multicultural diversity among the student body and faculty. Instead of continuing the studies and debates, within 30 days she instituted the "Madison Plan." It was responsive to the systemwide plan that called for aggressive efforts to recruit and retain minority and disadvantaged students and diversify the faculty by including more women and minorities. The idea was to have the campuses more closely resemble the demographics of the nation. Shalala was attacked by a group of faculty who claimed the plan would erode the quality of the institution. She did not budge in her resolve, and proved by example that the plan could be implemented and would work.

An example of her willingness to pay attention to her students: she became aware that some Jewish students felt alienated. Through the dean of students office, she created the Jewish Task Force to address the issues of concern.

Another example that has reached prominence was that ROTC discriminated against gay and lesbian students. Shalala advocated for her students and was an outspoken critic of federal policy, despite coming under fire from many.

She understood that language could send powerful signals. When a regent suggested at a board meeting that the state's prohibition against investing in corporations doing business in South Africa be rescinded, Shalala stood up and said, "No. Not until there is one person-one vote in South Africa." Her opinion was sustained by the attorney general.

Shortly after she arrived on campus, we met. I took the opportunity to explain to her that for over two decades, there had been efforts to establish an interdisciplinary program in Jewish studies. UW-Madison was one of the few major doctoral campuses in the United States without such a program. A brief time later, at her invitation, Professor George Mosse of the history department and I met with her. In typical Shalala style, she already knew that Mosse was among the most eminent scholars on the campus. She knew what I told her was correct, and she indicated her full support for the effort. Her charge to Mosse was to have the faculty develop and present a proposal. She pledged her support. The meeting lasted about 30 minutes. She had no trouble making up her mind and moving on to the next challenge. A faculty group met, a proposal was submitted, went through the proper committees, and the Center for Jewish Studies was established.

Goal: There was a need for more private sector funds if UW-Madison was to maintain its world-class status. Shalala understood that in order for public universities to stay world-class, they had to substantially increase private fund-raising. Before Shalala arrived, I had heard it said that a public university such as UW-Madison had difficulty raising money in the private sector because the large Wisconsin corporations and alumni felt they were giving because they were paying state income taxes. Shalala kept the goal in mind and successfully challenged all the previous assumptions. She reorganized leadership of the University of Wisconsin Foundation, the fund-raising arm of UW-Madison, and announced a goal that was ten times greater than any previous one. She immediately set about showing, by example, how her goal could be reached. She met with alumni all over the U.S. and as far away as the Orient. I have seen her in action. It is awesome to behold!

Goal: The needs of the infrastructure must be dealt with promptly. UW-Madison needed a massive infusion of funds to improve its research facilities. Time after time, the issue was discussed. Nothing happened. Hand wringing was the usual response. Undaunted by a lack of state funds, Shalala appointed a task force which identified the need for an additional $225 million. She told the board of regents she would raise $75 million from the private sector if the state would contribute $150 million. The board recommended the plan and the governor endorsed it. The plan is on target!

Goal: The university was a community within the greater community. Shalala did not believe in the separation of "town and gown." She reached out to civic and religious groups, and was a highly sought after speaker. For example, she joined with the Madison Jewish community in a public show of solidarity when Jewish buildings were defaced. Shalala believed that being chancellor of one of the world's great universities required her to speak out on the major social issues of society, and she did. She believed academic leaders must be engaged in the betterment of society. Scholarship alone was not acceptable. She was as comfortable wearing a university sweat shirt and rooting for the home team as she was hosting a campus-community reception for Bishop Desmond TuTu or Elie Weisel, conferring honorary degrees on distinguished alumni, or going toe to toe with political leaders in order to make the case for the needs of her campus.[1]

Since the announcement of her nomination, some pundits have proclaimed that Shalala has an agenda of political correctness, or P.C. as we know it — that diversity comes before quality. Those who make this argument leveled that same criticism at President Clinton for his choice of members of his cabinet. Earlier I described how those who opposed the regents' diversity programs leveled that same attack. Fortunately, those arguments are wearing thin and being ignored.

As all who have been in management know, proclaiming goals and acting upon them brings risk. Shalala was no different. As mentioned earlier, even before the Senate confirmation hearings, her detractors went public. Some said she was the princess of political correctness and invented the student conduct code that dealt with speech. Since I was president of the board at the time the code was adopted, I know that to be a false accusation. She did not invent the code. It came from the board only after consultation with constitutional scholars of the UW-Madison Law School, public hearing held by the board, and legislative approval. Shalala was in favor of the code, as were the other chancellors and the overwhelming majority of regents and Wisconsin legislators. Others accused her of building a large administrative cadre, that she was self-serving, etc., etc.

All of these comments are interesting because they ignore the main issue. Was she an effective administrator? My conclusions and those of many others are clear. Shalala was the consummate campus administrator. She not only understood but practiced solid management principles. That all too rarely takes place on campuses. She was committed to having the university play an important role in transforming our society so that it would become more inclusive. She brought to her position an enlightened view of social change, a superb intellect, a warm and caring heart, and a determination that everyone respected. While she will be sorely missed in Wisconsin, she will bring a breath of fresh air to the nation's capital.

Upon leaving UW-Madison for Washington, Shalala described herself by stating her views regarding qualifications of future campus leaders: "The new leaders of great institutions have to have more than great academic skills. They have to understand outside constituencies — the business community, minority groups and women's groups, social services, school systems. Wisconsin needs a leader who understands more than just the campus."[1]

Notes

Chapter 1

1. Board of Regents Resolution 5609, adopted October 5, 1990. Paraphrased from the introduction to *Planning the Future: Report of the Regents on the Future of the University of Wisconsin System*, December 1986.

Chapter 2

1. Agency Strategic Plan Programs and Services (Wisconsin Board of Vocational, Technical and Adult Education), January 1987: 8.

2. "Discussion Paper on Coordination with the University of Wisconsin System," prepared by the staff of VTAE for the VTAE Board Retreat, June 22-23, 1987.

3. *Ibid.*

4. *Fact Book for the University of Wisconsin System*, UW System Office of University Relations, 1990: 5.

5. *History Digest: Bulletin of the University of Wisconsin* (Madison: University News and Publications Service), 1971: 2.

6. Jacob O. Stampen, *Conflict, Accountability and the Wisconsin Idea: Relations Between Government and Higher Education in Wisconsin 1965 to 1978 (prepared for the Sloan Commission on Government and Higher Education, Cambridge, MA), December 1979.*

7. Jonathan Henkes, "Merger Twenty Years Later," *Wisconsin Ideas*, UW System, September 1991: 9.

8. *Fact Book for the University of Wisconsin System*, 1992: 56-57.

9. *Ibid.*, 55.

10. The UW System Board of Regents Briefing, July 1992: 1.

11. *Fact Book for the University of Wisconsin System*, 1992: 56-57.

12. *Wisconsin Week*, UW-Madison, September 1, 1992: 1.

13. "The Economic Impact of the U.W. Madison — An Update," Graduate School of Business, The School of Business, University of Wisconsin-Madison, April 19, 1991: 1. (For a more detailed study, see Monograph

No. 20, March 1985, Graduate School of Business, University of Wisconsin-Madison.)

14. *Fact Book for the University of Wisconsin System,* 1992: 20.

15. *Ibid.,* 65.

16. *Ibid.,* 33.

17. Wisconsin Statutes, Chapter 36.01(1) and 36.09(1).

18. *Planning the Future: Report of the Regents on the Future of the University of Wisconsin System,* December 1986: 1.

19. Wisconsin Statutes, Chapter 36.09 (1) (e).

20. Wisconsin Administrative Code, "Rules of Board of Regents of the University of Wisconsin System," UW System Board of Regents.

21. Wisconsin Administrative Code, Chapter UWS 2.02: 3.

22. Kenneth Shaw, letter to Jordan Marsh, University Affairs Director, Wisconsin Student Association, May 7, 1990.

Chapter 3

1. UW System Board of Regents Meeting Minutes, July 13, 1990: 2.

2. Resolution 5947, UW System Board of Regents Meeting Minutes, November 8, 1991: 9-10.

3. Attorney General, State of Wisconsin, James E. Doyle, letter to Judy Temby, Secretary, UW System Board of Regents, January 21, 1992.

4. Wisconsin Administrative Code, Chapter UWS 17: 63-74.

5. Richard Hofstadtler and Wilson Smith, ed., *American Higher Educational Documentary History,* 2nd ed., vol. 2, Chicago: The University of Chicago Press, 1968: 568-569.

6. Wisconsin Statutes, Chapter 36.12 (1).

7. Wisconsin Statutes, Chapter 38.23 (1).

8. Resolution 3757, Policy 87-16, UW System Board of Regents Meeting Minutes, February 2, 1990.

9. *Bylaws and Standing Orders of the Regents of the University of California,* with amendments to and including January 18, 1991.

10. *Ibid.,* 5.1[a].

11. *Ibid.,* 5.1[b]

12. *Ibid.,* 5.1[d].

13. *Ibid.,* 5.1[f].

14. *Ibid.,* 20.2.

15. *AGB Reports*, Association of Governing Boards of Universities and Colleges, May/June 1991: 12-15.

16. UW System Board of Regents Meeting Minutes, February 13, 1990: 4.

Chapter 4

1. "Faculty Governance — What It Means, How It Works," *Wisconsin Ideas*, UW System, December 1978.

2. Wisconsin Statutes, Chapter 36.09(4).

3. Michael H. Walsh, "Wimps Need Not Apply," AGB Reports, *The Journal of the Association of Governing Boards of Universities and Colleges*, September/October 1991: 30.

4. Margaret Atherton and Robert Schwartz, "Business no role model for universities," *Milwaukee Journal*, February 1, 1992.

Chapter 5

1. "Faculty Governance — What It Means, How It Works," *Wisconsin Ideas*, UW System, December 1978.

2. John J. Corson, "Trusteeship, 1977 Style," *AGB Reports*, January/February 1977.

3. Wisconsin Administrative Code, Chapter 5, "Layoff and Termination for Reasons of Financial Emergency," 5.01:15.

4. *Wisconsin State Journal*, September 8, 1991: A1.

5. Steve Shultze, "Bias Blocks Tenure for UW Women, NOW Says," *Milwaukee Journal*, September 4, 1991: B2.

6. Phil McDade, "Instructor Sues Over UW Tenure," *Wisconsin State Journal*, October 31, 1991: B1.

7. Wisconsin Legislative Audit Bureau Audit Report "UW Milwaukee Affirmative Action," March 1992, Report 92-11.

8. Wisconsin Administrative Code, Chapter UWS 4.01 (2), "Procedures for Dismissal." "A faculty member is entitled to enjoy and exercise all the rights and privileges of a United States citizen, and the rights and privileges of academic freedom as they are generally understood in the academic community. This policy shall be observed in determining whether or not just cause for a dismissal exists. The burden of proof of the existence of just cause for a dismissal is on the administration," 11.

9. *Achieving Faculty Diversity, A Source Book of Ideas and Success Stories*, UW System, March 1988.

10. *Ibid.*, 15.

11. "Report on Use of 1987-88 Instructional Positions and Reports for Release of 1988-89 Instructional Positions," UW System, March 1988.

12. *Planning the Future: Report of the Regents on the Future of the University of Wisconsin System*, December 1986: 4.

13. Wisconsin Legislative Audit Bureau, "An Evaluation of Faculty Positions Authorized in 1987, University of Wisconsin," April 1991, Report 91-7.

14. "Faculty Governance — What It Means, How It Works," *Wisconsin Ideas*, UW System, December 1978.

15. Wisconsin Statutes, Chapter 36.12(1).

Chapter 6

1. *Planning the Future: Report of the Board of Regents on the Future of the University System*, December 1986: 4.

2. Wisconsin Legislative Audit Bureau, "A Management Audit of the University of Wisconsin System Administration," November 1987, Report 86-38.

3. *Planning the Future*: Introduction.

4. *Ibid.*

5. Kenneth Shaw, "Design for Diversity," UW System, April 7, 1988.

6. Diane Hatton Bailiff, "The Role of Leadership in Mandated Academic Change: A History of University of Wisconsin System Leadership and AP #7.2, the Minority Retention and Recruitment Mandate," diss., UW-Madison, 1991.

7. Wisconsin Administrative Code, Chapter UWS 14, "Student Academic Disciplinary Procedures," 57.

8. Wisconsin Administrative Code, Chapter UWS 17, "Student Nonacademic Disciplinary Procedures," 63.

9. Wisconsin Administrative Code, Chapter UWS 17.06, 17.06(2)(a): 65-66.

10. Wisconsin Statutes, Chapter 36.09 (1)(b).

11. Vernon Carstensen, "The Origin and Early Development of the Wisconsin Idea," *Wisconsin Magazine of History*, Spring 1956: 182.

12. Emmalou Van Trilburg Norland, "Extension Is Not Just Service," *Journal of Extension*, Winter 1990, 3.

13. Report of the Special Regent Study Committee on Extension, submitted to the UW System Board of Regents, with proposed resolutions, April 9, 1982.

14. Resolution 2558, Policy Document 82-3, UW System Board of Regents "Report of Special Regent Committee on Extension," adopted April 9, 1982.

15. "President's Report to the UW Board of Regents on Integration of the Extension Function With the Other UW System Institutions," May 3, 1985.

16. Patrick G. Boyle, statement, UW System Board of Regents Hearing on Integration of the Extension Function, January 8, 1988.

17. *Fact Book for the University of Wisconsin System*, UW System Office of University Relations, 1991: 58-59.

18. Katharine C. Lyall, statement, *The Undergraduate Imperative: Building on Excellence*, UW System Board of Regents, December 5, 1991.

19. *The Chronicle of Higher Education*, July 25, 1990: A16.

20. *The Chronicle of Higher Education*, September 12, 1990.

21. *Ibid.*, A30.

22. *Ibid.*, A29.

23. Fredi-Ellen Bove, memo to Education Committee and All Regents, "Report on the Use of Teaching Assistants at the Doctoral Institutions," September 26, 1990.

24. Ernest L. Boyer, *College: The Undergraduate Experience in America*, The Carnegie Foundation for the Advancement of Teaching, New York: Harper & Row, 1987.

25. UW System Board of Regents, Resolution 1.1.g, February 8, 1991.

26. *Wisconsin State Journal*, March 10, 1991.

27. *The Chronicle of Higher Education*, March 13, 1991: A 15.

28. *Wisconsin Week*, UW-Madison, March 13, 1991: 1.

29. Stephen R. Portch, memo to UW System Board of Regents, May 7, 1991.

30. Resolution 5897, UW System Board of Regents Meeting Minutes, September 6, 1991: 7.

31. UW System Board of Regents Meeting Minutes, September 6, 1991: 11.

32. "The Undergraduate Imperative: Building on Excellence," presented to the UW System Board of Regents December 5, 1991: 11.

33. "Exploring post-tenure review," *Wisconsin Week*, UW-Madison, April 1, 1992: 11.

34. *Wisconsin Week*, April 15, 1992: 3.

35. *Ibid.*, 7.

36. "Future Directions: The University in the 21st Century," The Future Directions Committee, UW-Madison, 1989: 29.

37. UW System Board of Regents Meeting Minutes, May 8, 1992: Agenda Item 1.1.a.

38. Alice Kent, "Regents approve initial plans for tenure review," *Wisconsin Week*, UW-Madison, May 13, 1992: 1-5.

39. Mike Dorsher, "UW tenure review plan opposed," *Wisconsin State Journal*, May 1, 1992.

40. Mike Dorsher, "Regents to decide on speech, tenure," *Wisconsin State Journal*, May 7, 1992.

41. *Planning the Future, Report of the Regents on the Future of the University of Wisconsin System*, December 1986: 23.

42. Occasional Research Brief 91/5: "Trends in Enrollment," UW System Office of Policy Analysis and Research, August 1991.

43. Occasional Research Brief Update 92/3: "Trends in Enrollment," Fall 1991 Update, April 1992: 2

44. *Planning the Future*, 7.

45. *Ibid.*

46. Eugene P. Trani, Revision of the Structure and Responsibility of the Joint Administrative Committee on Continuing Education, proposal to the Education Committee and Other Regents, March 19, 1989.

47. Resolution 1.1.i [revised], University of Wisconsin System Board of Regents Meeting Minutes, April 7, 1989.

48. "Transferring Credits: Opportunities for Transferring Credits Between the Vocational, Technical and Adult Education System and the University of Wisconsin System," UW System, June 1, 1985.

49. "Student Transfer Policies and Practices," Wisconsin Association of Independent Colleges and Universities and Wisconsin Board of Vocational, Technical and Adult Education, 1986: 6.

50. "Agency Strategic Plan Programs and Services," Wisconsin Board of Vocational, Technical and Adult Education, January 1987: 66.

51. James Bortelt, "Merger of UW Centers, tech schools urged," *Green Bay Press Gazette*, May 15, 1987.

52. Mary Carole McCauley, "Governor opposes plan to revamp VTAE courses," *Milwaukee Journal*, June 18, 1987.

53. "MATC leader urges merger of system," *Milwaukee Journal*, July 28, 1988.

54. Roger A. Gribble, "Voc-school credit transfer unresolved," *Wisconsin State Journal*, July 29, 1988.

55. Cliff Miller, "Hassett: State and VTAE control needs study," *Appleton Post-Crescent*, July 7, 1988.

56. *Lifeline*, Wisconsin Vocational Association, March 1989: 2.

57. UW System Board of Regents Meeting Minutes, June 9, 1989: Exhibit A.

58. "Faculty Policies and Procedures, University of Wisconsin-Madison," February 3, 1992: section 7.20.

59. Resolution 5364, UW System Board of Regents Summary Minutes, November 10, 1989.

60. "Faculty Policies and Procedures, University of Wisconsin-Madison," February 3, 1992: section 7.20.

Chapter 7

1. *The Palm Beach Post*, February 18, 1992: A2.

2. Richard N. Ostling, "Big Chill on Campus," *Time*, February 3, 1992: 30-31.

3. Carolyn J. Mooney, "Death on Campus," *The Chronicle of Higher Education*, June 24, 1992: A13.

4. *The Chronicle of Higher Education*, August 26, 1992: A13.

5. Katharine C. Lyall, "UW System Quality Reinvestment Plan, 1992-93," UW System Board of Regents, February 6, 1992.

6. "Regents approve Quality Reinvestment Plan," *Wisconsin Week*, University of Wisconsin-Madison, February 19, 1992: 2.

7. Neil H. Shively, "UW regents back controversial reallocation plan," *Wisconsin State Journal*, February 7, 1992: 1.

8. *Ibid.*

9. Resolution 5609, UW System Board of Regents Meeting Minutes, October 5, 1990.

10. Glenn Jensen, letter to UW System Board of Regents "Administrative Costs," March 4, 1987.

11. Matt Pommer, "Campus merger talk inflammatory maybe inevitable," *The Capital Times*, April 23, 1992: A10.

12. UW System Board of Regents Meeting Minutes, October 9, 1992: 21.

13. *The Chronicle of Higher Education*, May 20, 1992: A 26.

14. Mark G. Yudof, "The Burgeoning Privatization of State Universities," *The Chronicle of Higher Education*, May 13, 1992: A 48.

15. Draft Report of the Higher Education Coordinating Board of the State of Washington.

16. Katharine C. Lyall, memo to UW System Board of Regents, February 4, 1991.

17. *The Wisconsin Taxpayer*, A Service of the Wisconsin Taxpayer's Alliance, December 1991: 5.

18. "Student Statistics Fall 1991," University of Wisconsin System, 1991: 11.

19. UW System Analysis of Comparative Funding Support Indicators, December 16, 1986.

20. Stephen R. Portch, letter to the Governor's Commission on Compensation, May 27, 1992.

21. *The Wisconsin Taxpayer*, A Service of the Wisconsin Taxpayers's Alliance, December 31, 1991: 7.

22. *Ibid.*, 5.

23. "State Appropriations for Higher Education," *The Chronicle of Higher Education*, October 21, 1992: A27.

24. Alicia Kent, "State orders $3.9 million budget cutback for campus," *Wisconsin Week*, UW-Madison, October 21, 1992: 1.

25. Joe Schoenmann, "State order may trip UW payroll," *The Capital Times*, October 9, 1992.

26. Jean Evangelauf, "Tuition at Public Colleges is Up 10% This Year, College Board Study Finds," *The Chronicle of Higher Education*, October 21, 1992: A36.

27. "Tuition and fees up 10% at public universities," *Milwaukee Journal*, October 14, 1992.

28. *Fact Book for the University of Wisconsin System*, UW System Office of University Relations, 1986: 56.

29. *Ibid.*, 47.

30. *Fact Book for the University of Wisconsin System*, 1992: 58.

31. *Ibid.*, 47.

32. *Ibid.*, 55.

33. Phil McDade, "UW officials, students rap bill to limit tuition boosts," *Wisconsin State Journal*, January 16, 1992.

34. Tom Vanden Brook, "UW students may face years of tuition increases near 10%," *Milwaukee Journal*, July 12, 1992: A1.

35. Phil McDade, "UW considers surcharge," *Wisconsin State Journal*, March 7, 1992: 13.

36. Steve Schultze, "Lyall assesses UW problems and solutions," *Milwaukee Journal*, April 9, 1992.

37. *The Capital Times*, March 7, 1992: 12.

38. *Wisconsin State Journal*, July 12, 1991: C1.

39. *The Capital Times*, March 7, 1992: 12.

40. *The Capital Times*, July 12, 1991: A3.

41. Thomas P. Wallace, "The Inequities of Low Tuition," *The Chronicle of Higher Education*, April 1, 1992: A48.

42. *The Capital Times*, December 12, 1991: C7.

43. W. Ann Reynolds, "Who Should Pay for Public Higher Education?" *The Chronicle of Higher Education*, April 29, 1992: B3.

44. John Elson, "Campus of the Future," *Time*, April 13, 1992: 55.

45. Occasional Research Brief 92/5: "Annual Status Report on Student Financial Aid," UW System, June 1992: 9.

46. Mike Dosher, "UW Madison tuition is unfairly low, regent says," *Wisconsin State Journal*, June 5, 1992: A1.

47. George K. Steil, Sr., address to UW System Board of Regents following his election as president of the board, June 5, 1992: 3.3

48. Katharine C. Lyall, memo to Ron Bornstein, "Re: Regent Weinstein's Request for Consolidated Tuition & Fee Information," November 2, 1990.

49. Resolution 1.2.b. [revised], "Long Term Tuition Policy," UW System Board of Regents Meeting Minutes, November 9, 1990.

50. *Student Statistics Fall 1991, The University of Wisconsin System Office of Policy Analysis and Research*, "Headcount Enrollment by Age — UW System," UW System, Table 43: 72.

51. *Ibid.*, "Total Headcount Enrollment According to Sex and Full-Time Status," Table 21: 32.

52. *Ibid.*, "Undergraduate Men According to Class," Table 16: 27; "Undergraduate Women According to Class," Table 17: 28.

53. Student Statistics Fall 1991: 32.

54. *The Chronicle of Higher Education Almanac*, August 26, 1992: 7.

55. Compiled by the Wisconsin Taxpayers Alliance from information from the U.S. Department of Commerce, 1991.

56. *The Wisconsin Taxpayer*, 1991: 8.

57. *Ibid.*

58. *Fact Book for the University of Wisconsin System*, 1992: 48.

59. *Taxes 1992*, Wisconsin Taxpayers Alliance, 6-7.

60. Report to the UW System Business and Finance Committee, 1.2.d, August 10, 1990: Appendix J.

61. "Tuition increase is 8 percent below national average," *Wisconsin Week*, October 23, 1991: 5.

62. Fredi-Ellen Bovi, memo to UW System Board of Regents, "Historical Student Share of Cost of Instruction," August 29, 1991.

63. Stephen R. Portch, letter to Governor's Commission on Compensation, May 27 1992.

64. *Ibid.*, 2.

65. Judith A. Temby, April 6, 1989, letter to UW System Regents. Chart enclosed appeared in the October/November 1988 *AGB Report*, the newsletter of the Association of Governing Boards. Source: College Board.

66. Occasional Research Brief 91/4: "Annual Status Report on Student Financial Aid in the UW System, 1989-90," UW System Office of Policy Analysis and Research, May 1991: 1.

67. Occasional Research Brief 91/4: 10.

68. Jim Zook, "Hope Fades for Cutting Reliance on Loans as Chief Component of US Student Aid," *The Chronicle of Higher Education*, October 28, 1992: A28.

69. Alan Guskin, "Middle Income Families Need Immediate Help in Paying for College," *Black Issues in Higher Education*, December 19, 1991: 84.

70. *Occupational Outlook Quarterly*, "Findings by education and occupation," U.S. Department of Labor, Bureau of Labor Statistics, Fall 1991: 36.

71. Eileen Zito, "Student Financial Aid & Major Choices Among Undergraduates: A National Study," diss., University of Minnesota, 1991.

72. *Wisconsin State Journal*, November 8, 1992: 7B.

73. *Wisconsin State Journal*, March 3, 1992: 14.

74. Katharine C. Lyall, memo to University of Wisconsin System Board of Regents, February 4, 1991.

75. *Wisconsin Week*, UW-Madison, November 4, 1992: 1.

76. *Milwaukee Sentinel*, July 12, 1992.

77. 1992 Report of the Governor's Commission on University of Wisconsin System Compensation, August 25, 1992: 5.

78. *Ibid.*, 25.

79. Matt Pommer, "Pair want UW tuition added to special session," *The Capital Times*, September 8, 1992.

80. Tom Vanden Brook, "UW-Madison students rap plan that could raise tuition 14.2%," *Milwaukee Journal*, September 3, 1992.

81. Daniel Bice, "Lyall's 8% tuition hike plan stirs legislator objections," *Milwaukee Journal*, October 30, 1992.

82. Tom Vanden Brook, "UW Madison students rap plan that could raise tuition 14.2%," *Milwaukee Journal*, September 3, 1992.

83. Joe Schoenmann, "UW budget draws quick protest," *The Capital Times*, October 29, 1992.

84. Richard Mial, "Commission: UW System in deep hole on pay scale," *La Crosse Tribune*, September 1, 1992.

85. 1992 Report of the Governor's Commission, 23.

86. Scripps-Howard News Service, "U.S. college tuition up again this year," *The Capital Times*, October 14, 1992.

Chapter 8

1. "Occasional Research Brief 92/1: "Access to the UW System; Patterns of Application, Admissions, and Enrollment of New Freshmen," February 1992: 3.

2. *Ibid.*, 1.

3. *Ibid.*, 2.

4. *Ibid.*, 2.

5. *U.S. News & World Report*, June 26, 1989: 45.

6. Resolution 5609, UW System Board of Regents Summary Minutes, October 5, 1990: Exhibit B.

7. *Money Guide*, "Best College Buys," 1992 edition.

8. "America's Best College Buys," *U.S. News & World Report*, June 5, 1992: 4-24.

9. Jack Gourman, *The Gourman Report, A Rating of Undergraduate Programs in American and International Universities*, 6th ed., Revised, 1988.

10. *Ibid.*, 180.

11. *Ibid.*, 262.

12. *Ibid.*, 127 and 145.

13. "UW ranks high in business survey," *The Capital Times*, June 29, 1992: B6.

14. Jeff Cole, "UW System rides high in exec poll," *Milwaukee Sentinel*, June 26, 1992.

15. Cliff Miller, "Education quality big concern for UW," *Appleton Post-Crescent*, May 24, 1992.

16. "Bulletin Board: Positions Available," *The Chronicle of Higher Education*, April 29, 1992: B38.

17. *Wisconsin Ideas*, "Faculty Governance — What It means, How It Works," December 1978: 7.

18. Clark Kerr, *Presidents Make a Difference, Strengthening Leadership in Colleges and Universities*, Report of the Commission on Strengthening Presidential Leadership, Association of Governing Boards of Universities and Colleges, 1984: 65.

19. *Ibid.*

20. Patricia A. Hollander, "Evaluating Tenured Professors," *The Chronicle of Higher Education*, June 17, 1992.

21. *Ibid.*, A44.

22. James Rhem, "It is time to rethink our values," *Wisconsin State Journal*, December 15, 1991: F1.

23. Phil McDade, "Top educators say schools need to alter their missions," *Wisconsin State Journal*, October 30, 1990.

24. Alicia Kent, "Faculty Share Commitment, Report: University must find ways to reward quality teaching," *Wisconsin Week*, November 4, 1992: 7.

25. Carolyn J. Mooney, "Professors Feel Conflict Between Roles in Teaching and Research, Say Students Are Badly Prepared," *The Chronicle of Higher Education*, May 8, 1991: A15.

26. Ibid, 17.

27. Bryan Barnett, "Teaching and Research Are Inescapably Incompatible," *The Chronicle of Higher Education*, June 3, 1992: A40.

28. *Ibid.*, A40.

29. Robert L. Jacobson, "Colleges Face New Pressure to Increase Faculty Productivity," *The Chronicle of Higher Education*, April 15, 1992: A1.

30. *Ibid.*, A17.

31. UW System Board of Regents Meeting Minutes, May 8, 1992: 11. *Fact Book for the University of Wisconsin System*, UW System Office of University Relations, 1992: 32, 64.

32. "Occasional Research Brief 92/7: "Trends in Faculty Teaching Assignments," UW System Office of Policy Analysis and Research, October 1992.

33. *The Student Voice*, UW-River Falls, April 28, 1989: 1.

34. Kenneth Shaw, letter to Regent Weinstein, "Comparative Data on Faculty Teaching Loads Educational Quality Mechanisms," March 7, 1989.

35. *Ibid.*, 3.

36. Robert J. Larson, News Release, April 18, 1989.

37. George Keller, *The Wisconsin Idea: Yesterday and Tomorrow*, Wisconsin Idea Commission, UW-Extension, Madison, Wisconsin, July 1986: 33.

38. *Ibid.*, 32.

39. *Ibid.*, 30.

40. Steve Schultze, "Wired for sense: System delivers education," *Milwaukee Journal*, February 24, 1992: C8.

41. "ECB Commission's technology needs study," Telelink, *News About Distance Learning Opportunities for Adults*, Wisconsin Educational Communications Board, March-April 1992: 1.

42. *Ibid.*, 1

43. Mark Robichaux, "Giving College Degrees for Watching TV," *The Wall Street Journal*, June 1, 1992: B1.

44. Mike Dorsher, "UW can't keep female faculty," *Wisconsin State Journal*, May 31, 1992.

45. "Feds may probe UW sex-bias claim," *Green Bay Press Gazette*, March 6, 1992: 18.

46. *Wisconsin Week*, December 4, 1991: 2.

47. Carolyn J. Mooney, "Critics Say Faculty Reward System Discounts the Importance of Service," *The Chronicle of Higher Education*, March 25, 1992: A16.

48. Jeffrey Boutwell, "Scholars Should Share Their Expertise on Key National Issues," *The Chronicle of Higher Education*, April 8, 1992: B3.

49. Carolyn J. Mooney, "Bok: To Avoid Bashing, Colleges Must Take a Leadership Role in National Problems," *The Chronicle of Higher Education*, April 8, 1992: A17.

50. Michael Quinn Patton, "To Educate a People," *Journal of Extension*, Winter 1986: 21.

51. UW System Board of Regents Meeting Minutes, December 8, 1989: 27.

52. Resolution 2558, Policy 82-3, UW System Board of Regents, April 9, 1982. Reaffirmed Regent Resolution 4042, P 88-5, May 6, 1988.

53. Resolution II.4.c.c., UW System Board of Regents, May 6, 1992: 2.

54. James O'Toole, "Tenure, A Conscientious Objection," *Change*, June-July 1978: 1-4.

55. *The Chronicle of Higher Education*, May 8, 1991: A15.

56. James A. Winn, "Thinking the Unthinkable About Tenure," *The Chronicle of Higher Education*, September 16, 1992: B1.

57. Wisconsin Administrative Code, Chapter UWS 34.01[1], 11.

58. *Ibid.*, Chapter UWS 4, 11-14.

59. *Ibid.*, Chapter UWS 4.02.

60. *Ibid.*

61. James O'Toole, "Tenure, A Conscientious Objection," *Change*, June-July 1978: 1-4.

62. UW System Board of Regents Meeting Minutes, September 6, 1991: 7.

63. Richard P. Chait and Andrew T. Ford, "Beyond Traditional Tenure," *Change*, July/August 1982.

64. *The Capital Times*, February 5, 1992: 1.

65. Neil H. Shively, "Two UW schools near $60,000 in faculty pay," *Milwaukee Sentinel*, January 9, 1992.

66. Kevin Murphy, "UW faculty salaries still haven't caught up," *Eau Claire Leader Telegram*, January 14, 1992.

67. Governor of Wisconsin Executive Order 138.

68. Steve Schultze, "UW System slips in pay comparisons," *Milwaukee Journal*, April 22, 1992.

69. Steve Schultze, "UW faculty pay is on target, says budget director," *Milwaukee Journal*, May 14, 1992.

70. Joe Schoenmann, "Faculty turnover called not that bad," *The Capital Times*, May 13, 1992.

71. Alicia Ken, "Faculty, staff raise salary concerns at public hearing," *Wisconsin Week*, UW-Madison, April 29, 1992: 1.

72. Wisconsin Statutes, Chapter 36.09[4m].

73. *Update on the Governor's Commission on UW System Compensation*, UW System Office of University Relations, May 13, 1992: 3.

74. *1992 Report of the Governor's Commission on University of Wisconsin System Compensation.*

75. Ibid., 4-6.

76. *The Capital Times*, August 28, 1992.

77. Allen M. Winkler, "Explaining What Professors Do With Their Time," *The Chronicle of Higher Education*, July 15, 1992: B1.

78. "Student Statistics Fall 1991," UW System, Table 6, 1991: 12.

79. Kenneth Shaw, letter to R. Dale Cattancach, State Auditor, April 17, 1991: 4.

80. "On Line," *The Chronicle of Higher Education*, April 29, 1992: A18.

81. *The Chronicle of Higher Education*, May 6, 1992: B3.

82. Harvey H. Kaiser, *Crumbling Academe*, Association of Governing Boards of Universities and Colleges, 1984: 13-16.

83. Minutes of the Wisconsin Foundation, March 9, 1992: 4.

84. Occasional Research Brief 93/2: "Table 1," UW System Office of Policy Analysis and Research, March 1993: 8.

85. *Factbook for the University of Wisconsin System*, 1986: 31.

86. Student Statistics Fall 1991, The University of Wisconsin SystemOffice of Policy Analysis and Research, "Total FTE Enrollment with 10-year Profile (Number and Percent Change), The UW System, Table 5: 10.

87. Terry Anderson, "Colleges face a balancing act," *Green Bay Press Gazette*, April 5, 1992.

88. "Occasional Research Brief 91/2: "Outcomes of New Freshmen Students: Retention, Graduation and Time to Degree," UW System Office of Policy Analysis and Research, March 1991.

89. "Number of UW Freshman hits lowest point since '71," *Wisconsin State Journal*, July 5, 1992: C3.

90. Vernon E. Lattin, "Competency and Proficiency Programs," memo to Laurence A. Weinstein, October 2, 1985: 3.

91. *Ibid.*, 5.

92. Resolution 5957, UW System Board of Regents Meeting Minutes, November 8, 1991: 17-19.

93. S. Frederick Starr, "Tuition Relief for the Middle Class," *The Journal of* the Association of Governing Boards of Universities and Colleges, January/February 1992: 34.

94. "What's Going on in the College Labor Market?" Editor's Note, *Occupational Outlook Quarterly*, U.S. Department of Labor, Bureau of Labor Statistics, Summer 1992: 3.

95. Dwight A. York, remarks to the Vocational, Technical and Adult Education Board, August 29, 1990.

96. *Assuring Wisconsin's Economic Future: Improving Occupational Options for Youth*, Report of the Joint VTAE/DPI Task Force on Implementing Occupational Options in Wisconsin, March 1991: 10.

97. Nora Roy, memo to Student Services Directors, May 26, 1992.

98. "*Milwaukee Sentinel's* 29th Forum for Progress," *Milwaukee Sentinel*, April 6, 1992.

99. Mary Glindinning, "UW schools face enrollment dilemma," *Wisconsin State Journal*, October 30, 1990.

100. *Dubuque Telegraph Herald*, April 6, 1992.

101. *La Crosse Tribune*, February 18, 1992.

102. *Milwaukee Journal*, March 29, 1992.

103. *Milwaukee Journal*, March 3, 1992: 27.

104. Phil McDade, "UW's anti-bias record attacked," *Wisconsin State Journal*, March 5, 1992.

105. Thomas B. Pfankuch, "Administration ponders gay bashing," *Eau Claire Leader Telegram*, October 8, 1992.

106. "The Annual Audit: Anti-Semitic Attacks Reach Record Numbers," *ADL on the Frontline*, Anti-Defamation League, March 1992: 1-2.

107. *The Chronicle of Higher Education*, March 25, 1992: A1.

108. Resolution 6073, UW System Board of Regents Meeting Minutes, April 10, 1992: 9.

109. Design for Diversity Progress Report, April 9, 1992.

110. *Ibid.*, Table 1.

111. *The Capital Times*, April 6, 1992.

112. *The Capital Times*, April 10, 1992.

113. Design for Diversity, Table 1.

114. *Ibid.*, Table 9.

115. *Ibid.*, Table 6.

116. Occasional Research Brief 92/4: "Minority Student Trends," UW System Office of Policy Analysis and Research, May 1992: 11.

117. *Wisconsin State Journal,* January 20, 1992.

118. *Wisconsin State Journal,* June 28, 1992: B3.

119 Alicia Ken, "Wiesel: 'People should know the real meaning of racism,'" *Wisconsin Week,* UW-Madison, April 1, 1992: 1 and 14.

120. *Janesville Gazette,* March 13, 1992.

121. Joni Finney, "Opening the Minority Pipeline," *AGB Reports, The Journal of the Association of Governing Boards of Universities and Colleges,* May/June 1991: 16.

122. "Commentary: Scrap hate rule" *Green Bay Press Gazette,* February 26, 1992.

123. Morris Dees, *A Season for Justice,* New York: Charles Scribner's Sons, 1991.

124. Phil McDade, "Regents O.K. limits on speech, *Wisconsin State Journal,* March 7, 1992: 6. Joe Schoenmann, "Regents approve controversial hate speech rule, 9-6," *The Capital Times,* March 6, 1992: 1.

125. *The Capital Times,* March 6, 1992: B3.

126. For a sampling of such editorials see: *The Capital Times,* March 12, 1992; *La Crosse Tribune,* March 9, 1992; *Milwaukee Sentinel,* March 7, 1992; *Wisconsin State Journal,* March 15, 1992.

127. "Free speech loses again," *The Capital Times,* May 11, 1992.

128. Sarah Bowen, "Can racist slurs be banned on campus?" *USA Today,* October 15, 1992.

129. Donald K. Stitt letter to Frank Horton, UW-Milwaukee, April 19, 1985.

130. "Minority and women faculty subjects of special study," *The UW-M Report,* October 29, 1985: 3.

131. *Milwaukee Journal,* May 5, 1990.

132. "Note Book," *The Chronicle of Higher Education,* June 10, 1992: A27.

133. John Lancaster, "U.S. study challenges military's ban on gays," *The Capital Times,* June 19, 1992: A1.

134. "Canadian military to end gay bias," *The Capital Times,* October 28, 1992: C4.

135. *Milwaukee Sentinel,* February 29, 1992: 27.

136. Liz McMillen, "Three Grant Makers Are Awarding Millions in Effort to Improve Racial Tolerance on College Campuses," *The Chronicle of Higher Education,* February 26, 1991: 7.

137. Steve Schultze, "Conservatives flex muscles at UW," *Milwaukee Journal*, December 15, 1991: 1.

138. Steve Schultze, "Regents may block hate-speech rule," *Milwaukee Journal*, February 27, 1992.

139. *Ibid.*

140. *Ibid.*

141. UW System Board of Regents Verbatim Minutes, November 8, 1991: 6.

142. New York Times Service, "Young Americans say race relations 'generally bad,' " *Palm Beach Post*, March 17, 1992: A3.

143. *Stevens Point Journal*, February 23, 1989.

144. Delmar E. DeLong, memo to Wisconsin Board of Vocational, Technical and Adult Education, July 5, 1989, given to the UW System Board of Regents.

145. *Superior Evening Telegram*, April 17, 1992.

146. Phil McDade, "Thompson: No UW campuses to close," *Wisconsin State Journal*, April 23, 1992: B1.

147. Steve Schultze, "Officials try to ease merger fears," *Milwaukee Sentinel*, April 16, 1992.

148. Steve Schultze, "Likely regents leader tones down rhetoric," *Milwaukee Journal*, May 3, 1992.

149. Stephen R. Portch, letter to Regent Davis, November 2, 1992.

Chapter 9

1. Joe Schoemann, "Pay, tuition hikes may hit lawmaker roadblock," *The Capital Times*, November 6, 1992: 3A.

2. Robert Birnbaum, *How Colleges Work,* San Francisco: Jossey-Bass Publishers, 1988: 6-7.

3. J. Victor Baldrige, *Academic Governance: Research on Institutional Politics and Decision Making*, McCutchan Publishing, 1971: 100.

4. Baldrige, 101.

5. *Ibid.*, 100.

6. Liz McMillen and Julie L. Nicklin, "In Tough Times, Some Colleges Find Conservative Management Pays Off," *The Chronicle of Higher Education*, June 5, 1992.

7. Clark Kerr, *Presidents Make a Difference, Strengthening Leadership in Colleges and Universities,* Report of the Commission on Strengthening Presidential Leadership, Association of Governing Boards of Universities and Colleges, 1984: 83.

8. *1992 Report of the Governor's Commission on University of Wisconsin System Compensation,* 1992: 4-6.

9. *Milwaukee Journal,* July 5, 1992.

10. Frank Newman, *Choosing Quality, Reducing Conflict Between the State and the University* (Education Commission of the States, 1987).

11. *Ibid.,* 45.

12. *Ibid.,* 83.

13. *Ibid.,* 97.

14. *Ibid.,* 98.

15. *Ibid.,* 100.

16. *Ibid.,* 87.

17. "Campus of the Future," *Time,* April 13, 1992: 54.

18. *Appleton Post-Crescent,* April 10, 1992.

19. Phil McDade, "Pivotal issues await Lyall," *Wisconsin State Journal,* April 5, 1992.

20. *Ibid.*

21. *Oshkosh Northwestern,* March 11, 1992.

22. *Racine Journal Times,* April 8, 1992.

23. *Ibid.*

24. *The Capital Times,* April 6, 1992.

25. "Lyall would like UW job," *Oshkosh Northwestern,* March 14, 1992.

26. Ibid.

27. *Ibid.*

28. *The Chronicle of Higher Education,* May 13, 1992: A48.

29. Mike Dorsher, "UW System rates high in statewide survey," *Wisconsin State Journal,* July 11, 1992.

30. *The Chronicle of Higher Education,* September 12, 1990: A31.

Chapter 10

1. *Wisconsin State Journal,* December 25, 1992: D8.

Index